THE
KEMBLE ERA

The Marvellous Boy:
The Life and Myth of Thomas Chatterton
The Young Romantics:
Paris 1827–37

The Kemble Era

*John Philip Kemble, Sarah Siddons
and the London Stage*

Linda Kelly

RANDOM HOUSE
New York

To Nigel

Copyright © 1980 by Linda Kelly
All rights reserved under International and Pan-American Copyright Conventions.
Published in the United States by Random House, Inc., New York. Originally
published in Great Britain by The Bodley Head, London.

Library of Congress Cataloging in Publication Data
Kelly, Linda, 1936-
The Kemble era.
1. Theater—England—London—History. 2. Kemble,
John Philip, 1757-1823. 3. Siddons, Sarah Kemble,
1775-1831. 4. Actors—Great Britain—Biography.
5. Theatrical managers—Great Britain—Biography.
I. Title
PN 2593.K44 1980b   792.09421   79-5537
ISBN 0-394-41034-3

Manufactured in the United States of America
2   4   6   8   9   7   5   3
First American Edition

ILLUSTRATIONS

1. Mrs Siddons as Isabella, Henry Siddons as her son, in *Isabella*.
2. The pit entrance to Drury Lane on a Siddons night.
3. Kemble as Hamlet, 1783.
4. Richard Brinsley Sheridan.
5. Kemble and Mrs Siddons as Mr and Mrs Beverly in *The Gamester*.
6. Garrick and Mrs Pritchard in *Macbeth*.
7. Macbeth and Lady Macbeth after the murder of Duncan.
8. Kemble and Mrs Siddons in *Macbeth*.
9. Mrs Jordan as Euphrosyne.
10. Mrs Jordan as Viola.
11. Priscilla Hopkins (later Mrs John Philip Kemble) as Peggy in *The Country Wife*.
12. Mrs Siddons by Gainsborough.
13. Mrs Siddons as the Tragic Muse.
14. Kemble as Coriolanus.
15. Mrs Siddons in 1797.
16. Kemble as Rolla in *Pizarro*.
17. Kemble on stage in *Pizarro*.
18. Michael Kelly.
19. William Henry Ireland.
20. Charles Kemble.
21. Master Betty as Young Norval.
22. Edmund Kean as Sir Giles Overreach.
23. Mrs Inchbald.
24. The Kembles in *Henry VIII*.
25. Maria Siddons.
26. Thomas Lawrence.
27. William Siddons.
28. Sally Siddons.
29. Kemble as Richard III.

The publishers are grateful to the following for their kind permission to reproduce the illustrations in this book: the Garrick Club: 8; the GLC

PREFACE

In the late eighteenth and early nineteenth centuries – the period when John Philip Kemble and his sister Sarah Siddons held sway on the London stage – the theatre was a centre of social and intellectual life to an extent unthinkable to later generations. 'Forty or fifty years ago', wrote Leigh Hunt, 'people of all times of life were much greater playgoers than they are now. They dined earlier, they had not so many newspapers, clubs and pianofortes; the French Revolution only tended at first to endear the nation to its own habits; it had not yet opened a thousand new channels of thought and interest, nor had the railroads conspired to carry people, bodily as well as mentally, into as many and analogous directions. Everything was more concentrated and the various classes of society felt a greater concern in the same amusements. Nobility, gentry, citizens, princes – all were frequenters of the theatre and even more or less acquainted personally with the performers. Nobility intermarried with them; gentry, and citizens too, wrote for them; princes conversed and lived with them.'[1]

The widespread interest in the theatre at that time makes it a period particularly rich in theatrical memoirs and anecdotes. Playwrights, actors and their admirers wrote their reminiscences; newspapers and pamphlets provided a more fleeting commentary. The diaries and memoirs of leading figures in other fields, painters, politicians and writers, yield a harvest of theatrical encounters. Theatre criticism, above all, was beginning to be taken seriously. By the end of the Kemble era, with the advent of such great critics as Hazlitt and Leigh Hunt, the old practice of 'puffing' according to the strength of the actors' influence with editors was losing its hold. The public were no longer contented with insipid paragraphs in which actors were 'charming' or 'excellent', houses 'crowded' and performances carried off with 'éclat' – such criticisms, as Leigh Hunt remarked, being no more than 'a draft upon the box office, or reminiscences of last Thursday's salmon and lobster sauce'.

7

In this fertile field of memoirs and criticism some of the most abundant material is provided by the writings of James Boaden, playwright and editor of the *Oracle* newspaper from its founding in 1789. A personal friend of Kemble and Mrs Siddons, as well as Mrs Jordan and the playwright and novelist Mrs Inchbald, whose lives he also wrote, his biographies of Kemble and his sister, diffuse and rambling, but full of first-hand impressions of their acting, give a vivid and comprehensive picture of the theatre of the day. Sometimes one could wish for a little more outspokenness. No hint of scandal enters his life of Mrs Siddons, while in his introduction to that of Kemble he writes: 'On a few, a very few points, in the exercise of, I hope, a sound discretion, I have ventured to baffle the search of the malignant.' One is left, I hope not too malignantly, to carry out the search elsewhere.

Kemble's theatrical journals, now in the British Museum, are another major source of information. He kept them intermittently from the day he took over as manager of Drury Lane in 1788 till his retirement from the stage in 1817. Towards the end of his career his entries are confined to a laconic record of takings and performances – during the period of the Old Prices riots, for instance, he makes no mention of the nightly uproar in the theatre – but earlier entries provide picturesque glimpses of a manager's problems and preoccupations. Some notes for the season of 1791–2 give an example of their range:

Always take care to have a Singer of the Deepest Bass; no matter how he speaks; the Gallery loves a Rumble . . .
Never let an old Actor of Merit want an Engagement on any Account – It is the true Interest of the Stage Monopoly not to suffer the Publick to think that there is not Room enough for everybody at the two Theatres.
Little Children have a very pleasing Effect in Pantomimes, Processions & c . . .
Whenever there is Danger of a Riot, always act an Opera; for Musick drowns the Noise of Opposition.

I have always been drawn to this period in the theatre, by its memoirs, prints and paintings, by its links with the world of Burke,

Pitt, Fox and Sheridan, with the royal Dukes and the Prince of Wales. Percy Fitzgerald in *The Kembles*, 1871, wrote a joint life of Kemble and Mrs Siddons. Since then there have been a number of biographies of Mrs Siddons, most recently the excellent life by Roger Manvell, 1970; and Herschel Baker's *John Philip Kemble*, 1942, remains a standard work. My aim has been to spread the net rather wider, and taking Kemble and Mrs Siddons as the central figures, to give a picture of the theatre of their day, and of some of the characters whose lives, professionally or privately, were linked with theirs. A great deal of research has been devoted to this period, most comprehensively in the last two volumes of *The London Stage, 1660–1800*, in which details of performances and players, together with contemporary comments of interest, are listed night by night for the London theatres. On these and on the work of other theatre historians, as well as on the writings of the period, I have drawn for this impression of the era and hoped to capture something of its richness and variety. But no one, in the words of Boaden, who concluded his life of Mrs Siddons with the wish that it should prove a fitting monument, 'can be more sensible than myself that our wishes are children of the imagination and that their execution must be bounded by our power'.

THE
KEMBLE ERA

I

'We wish we had never seen Mr Kean', wrote Hazlitt in 1816, two years after that tempestuous actor's début at Drury Lane. 'He has destroyed the Kemble religion; and it is the religion in which we were brought up.'[1]

Hazlitt was mourning the ending of an era. For more than thirty years John Philip Kemble, with his illustrious sister Sarah Siddons, had dominated the London stage, Mrs Siddons as the queen of tragedy, Kemble not only as her masculine counterpart and with her the arch-exponent of the grand manner in acting but also as the first of a line of great nineteenth-century actor-managers, reigning in turn at Drury Lane and Covent Garden.

The Kemble era opened sensationally in 1782 with Sarah Siddons' tear-compelling first performance as Isabella, in the tragedy of that name, at Drury Lane. The sobs and hysterics of the audience and the acclamations of the press next day confirmed the occasion as the greatest first night in the London theatre since Garrick's début as Richard III forty-one years earlier. From that moment to the end of her career Mrs Siddons knew no rival as a tragic actress and her image, whether as Lady Macbeth, the Tragic Muse, or Gainsborough's fashionable beauty, still haunts the imagination of posterity.

Sarah Siddons was born a Kemble. The daughter of strolling players, she had been brought up to the stage since childhood and at the age of eighteen, against the wishes of her parents who had hoped for better things for her, had married a fellow player, William Siddons. Siddons, a handsome, pleasant spoken man, eleven years her senior, was a competent if uninspiring actor who could turn his hand, it was said, to anything from Macbeth to Pantaloon and master the longest part in a day. 'So slight however perfect was the impression', noted a colleague however, 'that it escaped entirely his memory in as few hours as he had devoted to its acquisition.'[2] A better judge of acting than he was an actor, he took great pains in coaching his young wife, who from their earliest days together had attracted the attention of provincial audiences, as much for her dark dramatic beauty as her playing.

Her brilliant first night as Isabella had not been Mrs Siddons' first appearance at Drury Lane. Seven years previously, when she was still a humble strolling player, news of her talents had reached the ears of David Garrick, at that time nearing the end of his career both as an actor and as manager of Drury Lane. He had sent the actor Thomas King, a leading member of his company, to see her play in Cheltenham. King reported very favourably, but Garrick, busy and in indifferent health, made no immediate move to engage her. He kept an eye on her movements however and in the summer of 1775, when he was making plans for what would be his final season at Drury Lane, he sent a second emissary, the dramatist and critic Henry Bate, who was travelling in her neighbourhood, this time with a commission to offer her an engagement should he think her suitable.

Bate, an old friend and admirer of Garrick's, and a shrewd judge of the theatre, was happy to undertake the errand, the more so since he was hoping to have an opera produced at Drury Lane. He wrote to him from Cheltenham where Mrs Siddons was once more playing and where, 'after combatting the various difficulties of some of the cussidest cross roads in this kingdom', he had arrived to see her in the part of Rosalind. Mrs Siddons was six months pregnant and plainly ill suited to a 'breeches' part, but despite this Bate was greatly struck by what he saw:

'Tho' I beheld her from the side wings of the stage (a barn about three yards over and consequently under almost every disadvantage) I own she made so strong an impression upon me that I think she cannot fail to be a valuable acquisition to Drury Lane. Her figure must be remarkably fine . . . Her face (if I could judge from where I saw it) is one of the most strikingly beautiful for stage effect that ever I beheld: but I shall surprize you more, when I assure you that these are nothing to her action, and general stage deportment, which are remarkably pleasing and characteristic; in short I know no woman who marks the different passages and transitions with so much variety and at the same time propriety of expression . . .'[3]

He lost no time in approaching Mrs Siddons, spurred on by the news that the management of the rival Covent Garden were also taking an interest in her. She showed 'all that diffidence usually the first attendant upon merit', expressing herself happy to be brought to Garrick's notice and to accept whatever terms he thought appropriate. She had a wide range of parts to offer – 'nay beware yourself, Great Little Man', wrote Bate waggishly, 'for she plays Hamlet to the satisfaction of the Worcestershire critics'. As for her husband, 'a damned rascally player tho' seemingly a very civil fellow', he asked no more than to be found useful in some capacity or other at Drury Lane, and it should, thought Bate, be possible to accommodate him. With Garrick's agreement, and an advance to tide them over her confinement, it was agreed that the pair should come to Drury Lane, Mrs Siddons as a leading lady, as soon as possible after her baby had been born.

Mrs Siddons gave birth to a daughter, her second child, on November 5th, having begun her labour in the midst of a performance on the stage. By early December, still barely recovered, she had arrived in London with her family. The London theatre season, which ran from September to June each year, was already in full swing; the inconvenient date of her confinement had made it impossible for Garrick to introduce her, as he would otherwise have wished, as his opening attraction. But the prospects before her seemed golden enough. To play at Drury Lane, to play moreover opposite Garrick, the greatest actor of the age, was the summit of every actress's ambition; Mrs Siddons had achieved it at the age of only twenty-one. It was true that Drury Lane was dominated at that time by three jealous and quarrelsome leading ladies, to mortify whom, she was later convinced, had been Garrick's chief motive in employing her. ('If any lady begins to play at tricks', he had written to Bate, 'I will immediately play off my masked battery of Siddons against her.')[4] It was true, too, that her first main role, that of Portia in *The Merchant of Venice*, lacked the emotional appeal of the tragic or melodramatic parts in which she had been most successful, and that King, not Garrick, would be Shylock. But the part was one which she herself had underlined in a list of her best roles and Garrick's flattering behaviour off-stage – making much of her in the green-room, sending her places for his most sought-after performances – would have been enough to turn a wiser head.

Her début as Portia was disastrous. Drury Lane, crowded and imposing, was a far cry from the scenes of her provincial triumphs. Always diffident in private life, she was, at this first confrontation, overcome with nerves on stage as well. A critic next day described her terror-stricken entrance: 'On before us tottered, rather than walked, a very pretty, delicate, fragile-looking young creature, dressed in a most unbecoming manner, in a faded salmon-coloured sack and coat and uncertain whereabouts to fix either her eyes or her feet. She spoke in a broken tremulous tone; and at the close of a sentence her words generally lapsed into a horrid whisper, that was absolutely inaudible.'[5] She recovered herself later on, delivering the great trial speech with 'the most critical propriety', but it was too late to redeem the unfavourable first impression.

Despite this unpropitious beginning, Garrick continued to put her forward, influenced more perhaps by her beauty and his desire to check the presumption of his leading ladies than by any great faith in her talents. She played the part of Venus in his Shakespearean pageant, *The Jubilee,* the other actresses pushing forward to hide her from the audience till Garrick himself came and led her to the forefront of the stage. She played in Bate's opera *The Blackamoor Wash'd White*, she was Mrs Strickland to Garrick's Ranger in the comedy *The Suspicious Husband*, and finally, greatest honour of all, she was the Lady Anne to Garrick's Richard III. Garrick was now preparing to retire from the stage. Richard III, in which he had first amazed the theatrical world, was to be one of his farewell performances. On this occasion, said the critics, he surpassed even himself and his appearance beggared all description. Mrs Siddons was abashed by the fire and ferocity of his gaze, and the glance of reproach which he gave her when, forgetting his instructions always to place herself so that he should face the audience when he spoke to her, she forced him to turn his head, was something she never forgot.

Shortly after, amidst scenes of great emotion, Garrick left the stage and the management of Drury Lane for ever. With the ending of the London season the Siddonses left for a summer engagement in Birmingham, secure as they thought in Garrick's assurances that he would see that his successors re-engaged them for the autumn. But either Garrick failed to press their claims or the new management, unimpressed by Mrs Siddons, overrode him, for towards the end of their stay in Birmingham to their amazement and dismay they received a letter from the prompter at Drury Lane dispensing with their services. For Mrs Siddons, whose hopes and ambitions had been fed by Garrick's flattering attentions, it was a stunning blow, her humiliation compounded by fears for their very survival, for the summer was already well advanced and she and her husband had no alternative arrangements. For the rest of her life she would blame Garrick for her rebuff, the shock of which, she wrote, came near to destroying her, plunging her into a depression from which only necessity and the thought of her children eventually aroused her. But it seems unlikely that Garrick was much to blame. He was no longer in control at Drury Lane and was guilty at most of what Mrs Siddons' biographer, Thomas Campbell, describes as 'that thought-lessness which the French call *une heureuse légèreté*' in promising more than he could perform. It is also unlikely that either to Garrick or the management of Drury Lane Mrs Siddons had given any real inkling of what she was to become. In the words of an earlier biographer, James Boaden: 'No doubt all those fiery markings of her intellect, those divine sparks that illuminated her maturer age, slept unawaked under an exterior of modest beauty, from which such signs of confidence were banished alike by timidity and prudence.'[6]

*   *   *

Six years later, on October 10th, 1782, Mrs Siddons reappeared at Drury Lane and in one night established herself as the greatest player it had seen since Garrick. During the intervening years she had become famous, having made her name at the Theatre Royal, Bath, at that time second only in importance to the two main London theatres. She had become the idol of fashionable and literary society in Bath and had made many friends among the latter. Critics and theatre-lovers would travel specially from London to see her play and since 1781 the management of Drury Lane had been making tentative advances to her. Caution might well have counselled her to stay in Bath where her success and her position were assured; ambition and the desire to triumph where she had once been humiliated led her to accept their first firm offer.

The management of Drury Lane was now in the hands of Richard Brinsley Sheridan. His meteoric career as a playwright already all but over, he had turned his energies towards a career almost equally brilliant in politics. Drury Lane, in which by various complicated transactions he had acquired a controlling interest, was chiefly regarded by him as a source of income to be pillaged at will for the furtherance of his political ambitions. Under these circumstances the theatre, which Garrick had left as a disciplined and thriving enterprise, was falling into disarray. Many of its best players had left, either to retire or to the rival Covent Garden; the rest were demoralised by the irregularity of their payments, the frequent changes of plan and the caprice and carelessness with which their affairs were run. Mrs Siddons' arrival at a time when receipts were beginning to reflect the confusion behind scenes would bring a welcome upsurge to the theatre's fortunes.

For the moment Sheridan seemed scarcely aware of the treasure which he had acquired. A year before, his delightful farce *The Critic*, by making fun of contemporary tragedies (almost always heroic, historical and in blank verse), had, so it seemed, cast a blight on the public's appetite for them. The season opened with a comedy, *The Clandestine Marriage*, preceded by a prologue in which the actor Thomas King, who was taking on the thankless task of manager, introduced himself to the public in that capacity; and it was not until nearly a month later that Mrs Siddons made her first appearance.

Isabella, adapted by Garrick from Southerne's tragedy *The Fatal Marriage*, was a well tried favourite in Mrs Siddons' and the theatre's repertoire. She had been guided in her choice of role by Sheridan's father, Thomas, a veteran of the stage, who had seen her in the part in Bath. Dubiously immortalised by Dr Johnson – 'Why Sir, Sherry is dull, naturally dull, but it must have taken him a great deal of pains to become what he is. Such an excess of stupidity is not in nature' – he showed himself inspired on this occasion. The role of Isabella, with its blend of pathos, maternal love and grief-induced madness, provided Mrs Siddons with an unrivalled opportunity to display her powers; not till she played Lady Macbeth, three years later, would she go beyond it.

Isabella, a widow when the play commences, is faced with destitution. Turned away by her proud and worldly father-in-law, who will help her only at the price of giving up her little son, she accepts the hand of Villeroy, who has long been in love with her, for the sake of her child. Scarcely has the marriage taken place than Biron, her first husband, who has been falsely reported as dead, returns. Despair at her predicament and Biron's subsequent death in a brawl unhinge her reason and she kills herself.

Mrs Siddons began the first rehearsal in a state of extreme apprehension. Gradually, as she became absorbed in her part, she forgot her fears, and the tears of her fellow actors as the play proceeded emboldened her still further. At the second rehearsal her little boy Henry, who was to act the part of her son in the play, was so affected by her acting that he burst into uncontrollable sobs, an incident that Sheridan, well versed in the arts of his own Mr Puff, was quick to pass on to the press.

The morning of October 10th was bright and sunny. Mrs Siddons, who for the last few days had been afflicted with a nervous hoarseness, greeted the sunshine as a happy omen, the more so since she found that her voice was completely recovered. Her father, who had arrived to support her in her ordeal, escorted her to the theatre that evening; William, her husband, completely unnerved, remained at home. Left in her dressing-room, Mrs Siddons, in one of what she called her 'desperate tranquillities', completed her dress, to the astonishment of her attendants, without uttering a word, though often sighing deeply.

'At length', she wrote, 'I was called to my fierey trial . . . The awful consciousness that one is the sole object of attention to that immense space, lined as it were with human intellect from top to bottom, and on all sides round, may perhaps be imagined but cannot be described, and never never to be forgotten . . .'[7]

The theatre was packed to overflowing. Mrs Siddons' Bath reputation had gone before her and public expectation, heightened by Sheridan's judicious puffing, had reached such a pitch that cynical critics had expressed their doubts that any performance, however good, could match the eulogies bestowed upon it in advance.

The evening dispelled all doubts. Mrs Siddons returned home when the performance was over with the echoes of unbounded applause in her ears and the consciousness that her triumph and her vindication were complete.

'I was half dead', she wrote, 'and my joy, my thankfulness, were of too solemn and overpowering nature to admit of words or even tears. My Father, my husband and myself sat down to a frugal, neat supper uninterrupted except by joyful exclamations from Mr Siddons. My Father enjoyed his refreshments, but occasionally stop'd short, and laying down his knife and fork, and lifting up his beautiful and venerable face, which was partly shaded by his silvered hairs hanging about it in luxuriant curls, let fall such abundant showers of delicious tears, that they actually poured down into his plate. We soon parted for the night, and I, worn out with continued broken rest, anxiety and laborious exertion, after an hour's introspection (who can conceive the intenseness of that reverie), fell into a sweet and profound sleep; which continued to the middle of the next day.'

* * *

One of the most striking descriptions of Mrs Siddons as Isabella is given by Madame de Staël, who saw her in the part that autumn and recalled it in her novel *Corinne*:

The noble face and profound sensibility of the actress so captivated Corinne that during the first act her eyes did not leave the stage. English declamation, when a great talent makes its power and originality felt, is more fitted than any other to stir the soul. There is less art, less calculation than in France; the impression it produces is more immediate . . .

In England one may risk anything if nature is the inspiration. Those long groans which seem ridiculous when one describes them make those who hear them shudder. The noblest of actresses, Mrs Siddons loses none of her dignity when she flings herself full length upon the ground . . .

At last comes the terrible moment when Isabella, having broken

20

free from her women, who wish to prevent her from killing herself, laughs, as she stabs herself, at the uselessness of their efforts. The effect of this laugh of despair is the most extraordinary and difficult achievement of dramatic art; it is far more moving than tears; misery finds its most heart-rending expression in its bitter irony. How terrible the anguish of the heart must be when it inspires such ferocious joy, when it shows, at the sight of its own blood, the fierce contentment of a savage enemy who tastes revenge.

Mrs Siddons' second part that season – Euphrasia in Murphy's *The Grecian Daughter* (memorable for its scene, off-stage, where the heroine suckles her starving father) – was more vehement and more heroic. The suffering innocence of Isabella gave place to the righteous anger of a daughter incensed at her father's wrongs. Mrs Siddons' entry on stage, rushing in, veils streaming behind her, exhorting the Grecian warriors to revenge:
'War on, ye heroes!'
was a moment which raised the play from near pantomime to epic dimensions. Mrs Piozzi described her in the part as one of 'the noblest specimens of the human race I ever saw'; and Brereton, the actor playing opposite her, was so overcome by her pleading for her father in the second act that he burst into tears and was scarcely able to finish the scene.

'Siddonian idolatry' had now reached fever-pitch. Drury Lane, no longer in the doldrums, was enjoying the highest receipts it had had for years. Takings on Siddons nights were £200 more than on other evenings. Mrs Siddons had been engaged at a modest £10 weekly but her real rewards would come from her benefit nights when all the evening's takings were assigned to her. The management, in gratitude, gave her two benefits instead of the usual one that season, and waived the theatre charges that would customarily be subtracted from the total. In one evening alone she made more than £800, the sum including a presentation purse of a hundred guineas as a token of admiration from the gentlemen of the Bar.

Honours flowed as fast as money. The cream of London society, fashionable and intellectual, crowded to her performances. Sir

Joshua Reynolds, trumpet to his ear, could be seen in the orchestra; there too – 'O glorious constellation!', wrote Mrs Siddons – sat Gibbon, Burke, Sheridan, Windham and Charles James Fox, the latter frequently in tears. The Prince of Wales came to see her in her dressing-room. George III, forgetting his disapproval of Sheridan's politics as a Whig and a supporter of the Prince of Wales, came with the royal family to see her in all the characters she played.

The king hid his tears behind his eye-glass, while the queen, as she told Mrs Siddons, was at times so overcome that her only refuge was to turn her back upon the stage, protesting that it was 'indeed too disagreeable'. Before long Mrs Siddons was summoned to read before the king at Buckingham House and Windsor and found in him a sympathetic and perceptive critic. He admired especially, he told her, her repose in certain situations – a quality which Garrick had lacked. 'He never could stand still', he said. 'He was a great fidget.'

Garrick had died three years before. His death, in Johnson's famous phrase, had 'eclipsed the gaiety of nations'; the magnificence of his funeral and his burial in Westminster Abbey were a tribute to the achievement of one who, in the equally famous words of Burke, had 'raised the character of his profession to a liberal art'. For Mrs Siddons, whose path had crossed his so briefly, one of the greatest moments following her success in *Isabella* had been her removal from an inconvenient upstairs dressing-room to one that had once been Garrick's. 'It is impossible to imagine my gratification', she wrote, 'when I saw my own figure in the self same glass which had so often reflected the face and form of that unequalled Genius, not perhaps without some vague, fanciful hope of a little degree of inspiration from it.'

Mrs Siddons played eighty times, in seven different parts, in her first season, though the strain of such continued exertion was so great that she frequently fainted at the end of a performance. This was nothing to the effect on her audiences; faintings and hysterics among the sensitive, and those who wished to be thought so, were commonplace. So accustomed did she become to playing amidst these disturbances that when, some time later, she was asked whether the frequent altercations which took place when late arrivals tried to force their way in did not disturb her, she replied that she was so used to playing amidst shrieks and groans that she scarcely noticed any further noise. The rush to get seats for her performances would start at breakfast time, the crush when the doors opened at six was almost unbearable, but those who managed to fight their way through to a place felt themselves amply rewarded from the first thrilling moment when she appeared. Never had a triumph in the theatre been so complete; never had the Tragic Muse gained such an ascendancy on the London stage.

II

The end of Mrs Siddons' first season might well have seen her in a mood to catch a respite from her exhausting labours. But Mrs Siddons, then, as for the rest of her career, was indefatigable in her quest for money; driven on perhaps by memories of early hardships, she was determined to make the most of her success in financial terms. Given this sense of insecurity and the energy with which she drove herself, it must have been galling, over the years, to see her hard won earnings squandered in unprofitable investments by her husband – William Siddons, unable to compete as an actor, was moving into the role of her business manager.

Unflagging therefore in her exertions, Mrs Siddons engaged herself to play at the Smock Alley Theatre in Dublin for the summer. Dublin society, revolving round the vice-regal court, considered itself as brilliant and fashionable as its London counterpart. Mrs Siddons' arrival had been eagerly awaited and the houses of the nobility were thrown open to her, but the Dublin critics, if only to assert their independence, were by no means all favourable. An anonymous account of her first night as Isabella made mock of her reception:

> On Saturday Mrs S –, about whom all the world has been talking, exposed her beautiful, adamantine, soft and lovely person, for the first time, at Smock-Alley theatre . . . She was nature itself! She was the most exquisite work of art! . . . Several fainted, even before the curtain drew up . . . The very fiddlers in the orchestra, 'albeit unused to the melting mood', blubbered like hungry children crying for their bread and butter . . . One hundred and nine ladies fainted! forty six went into fits! and ninety seven had strong hysterics! the world will scarcely credit the truth when they are told, that fourteen children, five old women, one hundred taylors and six common councilmen, were actually drowned in the inundation of tears that flowed from the galleries, lattices and boxes, to increase the briny pond in the pit.[1]

Mrs Siddons disliked ridicule; she disliked James Daly, the dissolute manager of the theatre who in his turn found her haughty and forbidding; and she disliked Dublin and its inhabitants. It was, she told a friend that summer, 'a sink of filthiness', while the people were all ostentation and insincerity, 'in their ideas of finery very like the French but not so cleanly'.[2] But she cleared more than a thousand pounds from her visit and when she returned to London she brought, as it were in her wake, her brother, John Philip Kemble, who for two years had been the leading actor at Smock Alley and now, with the way made open by his sister, was to make his début at Drury Lane.

*   *   *

John Philip Kemble, two years younger than his sister, had shared with her a strolling player's childhood though his parents, having higher ambitions for him, had sent him away at the age of twelve to train for the priesthood at the Roman Catholic college of Douay. (Kemble's father was a Catholic, his mother a Protestant, and according to the custom of the time he had been reared in his father's faith while his sisters were brought up in their mother's.) He had returned from France in 1775 with a classical education behind him and an unshakeable determination, whatever his parents' wishes, to make his career on the stage. He got no encouragement from them, indeed his father promptly turned him out, and the story of his early wanderings, at a time when strolling players were still legally classified with rogues and vagabonds, is one of hardships and humiliations. More than once – 'there are gripes and indigestion at the very thought', wrote Walter Scott in his essay on the actor – he was driven by hunger to make his supper on turnips in the open fields; and his tiffs with landladies and pursuit by angry creditors became the stuff of numerous derogatory and often, no doubt, apochryphal anecdotes. But in the words of Boaden, the indefatigable chronicler of the eighteenth-century theatre, 'we seldom find that feet which have once entered the charmed circle of the stage can avoid lingering about its limits', and there is something spirited and admirable in the way that Kemble rose above his circumstances. We read, for instance, how, being cast in the role of Ventidius in *All for Love*, he found himself embarrassed by his laundress's refusal to return his shirt until –

which was impossible – he had paid her bill. 'The rest of the company could boast no more than a lace ruffle between them, which he pinned to his right hand and wrapping his left hand in his substitute for a Roman cloak he went through the first act with great éclat; but justly supposing that his audience would conceive he could only use his right hand, he transferred the ruffle to the left in the next act; and so he went on, using either hand alternatively.'[3]

By the time he had reached Dublin, Kemble was long past such shifts. Thanks partly to his sister's influence, he had progressed by stages to the Yorkshire-based troupe of Tate Wilkinson, the best known of provincial actor-managers. During his years with Wilkinson, Kemble had not only studied his own art deeply but had tried his hand at authorship, composing verses, adapting plays and writing a full-fledged tragedy, *Belisarius*, in which he played the leading role along the Yorkshire circuit. Tall, roman-nosed, with a full share of his sister's classical good looks, he had a commanding presence on the stage and was noted already for his studied and intellectual approach to his parts. 'He never pulls out his handkerchief', wrote Leigh Hunt later, 'without a design upon the audience.'[4]

In Dublin, where he was engaged at a 'star' salary of £5 weekly, Kemble confirmed the reputation he had made in Yorkshire and was soon the most popular young actor in the place. Thanks to his friendship with the playwright Robert Jephson, who was attached to the vice-regal court and in whose play *The Count of Narbonne* (based on Horace Walpole's *The Castle of Otranto*) he had acted with conspicuous success, he was introduced to many of the local notables, his gravity and dignity and his reputation as a classical scholar ensuring his acceptance where other actors would have been looked at askance. The news of his sister's phenomenal success in London had shed further lustre on him and at a banquet given before her arrival in Dublin he had been gratified to hear the Earl of Inchiquin give the toast, 'The matchless Siddons!', and pass down a ring in which her likeness was set in diamonds, for his inspection.

Mrs Siddons had already introduced two of her sisters to Drury Lane, but though she could find them places, comments a theatrical historian, she could not make them actresses and they had met with little success. Her brother was a different matter; in John Philip

Kemble, they would have an actor of proven ability. Meanwhile Covent Garden, hoping to cash in on the Kemble fame, had engaged another of Mrs Siddons' brothers, Stephen, who was also acting at Smock Alley, but since he was very fat – he is best remembered by posterity for having played Falstaff without the stuffing* – rumour had it that they had mistaken the *fat* Mr Kemble for the *great* one.

*   *   *

From the memoirs of a fellow actor, John Bernard, we catch pleasing glimpses of Kemble's stay in Ireland. We see him helping Bernard, whose wife had fallen ill, with a loan of five pounds; we hear of his gallant rescue of a fellow actress, Miss Phillips, whom a group of drunken officers were trying to abduct from her dressing-room. We follow him, with the rest of Daly's company, on tour in Cork and Limerick and catch his tone of measured reproof when Bowles, the jester of the party, produced a skull which he had stolen from the local churchyard as a property for *Hamlet*, from under his waistcoat at supper: 'Really – er – Mr Bowles – if you go on in this manner – it will be – dan – ger – ous to travel with you.'

Shortly before his departure from Dublin Kemble bade farewell to his fellow actress, Elizabeth Inchbald, who had been spending the summer season at Smock Alley and had fallen foul of Daly half way through. The manager's assumption that he had *droits de seigneur* over the ladies in his company, and his determination to assert them, by blackmail if necessary, made him a dangerous employer. (Only a year before Dorothy Francis, later the celebrated Mrs Jordan, whom he had seduced and made pregnant, had fled to England to escape him.) Mrs Inchbald had indignantly rejected his approaches and had found herself jobless in mid-season. A fervent Catholic, she was resolutely virtuous and would spend much of her time rejecting the dis-honourable proposals of her numerous admirers – enamoured but unwilling to marry a penniless actress. In any case, she was in love, and had been for some time, with John Philip Kemble, and he him-self, though never, she declared, her lover, had 'knelt at her shrine

* 'We see no more reason why Mr Stephen Kemble should play Falstaff', commented Hazlitt when he played it in 1816, 'than why Louis XVIII is qualified to fill a throne because he is fat and belongs to a particular family.'

and felt her dazzling power'.[6] The hero of her best known novel, *A Simple Story*, was said to have been drawn from Kemble, and though the novel was not completed until 1791, its early chapters, in which the hero is introduced, were written soon after she first met him. She describes him thus:

His figure was tall and handsome, but his face, except for a pair of bright dark eyes, a set of white teeth and a graceful fall in his clerical curls of brown hair, had not one feature in it to excite admiration – he possessed notwithstanding such a gleam of sensibility diffused over each that many mistook his face for handsome and almost all were more or less attracted by it – in a word the charm that is here meant to be described is a countenance – on his countenance you beheld the feelings of his heart – saw all its inmost workings – the quick pulses that beat with hope or fear, the placid ones that were stationary with patient resignation.

She herself, some four years older than Kemble, was a figure no less attractive. Sprightly and very pretty, with reddish gold hair and fair, lightly freckled skin, she was, in the opinion of Charles Lamb, the only tolerable clever woman he had ever met. Her magnetism owed nothing to conventional aids to beauty; but though plainly, indeed shabbily dressed, for she was badly off and skimped herself to help a needy family, she was the despair of other women who found themselves deserted by the men at any gathering where she was present. On stage, despite her looks, she did not shine, her main impediment to success being a stammer which she had subdued but never wholly overcome.

She was now a widow and childless, though when Kemble first met her in 1778 she was still married and she and her husband, together with Sarah and William Siddons, had been acting in Liverpool. The five of them spent much time together, Mr Inchbald, a scene-painter and portrait-painter as well as an actor, occupying his spare moments with painting, Kemble reading and studying French with Mrs Inchbald, Mrs Siddons, laying aside her tragic majesty, washing and ironing for her children and in the evening playing cards or singing duets with her brother. Mrs Inchbald's journal at this time,

Boaden tells us, recorded almost daily altercations with her husband and visits no less frequent from Kemble.

When Inchbald, who was twenty years older than his wife, died of a heart attack, Kemble composed a funeral ode and an elaborate Latin inscription for his tomb, but though he continued to call on Mrs Inchbald and rumour linked their names together, he showed no signs of proposing. She would certainly have accepted him. 'Dear heart, I'd have j-jumped at you', she said with her charming stammer when he asked her jocularly years later if she would have thought of marrying him. But Kemble's chief interest, then as always, was in his career. Just as Dorriforth, the hero of her novel *A Simple Story*, a priest who is released from his vows in order to marry and perpetuate an ancient Catholic title, is severe and inflexible in the pursuit of his religion, so Kemble allowed nothing to divert him from his ambitions in the theatre. Mrs Inchbald was too spirited and too independent-minded to be the kind of wife he needed. As if she sensed the incompatibility between their temperaments, the marriage between Miss Milner, the headstrong heroine, and Dorriforth is shown to end disastrously.

Mrs Inchbald was on the brink of a successful career as a novelist and playwright. Kemble admired her talents and encouraged them. 'Now to *your* writings', he wrote in an early letter. 'Pray how far are you advanced in your novel? – what new characters have you in it – what situations? how many distressed damsels and valorous knights? how many prudes, how many coquettes? what libertines, what senti-mental rogues in black and empty cutthroats in red? . . .'[7]

From her in his apprentice days he sought advice on acting. Eager to improve himself, he would discuss the playing of a role down to the details of dress. Preparing to play the part of Sir Giles Overreach in *A New Way to Pay Old Debts*, in which she had appeared with Henderson, the leading actor at Covent Garden, he wrote:

What kind of hat does Mr Henderson wear? What kind of Wig? – of Cravat? – of Ruffles? – of Cloaths? – of Stockings, with or without embroidered Cloaks? – Square or round-toed shoes? I shall be uneasy if I have not an Idea of his Dress, even to the shape of his Buckles and what Rings he wears on his Hands.[8]

He had the highest opinion of her judgment, whether on acting or business matters, about which he frequently consulted her. But he backed away from any closer connection, and during their time in Dublin there seems to have been some awkwardness between them. From her diary for that year, writes Boaden, 'there appear some ingenuous wishes on her part that he would declare himself in form. She reads his books; writes to him; has notes, sometimes beautiful and at others *strange*. When he calls she either welcomes him or refuses him admittance; he yields to her humour for a while but returns and is again in favour . . .'[9]

They remained good friends enough, however, for Kemble to take temporary possession of her lodgings when he first arrived in London. 'You know, I imagine before now,' he wrote en route from Ireland, 'that I shall be Lord of your Tenement in about a fortnight – I understand moreover, that I am to enter it just as it is – you won't surely be so cruel as to be aiding or consenting to the removal of any Part of the Furniture . . .'[10]

He continued to pay his fair friend many compliments, reported Boaden, but ambition had now taken full possession of him. His début at Drury Lane, the most important moment of his career till then, was due to take place on September 30th. The play was *Hamlet*, and in the quiet of his borrowed lodgings he set himself to study for it, determined if he could to emulate his sister's fame.

III

Drury Lane, at the time of Kemble's arrival, shared with Covent Garden the monopoly of spoken drama in London by patents deriving from the reign of Charles II and reconfirmed in 1737. A third theatre, the Theatre Royal in the Haymarket, was allowed by royal concession to play straight drama in the summer months during the time the other two theatres were closed. Of the two main theatres, Drury Lane, despite Sheridan's erratic rule, had the commanding position, a position whose importance in the life of the capital it is hard to over-estimate. 'The theatre engrossed the minds of men to such a degree', wrote Arthur Murphy in his life of David Garrick, '. . . that there existed in England a *fourth estate*, King, Lords and Commons and *Drury Lane Playhouse*.' As a social centre for all classes except the very lowest, it drew a cross-section of London society whose divisions, in the theatre itself, were roughly defined – in the boxes the aristocracy, above them merchants and prosperous tradesmen, in the upper gallery the working classes, in the pit an indiscriminate collection that ranged from footmen to young bloods and professional men. As a source of entertainment and excitement it rivalled and often outstripped politics, though it is true to say that in an age of great oratory in Parliament and heroic declamation on the stage the differences between the two had never been less.

The theatre's repertoire, like that of Covent Garden, was as catholic as the composition of its audiences. On each evening there would be a main piece, lasting two to three hours, followed by an after-piece, usually of a light or humorous nature and often accompanied by music and dancing. It was perfectly normal to see, say, *King Lear* and a pantomime in a single evening's entertainment, though those who thought that five hours in the crowded and uncomfortable conditions of the pit were too much might come in after the second act of the main piece for half price. On Siddons nights, the theatre tended to empty after her performance was over and the spirits of those who remained, complained the comedians who followed her, were so depressed that all their efforts were in vain.

Operas sung in English, the music often linked by spoken dialogue, alternated with straight drama at Covent Garden and Drury Lane; and a fourth theatre, the King's Theatre in the Haymarket, presented exclusively Italian opera and ballet. In drama Shakespeare still held pride of place, though it was a Shakespeare so altered and 'improved' by later writers that it was sometimes scarcely recognisable. Tragedy, Shakespeare apart, tended to be Augustan and heroic, the blank verse in which it was written being used, rather as music is in opera, to heighten emotion. Less declamatory, and showing the first glimmerings of romantic feeling, were gothic plays such as Jephson's *The Count of Narbonne,* in which hermits, ruins and mysterious apparitions were staple ingredients. In comedy the golden years which had brought forth Sheridan's *The School for Scandal* and Goldsmith's *She Stoops to Conquer* were over, but they continued, as they have done ever since, to hold the stage. Beneath these two summits of achievement were a number of well constructed comedies, usually in the sentimental genre, in which virtue was rewarded after three acts of false situations and mistaken identities. In both tragedy and comedy the proportion of new works to established favourites was relatively small. It was the actor, rather than the novelty of the work, which drew the town.

A sense of intimacy between actors and audiences was fostered by the construction of the theatre, with a forestage jutting well out into the audience and boxes above the side exits, and by the fact that stage and auditorium remained fully lit and thus not differentiated from each other during performances. It was not long since Garrick had abolished the presence of spectators on the stage itself, their familiarities and interruptions having become intolerable – on one occasion, in Dublin, when Garrick was playing Lear, a drunken gallant had thrust his hand into the bosom of the dying Cordelia, and had been so incensed by Garrick's look of indignation that he had searched for him through the house to chastise him after the performance. It was a tribute to the ascendancy Garrick had won for himself that he was able to put an end to such things but it had not been done without strong opposition and the audience, though dismissed from the stage itself, still considered themselves very much the arbiters of what went on in the theatre. They had responded to Mrs Siddons with ecstatic enthusiasm; they were equally likely to greet a play or actor they disliked with riotous disapproval. The actors, in their turn, would sometimes answer back; at the first night of *The Rivals*, for instance, when the actor playing Sir Lucius O'Trigger, amid violent barracking from the Irish section of the audience, was hit by an apple from the pit, he stepped forward and without abandoning his brogue exclaimed, 'By the powers, is it personal? Is it me or the matter?' But too much spirit on an actor's part was not advisable. Even Garrick had been forced to his knees by a rioting audience; and in the end actors and managers had to comply with the fundamental law expressed by Johnson in a prologue written for Garrick's opening night as manager of the theatre:

> The drama's laws the drama's patrons give,
> For we who live to please must please to live.

In 1775 Drury Lane had been remodelled and redecorated by Robert Adam and the auditorium in pale green, pink and bronze-green vied with the stage in the splendour of its effect. Scenery itself was confined to a shallow stage behind the proscenium, or forestage, and consisted usually of a painted backcloth and a series of flats which were slid into place along grooves in the floor and superstructure of the stage. During his period as manager Garrick had introduced distinguished artists such as de Loutherbourg whose romantically naturalistic scenery – rigid side-wings replaced by broken irregular shapes, and the use of transparencies and lighting to create such dramatic effects as moonlight, fire and volcanoes erupting – marked a striking advance in stage design. Garrick himself, after a visit to Paris, had reorganised the lighting of the stage, replacing the circular overhead chandeliers which so often incongruously lit the forest of Arden or a blasted heath by lines of oil lights behind battens which lit the stage from the wings and front of the proscenium. In costume, though de Loutherbourg and other scenic artists were beginning to aim at authenticity in their settings, there was still no attempt at historical accuracy. Fanny Kemble, in her memoirs, describes her aunt Mrs Siddons playing the Grecian

Euphrasia in full panoply of feathers, powdered hair and vast hooped skirts; Garrick played Macbeth in the scarlet and gold of an officer of the Grenadier Guards; and Kemble, when he made his début as Hamlet, was dressed, according to Boaden, in 'modern court dress of rich black velvet, with a star on the breast, the garter and pendant ribband of an order – mourning sword and buckles, with deep ruffles: the hair in powder; which, in the scenes of feigned distraction, flowed dishevelled in front and over the shoulders'.

* * *

'How very like his sister!' was the most frequently repeated comment when on September 30th, 1783 Kemble made his first appearance at Drury Lane. Clad in black velvet as described, and wearing upon his brow 'the burden of intolerable woe', his performance was studied, graceful, suffused with sensibility. For some critics it was over-studied: his courtly graces, said one, were more suited to a dancing master than a prince. He was criticised, too, for pedantry: great play was made of his 'new readings' of certain lines. Shakespearean idolatry, which Garrick had done so much to forward, was at its height; Shakespearean commentary was a prestigious occupation in learned circles and a wealth of controversy was engendered, for instance, by Kemble's change of emphasis from the commonly accepted, 'Did you not *speak* to it?' when questioning Horatio about the ghost to, 'Did *you* not speak to it?'. Such debate, however, only served to under-line the feeling that Kemble was an actor to be taken seriously, and his début, though less sensationally successful than his sister's, immediately established him in the forefront of his profession.

Comparisons were inevitably made with Garrick, though as yet the young actor could not compare with his predecessor. Garrick had sprung to fame, as it were, fully armed; Kemble's acting, based on study and reflection, was in a continual state of improvement throughout his career. Nor could there have been a greater contrast in manner and appearance between the two.

'Garrick', wrote Walter Scott, 'was short though well formed, airy and light in all his movements, possessed of a countenance capable of the most acute or the most stolid, the most tragic or most ridiculous expression. Kemble, on the contrary, was tall and stately,

34

his person on a scale suited for the stage and almost too large for a private apartment, with a countenance like the finest models of the antique and motions and manners corresponding to the splendid cast of his form and features. Mirth, when he exhibited it, never exceeded a species of gaiety chastened with gravity; his smile seemed always as if it were the rare inhabitant of that noble countenance.'[1]

Kemble had to contend with other rivals than Garrick's shade, however, before he could achieve the unassailable position that was his sister's. At Covent Garden John Henderson, who since Garrick's death had been regarded as the first actor of the day, carried on the tradition of spontaneous, fiery playing which the grander, more declamatory style of Kemble would supersede, and which would be revived again with the arrival of Edmund Kean. Even Garrick, it was said, had been jealous of Henderson. His untimely death in 1785 would remove Kemble's most serious rival; but though Kemble's superiority in talent would be less and less in question, his inferiority in precedence and age – he was twenty-six at the time of his début – was a considerable disadvantage at Drury Lane where the established actors, Smith, Palmer and Brereton, were unwilling to give up the major parts they were accustomed to play and by tradition could not be deprived of them.

His best opening lay in parts not already bespoken, playing opposite Mrs Siddons, whose patronage of her relations, however, was beginning to provoke a counter-reaction in the press:

With Kembles on Kembles they've choked Drury Lane.
The family rubbish have seized public bounty
And Kings, Queens and Heroes pour forth from each county.
The barns are unpeopled – their half famished sons
Waste the regions of taste like th'irruption of Huns.[2]

No less than five members of the Kemble family were playing on the London stage that season. Frances and Elizabeth, Mrs Siddons' sisters, though they had something of her beauty had none of her talents; criticism and their lack of success, already noticed, would soon drive them from the boards of Drury Lane, Frances into the arms of the Shakespearean scholar and commentator, Francis Twiss, Elizabeth to the United States where, married to a theatre manager, she made a name for herself as Mrs Siddons' sister. Stephen Kemble had made his début as Othello at Covent Garden a day before his brother John who, together with Mrs Siddons, had loyally attended the performance. The evening had not gone well; Stephen Kemble, said the *London Magazine*, had 'seemed to labour earnestly but in vain'. Before long he, too, would leave London to become the manager of the Theatre Royal in Edinburgh.

Meanwhile Kemble and Mrs Siddons had made their first joint appearance in *The Gamester*, a moralising domestic tragedy, on November 30th. Kemble's Beverley, wrote the *Public Advertiser*, 'was all we could wish; his manner peculiar as it was, gave us some home Sensations'. Mrs Siddons, as Mrs Beverley, gave a heart-rending performance. Leigh Hunt, years later, described 'the widow's mute stare of perfected misery by the corpse of the gamester Beverley'[3] as one of the sublimest pieces of acting on the English stage, and Macready, playing with her at the end of her career, gives a vivid description of the same scene:

> The climax to her sorrows and sufferings was in the dungeon, when on her knees, holding her dying husband, he dropped lifeless from her arms. Her glaring eyes were fixed in stony blankness on his face; the powers of life seemed suspended in her; her sister and Lewson gently raised her and slowly led her unresisting from the body, her gaze never for an instant averted from it; when they reached the prison door she stopped, as if awakened from a trance, uttered a shriek of agony that would have pierced the hardest heart, and rushing from them, flung herself as if for union in death, on the prostrate form before her.[4]

Less immediately successful, but ultimately one of their great performances in partnership, was their playing of Constance and King John in Shakespeare's *King John*. Mrs Siddons' notes, penned some years later, give a striking insight into the concentration which she brought to any major role:

> Whenever I was called upon to personate the character of Constance, I never, from the beginning of the play to the end of my part in it, once suffered my dressing-room door to be closed,

in order that my attention might be constantly fixed on those distressing events which I could hear going on upon the stage, the
terrible effects of which progress were to be represented by me.
Moreover, I never omitted to place myself, with Arthur in my
hand, to hear the march, when, upon the reconciliation of England
and France, they enter the gates of Angiers to ratify the contract
of marriage between the Dauphin and the Lady Blanche; because
the sickening sounds of that march would usually cause the bitter
tears of rage, disappointment, betrayed confidence, baffled ambition, and above all, the agonising feelings of maternal affection, to
gush into my eyes. In short, the spirit of the whole drama took
possession of my mind and frame, by my attention being per-
petually riveted to the passing scenes.[5]

*   *   *

In an age when the grand manner of Reynolds dominated English
painting it was fitting that Mrs Siddons, who with her brother came
to epitomise the same lofty style in acting,* should be the subject of
one of his most celebrated paintings – his portrait of her as the
Tragic Muse. She sat to him during the autumn of 1783, and the
pose, suggestive of one of Michelangelo's Sibyls, was of her own
choosing. At her first sitting, she recalled in her reminiscences, 'after
many more gratifying encomiums than I dare repeat, he took me by
the hand, saying, "Ascend your undisputed throne and graciously
bestow upon me some grand Idea of the Tragick Muse." I walked up
the steps and seated myself instantly in the attitude in which she now
appears.' When the canvas was completed and framed Reynolds
signed his name on the edge of her dress, for, he told her gallantly,
'I have resolved to go down to posterity on the hem of your
garment.'[6]

Reynolds had the highest admiration for Mrs Siddons. As a painter
he particularly approved of the simplicity of her dress and the way
she did her hair. Though for a time she followed current fashions on

* Boaden quotes Reynolds' thirteenth Academy 'Discourse' on the grand style in acting
– the necessity for the actor to pitch his performance on a higher plane than that of
everyday life, the subordination of parts to a harmonious whole – as summing up the
lifelong principles on which Kemble strove to base his art.

the stage, she was one of the first to move from wide hoops and long stiff stays to dresses that were high-waisted, loose and flowing. She was one of the first, too, to wear her hair unpowdered, braided into a small compass so as to show the shape and size of her head, rather than piled high in pomatum-plastered curls.

During this autumn, too, she made the acquaintance of Dr Johnson, who though too old and infirm to see her act, pronounced himself most favourably impressed by her. 'She behaved with great modesty and propriety', he wrote to Mrs Thrale, 'and left nothing behind her to be either censured or despised. Neither praise nor money, those two great corruptors of mankind, seem to have depraved her. I shall be glad to see her again.'[7]

Kemble, as a rising if not yet risen star, was also favoured with an invitation to take tea with the Doctor, who, despite the celebrated dictum of his earlier days that players were no better than dancing dogs, still took a lively interest in the affairs of the theatre. Speaking of acting to Kemble, he asked him whether he was one of those enthusiasts who felt himself transformed into the very character he was acting. Kemble replied that he had never felt so strong a conviction himself. 'To be sure, Sir', said Johnson, 'the thing is impossible. And if Garrick really believed himself to be that monster Richard III he deserved to be hanged every time he performed it.'[8]

The social progress of both the Kembles kept pace with their theatrical success. Kemble, less established than his sister, moved chiefly in learned circles, and held his own as a scholar and a commentator on his favourite Shakespeare. Mrs Siddons, though her children and her acting left her little time to attend great gatherings, was courted and adored by the aristocracy. 'Perhaps no actress before or since', commented Boaden admiringly, 'ever possessed an equal intimacy with fashionable life.' It is hard now to imagine the extraordinary deference shown to the nobility in those days, a deference that took account of the power and influence then wielded by the great landed families, and it would be easy to mock Mrs Siddons and her brother for their cultivation of the great. But they made themselves respected, as no actors before them had been, in return. It was not long since the Duchess of Devonshire had been in doubt whether Sheridan, as the son of an actor, should be invited to her house and even Garrick, who had done so much to raise the standing of his profession, was accepted more as an entertainer than an equal. Mrs Siddons, whom shyness and an incapacity for small talk made especially aloof, was more than accepted, she could overawe her aristocratic company: Northcote, the painter, speaks of seeing 'young ladies of the quality, Lady Marys and Lady Dorothys, peeping into a room where Mrs Siddons was sitting, with all the same timidity and curiosity as if it were some praeternatural being'.[9]

IV

Mrs Inchbald had greeted the success of Kemble's début with genuine pleasure though her mood at the time was unhappy* and her own theatrical career was in the doldrums. Four years before, with high hopes, she had joined the company at Covent Garden under the management of Thomas Harris, who like so many others was quick to succumb to her charm. Mrs Inchbald had repulsed his too forthright advances by pulling his hair – 'I don't know what I would have done if he had w-worn a w-wig',[1] she commented, but neither she nor Harris took offence. There was nothing of the prig about her; it would have been hard to be one in the atmosphere of the time when to have fixed the shades of virtue among the ladies of the theatre, as she observes in a fragment of autobiography, would have been employment for an able casuist:

'One evening about half an hour before the curtain was drawn up, some accident having happened in the drawing room of one of the actresses, a woman of known intrigue, she ran in haste to the dressing room of Mrs Wells, to finish the business of her toilet. Mrs Wells, who was the mistress of the well-known Captain Topham, shocked at the intrusion of a reprobated woman, who had a worse character than herself, quitted her own room and ran to Miss Farren's crying, "What would Captain Topham say if I were to remain in such company?" No sooner had she entered the room, to which as an asylum she had fled, than Miss Farren (the mistress of the Earl of Derby) flew out at the door repeating, "What would Lord Derby say if I were to remain in such company?" ' – the chain reaction continuing to the dressing-room of a lady supposed, 'but not very accurately', to be respectably married.[2]

Mrs Inchbald had never advanced beyond the second rank as an actress at Covent Garden. Her salary varied between a humble two

---

* A memorandum in her papers headed 'An Account of my Septembers' gives a yearly barometer of Mrs Inchbald's state of mind. The entry for 1783 reads, 'Unhappy'; that for the following year, after her success as a playwright, 'Happy'.

and three pounds a week, she was humiliated by having to play walk-on parts in pantomime and her roles in more exalted works were few and far between. But she was still continuing to write. Her novel, with its portrait of Kemble, had been temporarily set aside – the Gordon riots with their cry of 'No Popery' three years earlier may well have convinced her that the time was not ripe for a novel with a Catholic hero. But she had had a farce accepted by Harris for which, though it was not performed, he had paid her £20. In the spring of 1784, she sent another, *A Mogul Tale*, to George Colman, the owner of the Haymarket Theatre. Its theme had been suggested by the contemporary craze for ballooning, and it followed in a light-hearted fashion the adventures of a party of balloonists, wafted from Wapping to the seraglio of the Grand Mogul. The piece took Colman's fancy: he paid her a hundred guineas for it, and since she herself was engaged at this theatre for the summer season, she was able to take part in it when it opened on July 6th. The name of the author was not revealed, but so great was her emotion when she first had to speak on stage that she was struck dumb by terror and met her cue with a protracted silence. At last, very slowly and in sepulchral tones, she stammered out her words – 'H-hyde Pa-ark Co-orner' – to the astonishment, and then as her own relieved laughter set them off, to the merriment of the audience. The play, enlivened with music and dancing, was an immediate success. Mrs Inchbald's authorship did not remain a secret for long; suddenly and to her great delight she found herself a celebrity, sought after and made much of in the small world of the London theatre.

From Liverpool, where Kemble was spending the summer season, he wrote to congratulate her in a letter characteristically self-absorbed and for the moment almost rueful. Despite his *Belisarius* and a published volume of 'fugitive verses', he knew his own literary talent to be slight:

My dear Madam,
Next to yourself, nobody could be more inclin'd to think highly of your Productions than I am; but alas! my poetical days I believe, are gone by – in my best Pretensions, I was but an indifferent Rhymer; nor in my vainest Moments ever thought

41

anything I did fit to be call'd Poetry – I have ransack'd my Brains for apt Parallels – but to no Purpose – I cannot pay you a Compliment in verse too high for what I truly think of you in Prose – and I might tell you, that Poetry is too essentially fictitious to answer the Purposes of real Esteem, and to express deserved Praise – The Fault however at present is in me, not in the Art – I repeated you some Lines of my Translation from Ovid, when I was in Town – I thought to have finished the Epistle in the Country – but no such thing – I have labour'd and labour'd so long in vain at it, that it is now thrown aside from an absolute Conscience of wasting so much time to no manner of Purpose. The Truth is, my Health declines every day – I have neither Spirits, in which I never abounded – nor Genius, of which Inclination, perhaps, wholly supply'd the Place – to attempt anything for my Improvement in polite letters – you know me, I believe, well enough to feel for me, when I say, that with all my Ambition I am afraid I shall live and die a common Fellow . . . If I cou'd write, I wou'd – I cannot – so you must receive Esteem instead of Flattery and Sincerity for Wit, when I swear there is no Woman I more truly admire, nor any Man whose abilities I more highly value.[3]

*   *   *

While Kemble, temporarily discouraged, spent the summer in Liverpool, Mrs Siddons set out in pursuit of new triumphs in Edinburgh and Dublin. In Edinburgh her arrival produced the usual sensation and only the theatre manager – with whom, through her husband, she drove so hard a bargain that his takings at the end of her stay were only a third of hers – was not enraptured by her. So great were the crowds at the theatre, and so frequent the cases of collapse from the heat and hurly-burly there, that the doctors spoke of 'Siddons fever' as a current summer ailment. As Lady Randolph in *Douglas*,* and then in *Isabella*, she played to a chorus of shrieks and groans; at one performance of the latter a certain Miss Gordon of

* By the Scottish playwright John Home. One of the most popular tragedies of the eighteenth and early nineteenth centuries, it was a source of great national pride – at its first night, in 1756, a voice from the audience had cried, 'Whaur's yer Wully Shakespeare noo?'

Gight was so overcome by Mrs Siddons' piteous cry of 'Oh my Biron! My Biron!' that she was carried out in hysterics, repeating the words again and again – an omen perhaps of her marriage, two years later, to Captain Jack Byron, and the birth of their son, the poet.

From Edinburgh, at the end of June, Mrs Siddons set sail for Ireland, and here, though her summer included such social delights as a visit to Shane's Castle where the luxury of the establishment, she wrote, 'inspired recollections of an Arabian night's entertainment',[4] the good luck which had followed her through the last two years, years to which she would always look back with wonder and delight, deserted her. The fault was partly hers, partly that of a malicious press, but above all perhaps the fickle public's, for whom no figure, however admired, can remain an idol for too long.

Mrs Siddons' phenomenal success had not been achieved without making enemies in her profession. Her patronage of her family was resented, her natural reserve off stage could be taken for arrogance and hauteur. Already, during the previous season, there had been signs that a cabal, mounted by her theatrical enemies, was preparing in the press. With her genius and her virtue beyond question, it was on the grounds of her supposed close-fistedness in money matters that she was attacked. Thoroughly professional, Mrs Siddons never short-changed a manager or an audience over a performance, but with four children, and the prospect of future pregnancies ever in her mind, she was eager to make all the money she could. In the eyes of her critics she was over-eager, even ruthless, an impression which gained seeming support from two episodes in Dublin, each hinging on her appearance or non-appearance in the benefit performance of a fellow actor.

The first of these, William Brereton, had acted Jaffier to Mrs Siddons' Belvidera in *Venice Preserved* and had been so carried away by his role as her lover that, in the words of Boaden, 'in kindling his imagination the divinity unsettled his reason and in clasping the goddess he became sensible of the charms of the woman'[5] – or, more simply, he had fallen in love with her. Mrs Siddons, except on stage, had been unresponsive, and the arrival of her brother the following season and her preference for him as a partner had changed Brereton's feeling to ill-concealed resentment, intensified by growing mental instability – he would be confined to an asylum after a suicide attempt not long afterwards. Mrs Siddons had agreed to play in his benefit performance, when the evening's takings, by arrangement with Daly, would go to him; her presence, as a certain draw, would ensure the success of the occasion. In the event, however, she fell ill, and having been confined to bed for a fortnight with an inflamed throat and high fever, felt obliged to cancel the performance on the grounds that, already committed by her contract to play three nights that week for Daly, her health was not equal to a further appearance. Brereton, who had been relying on the benefit to make his visit to Dublin profitable, made no secret of his resentment, and almost immediately the rumour, which he did nothing to deny and probably fostered, that she had unreasonably refused to play for him, or alternatively, that she had demanded an exorbitant fee for doing so, began to circulate in the press.

The second episode concerned a veteran actor, West Digges, who suffered a paralytic stroke half way through the season. Mrs Siddons had been asked to appear in a performance to raise money for him and had at first refused, having promised her only available evening for a charity performance in aid of the Marshalsea prison. Later, thinking Digges' case the more deserving, she changed her mind and appeared for him *gratis* at the end of the season in *Venice Preserved*. By the time the performance took place, however, the Smock Alley company had left Dublin to go on tour, and she and her husband had been obliged to do the best they could with a makeshift company of supporting actors. The receipts and the performance had suffered accordingly and since West Digges was too ill or unwilling to acknowledge his obligation to her publicly, she got no credit for her tardy generosity but was accused instead of having demanded money from him before agreeing to play.

Mrs Siddons returned to London, where only a few weeks before she had been the object of universal admiration, to meet a storm of criticism in the press. She was accused of avarice and callous indifference to the misfortunes of her fellow actors; she was dared to show whether, in her entire career, she had ever done a generous action. In vain her husband sent an open letter to the papers, explaining the circumstances in each case; his letter, detailing her nightly payment – £50 in Dublin, and the reduced fee, £20, which she would have charged to Brereton – lacked the dignity of a straight denial; and a letter from Brereton exculpating her was so curtly and coldly expressed as to carry no conviction. From West Digges, for the time being, there was no word, the mails from Ireland having been held up by storms in the Irish Channel.

Matters had reached this point when on October 6th Mrs Siddons made her opening appearance of the London season. The play was *The Gamester*, and Kemble, as before, was Beverley to her Mrs Beverley – she had chosen the play perhaps to have his support in her ordeal. Brereton and his wife were also taking part and Mrs Brereton, as Beverley's sister, was to appear with Mrs Siddons in her opening scene. In the furious uproar which greeted Mrs Siddons when she first appeared, Mrs Brereton, noted a spectator, 'was mean enough to sneak off and leave her to face the insults of a malicious party, tho' she knew the whole disturbance was on her account and her husband at least had been obliged to contradict the reports that concerned him.'[6] Alone in the midst of the stage Mrs Siddons made several vain attempts to speak. 'At length', she recalled with a gratitude still vivid when she came to write her memoirs forty years later, 'a Gentleman stood forth in the middle of the front of the pit impelled by benevolent and manly feeling for the oppressed, who, as I advanced to make my last attempt at being heard, accosted me in these words: "For heaven's Sake, madam, do not degrade yourself by an apology for there is nothing necessary to be said." '[7] His words were followed by a clamour so prolonged that Kemble, indignant at his sister's treatment, came forward to hurry her from the stage; Mrs Siddons, self-possessed until that moment, no sooner left it than she fainted in his arms. The audience, left to themselves, gradually began to quieten down while behind the scenes, as soon as she had somewhat recovered, Mrs Siddons was urged by her brother, her husband and the anxious Sheridan to go and confront them once more – 'that audience by whom I had been so cruelly and unjustly degraded and where, but in consideration of my children, I never would have appeared again.

'Great and pleasant was my astonishment', she continued, 'to find myself on the second rising of the curtain, received with a silence so profound that I was absolutely awestruck, and never yet have I been able to account for this surprising contrast; for I really think that the falling of a pin might then have been heard upon the stage.'

She had come to the theatre expecting trouble, with a speech already prepared, in which her brother, a more skilful writer than her husband, had had a hand:

'Ladies and gentlemen, the kind and flattering partiality which I have uniformly experienced in this place, would make the present interruption distressing to me indeed, were I, in the slightest degree, conscious of having deserved your censure. I feel no such consciousness. The stories which have been circulated against me are calumnies; when they shall be proved to be true my aspersors will be justified. But till then my respect for the public leads me to be confident that I shall be protected from unmerited insult.'

This speech, with its appeal to the chivalry of the audience, was received with repeated bursts of applause, but Mrs Siddons was close to collapsing again as she left the stage, and so great was her agitation that King, the stage manager, came forward to beg a few moments' indulgence before the play began. 'She was soon sufficiently composed', wrote Boaden, who had witnessed the whole event, 'to throw her whole mind into the character of Mrs Beverley and perhaps never produced greater effect.'[8]

The shock of this evening had a profound effect on Mrs Siddons. A second letter to the papers from Brereton, alarmed at the furies he had unleashed, and one from Digges soon after, sufficiently cleared her of the charges against her and though the disturbances in the theatre continued on a lesser scale for some nights, she was soon restored to her position in the public favour. But for a long time after, she told a friend, her joy in her profession left her, and she sickened at the thought of being an actress. Nonetheless, it was from this mood, and with a courage steeled by her recent ordeal, that she was to rise to the role of Lady Macbeth, the greatest achievement of her career.

*   *   *

Years later, in a note for her biographer Thomas Campbell, Mrs Siddons described:

It was my custom to study my characters at night, when all the domestic cares and business of the day were over. On the night preceding that in which I was to appear in this part for the first time, I shut myself up as usual, when all the family were retired, and commenced my study of Lady Macbeth. As the character is very short, I thought I should soon accomplish it. Being then only twenty years of age, I believed, as many others do believe, that little more was necessary than to get the words into my head; for the necessity of discrimination, and the development of character, at that time of my life, had scarcely entered into my imagination. But to proceed. I went on with tolerable composure, in the silence of the night (a night I never can forget), till I came to the assassination scene, when the horrors of the scene rose to a degree that made it impossible for me to get farther. I snatched up my candle, and hurried out of the room in a paroxysm of terror. My dress was of silk, and the rustling of it, as I ascended the stairs to go to bed, seemed to my panic-struck fancy like the movement of a spectre pursuing me. At last I reached my chamber, where I found my husband fast asleep. I clapt my candlestick down upon the table, without the power of putting the candle out; and I threw myself on my bed, without daring to stay even to take off my clothes.[9]

Since arriving at Drury Lane Mrs Siddons had played in only two Shakespearean parts – Isabella in *Measure for Measure* and Constance in *King John* – and her detractors had murmured that she dared not trust herself to Shakespeare's greatest roles. In choosing Lady Macbeth, as she did for her benefit performance that February, she not only aimed at the dramatic heights but challenged the memory of Mrs Pritchard, the greatest of Lady Macbeths, whose performance, with Garrick as Macbeth, had become a legend; after her death in 1766, save once at the request of the King of Denmark, Garrick never played the part again. Kemble once compared Garrick and Mrs Pritchard in Zoffany's famous painting of the dagger scene to a cook and butler quarrelling over a kitchen knife and Mrs Siddons could find some consolation too in Dr Johnson's comments on Mrs Pritchard when she had visited him the previous year. 'Madam', he said, 'she was a vulgar idiot. She never read any part of the Play except her own part, and she said *gownd*.'[10] Nonetheless, with the recent disturbances in the theatre still fresh in the public memory and her position as favourite not long restored, a failure as Lady Macbeth could prove near fatal to her career.

She prepared for the role, she wrote, with the greatest diffidence and terror, to which the fear of Mrs Pritchard's reputation added. On the evening of the benefit, when she had finished dressing and was composing herself, as her custom was, before the performance, she was disturbed by Sheridan who insisted urgently on seeing her. He had heard, he said, that she was intending in the sleep-walking scene to act without carrying the candle in her hand; he had come to remonstrate with her and beg her to change her plan. To Mrs Siddons' protests that the action of washing her hands to rid herself of the 'damned spot' would then be impossible, he replied that Mrs Pritchard had always played the part with a candle and that it would be considered a presumptuous innovation by the audience. But Mrs Siddons' mind was made up; in her agitation before the performance it was too late to change it, though such were Sheridan's persuasive powers that had he asked her earlier she would have done so against her better judgment.

In the triumphant evening that followed, the sleep-walking scene was her most applauded moment. It was true that her dress, a sweeping white garment half way between a nightgown and a robe, was criticised. 'Lady Macbeth is supposed to be *asleep* and not *mad*', wrote the *Morning Post* next day, 'so that custom itself cannot be alleged as a justification for her appearance in white sattin.'* But her actions on entering the stage – setting down the light and washing her hands, pouring water from an imaginary ewer as she did so – established a tradition for generations of Lady Macbeths, and the audience, enthralled, accepted them at once.

'Behold her now', she wrote later in her own notes on the role, 'with wasted form, with wan and haggard countenance, her starry eyes glazed with the ever-burning fever of remorse . . . whether waking or asleep the smell of innocent blood incessantly haunts her

* White, by tradition, was the colour associated with madness on the stage – thus Sheridan's famous stage direction in *The Critic:* 'Enter Tilburnia stark mad in white satin.'

48

imagination: "Here's the smell of blood still: all the perfumes of Arabia will not sweeten this little hand".'[11]

These last words, recalled a spectator, were accompanied by a sigh, 'a convulsive shudder – very horrible. A tone of imbecility audible in the sigh.'[12]

For Hazlitt, who first saw her some years later, Mrs Siddons' performance was something 'above nature'.

> . . . It seemed almost as if a being of a superior order had dropped from a higher sphere to awe the world with the majesty of her appearance. Power was seated on her brow, passion emanated from her breast as from a shrine; she was tragedy personified. In coming on in the sleeping-scene, her eyes were open, but their sense was shut. She was like a person bewildered, and unconscious of what she did. Her lips moved involuntarily – all her gestures were involuntary and mechanical. She glided on and off the stage like an apparition. To have seen her in that character was an event in everyone's life, not to be forgotten.[13]

As soon as the play was ended Sheridan hastened round to Mrs Siddons' dressing-room to congratulate her – 'most ingenuously', she wrote – upon her obstinacy. When he had gone, she began to undress and standing in front of her mirror, her mind still full of the emotions of the evening, repeated aloud in the tones she had used on the stage, 'Here's the smell of blood still', to the amazement of her dresser who innocently exclaimed, 'Dear me, ma'am, how very hysterical you are tonight; I protest and vow, ma'am, it was not blood but rose pink and water, for I saw the property man mix it with my very eyes.'[14]

V

Kemble had supported his sister in her ordeal as Mrs Beverley; he would have given much to share her triumph in *Macbeth*. But the part of Macbeth had been pre-empted by the actor William Smith, to whom it belonged by tradition, and no pressure from Kemble's admirers could prevail on him to give it up. Best suited to comedy, Smith had been ill received in the part, and his known 'convivial habits', in contrast to Mrs Siddons' frugal ways, provoked the malicious comments of the Shakespearean scholar George Steevens on their performance in the banquet scene:

> Mr Smith who, during his college life and since, is known to have been an utter enemy to all convivial meetings and prodigalities of entertainment, gave his welcome to the nobles of Scotland with a coldness that might have been expected from one who has been compelled to counterfeit an office, from which, had it been real, his heart would have revolted. The consequence was obvious, not a knife or fork was lifted at his bidding. The soul of Mrs Siddons on the contrary (Mrs Siddons whose dinners and suppers are proverbially numerous) expanded on this occasion. She spoke her joy on beholding so many guests, with an earnestness little short of rapture . . . Her address seemed so like reality, that all the Thanes about her seized the wooden fowls & c. in hopes alas! to find every dish as warm and genuine as her invitation to feed on it.[1]

Kemble, cast back on lesser roles, had no intention of wasting his time. Over the next few years, spending largely in relation to his means, he would lay the foundations of a library devoted to drama and works of dramatic criticism. Paying little attention to current affairs – according to Boaden, he never read a newspaper – he devoted himself wholeheartedly to the study of the theatre and its history, and above all to his idol Shakespeare. If he could not yet have the part of Macbeth (except on a single evening when he chose it for his benefit) he could study it and write on it. A pamphlet written that autumn under the title *Macbeth Reconsidered*, and dedicated to the great Shakespearean scholar Edmond Malone, enhanced his reputation in learned circles. For Sheridan, who already had an eye on him as a possible successor to King, he set his hand to pruning and adapting earlier plays – his adaptation of Dryden's *King Arthur*, under the title of *Arthur and Emmeline*, appeared that autumn, he himself playing Arthur in 'most chivalrous style'. He was continuing his classical studies too and writing letters such as this to Mrs Inchbald:

> I have been hunting above an Hour for the second vol. of Ovid, and cannot light upon it, high or low –What can be become of it I can't imagine, I had it in my Hands a day or two ago –
>
> I send my Compts. to Mrs Whitfield, and return her Lord and Master his two Books. They told me Randolph was a poet – God help [us] – Some men are strangely fortunate – I have read his Works twice over, and for the Life of me, I have not been able to make out his Title to anything more on Parnassus, than a very small Plot, and that's at its Foot, thinly sprinkled with a few gay, but common Flowers, and for the most part overgrown with Weeds and Brambles.[2]

Mrs Inchbald was enjoying a continuing success. A second play had been accepted by the Haymarket, a sentimental comedy in which the beautiful Miss Farren, the leading comic actress at Drury Lane, was to play when she transferred to the Haymarket for the summer season. Colman, the proprietor, a well known playwright himself, had suggested its title in a note:

'The Licenser wants a title for your play: I have thought of a whimsical one that I think will not displease you; and if you will favour me with a call about eleven in the forenoon tomorrow or next day "I'll Tell You What".'[3]

I'll Tell You What the play became; it heralded a string of popular comedies over the next few years. Mrs Inchbald prudently invested her earnings in government bonds; family commitments, among them to her stepson George, an unsuccessful actor, forced her to live as economically as ever, but her beauty, her charm and her growing reputation gained her the entrance to a wide and interesting circle, ranging from figures such as William Godwin – who called her 'a piquant mixture between a milkmaid and a lady' – to the elegant Sir Charles Bunbury, formerly the husband of the Lady Sarah Lennox with whom George III had been so much in love before duty forced him to marry his German queen. Mrs Inchbald, though her heart, as she always maintained, belonged to Kemble, might have been happy to accept the consolation of a fashionable marriage. But Sir Charles did not propose though she, continuing to hope, let other offers slip by. He was too worldly, as Kemble was too prudent and ambitious, to think of marrying her. Mrs Inchbald would accept him on no other terms; refusing all pleas and inducements, she remained devoted, as Harris put it, 'to virtue and a garret'.

*　　*　　*

Mrs Siddons, stiff and shy in company with those she did not know, was expansive with her closest friends, seeking perhaps in their affection some substitute for the warmth she lacked in her marriage. Dr Whalley, a literary dilettante, and his wife, whom she had met in Bath, were especial confidants, and to them, when her troubles with Digges and Brereton were over, she wrote to express the feelings which in public and in conversation with her fellow actors she had concealed:

> I have been very unhappy, but now t'is over I will venture to tell you so, that you may not lose the 'dues of rejoicing'. Envy, malice, detraction, all the fiends of hell have compassed me round about to destroy me . . . I have been degraded; I am now again the favourite servant of the public and I have kept the noiseless tenor of my temper in these extremes; my spirit has been grieved but my victorious faith upholds me. I look forward to a better world for happiness, and am placed in this in mercy to be a candidate for that. But what makes the wound rankle deeper is that ingratitude, hypocrisy and perfidy have barbed the darts. But it is over, and I am happy. Good God! What would I give to see you both, but for an hour! how many times do I wish myself with you and long to unburthen my heart to you.[4]

To the Whalleys too Mrs Siddons confided her domestic news. She had moved to a house in Gower Street, Bedford Square, its back 'effectually in the country and delightfully pleasant'. Her children were all well: 'Sarah is an elegant creature, and Maria is as beautiful as a seraph. Harry grows very awkward, sensible and well disposed'. But a certain Mary, presumably the housekeeper, had proved to be 'a very viper': 'She has lately taken to drinking, has defrauded us of a great deal of money given to her to pay the tradespeople, and in her cups abused Mr Siddons and me beyond bounds.'[5]

This same Mary, it seems, had been spreading stories that Mr Siddons ill-treated his wife, rumours that Mrs Siddons strongly denied. Nonetheless it appears that already all was not perfect in the Siddons ménage. William Siddons, obscured by his wife's fame, may have sought solace for his self-esteem elsewhere – there was a suggestion that he had a mistress in Chelsea – and he was often irritable and overbearing. Mrs Siddons would have done her best to hide dissension. Socially and psychologically her position as a perfect wife and mother, unsullied by intrigue, was of the first importance to her. Her immense emotional energies were channelled into her acting; off stage her virtue seemed impregnable. Some years later Sheridan was discussing her with Samuel Rogers. 'Your admiration of Mrs Siddons is so high', said Rogers, 'that I wonder you do not make open love to her.' 'To her!' said Sheridan. 'To that magnificent and appalling creature! I should have soon have thought of making love to the Archbishop of Canterbury.'[6]

*　　*　　*

For three years Mrs Siddons had virtually eclipsed the Muse of Comedy in the London theatre. At Covent Garden Mrs Abingdon, one of the great comic actresses of Garrick's day and the first Lady Teazle in *The School for Scandal*, was past her meridian, while at Drury Lane only Miss Farren, excelling, as her relationship with Lord Derby might lead one to expect, in playing fine ladies, had any real claim to distinction. Mrs Siddons' attempts at comedy were almost always unsuccessful and seldom more so than when, late that season, she followed her Lady Macbeth with Rosalind in *As You Like It*. Henry Bate had been enchanted when he saw her playing the part as a girl of twenty, but Mrs Siddons was thirty now and the mother of four children. She had grown too stately for comedy; though possessed of a fund of quiet humour in private life she lacked vivacity on stage. Even her looks were against her – 'how could such a countenance be arch?' said a fellow actor – and the mysterious nondescript garments, neither male nor female, which for reasons of modesty she chose to wear in masculine disguise, excited universal derision. 'Her hussar boots', wrote the *Morning Post*, 'with a gardener's apron and petticoat behind, gave her a most equivocal appearance which rendered Orlando's stupidity astonishing in not making a premature discovery of his mistress.'

Decidedly comedy was not Mrs Siddons' genre. But whereas Kemble, though held back for a time by those in possession of the classic roles, bid fair to be a tragic actor of the stature of his sister, it was in comedy that the other leading players, with King at their head, were at their best, and while Mrs Siddons harrowed the public with pity and terror they had waited, so far vainly, for some actress to redress the balance in the comic field. By the summer of 1785 redress was close at hand: Dorothy Jordan, as dazzling a star in her way as Mrs Siddons, was waiting in the wings.

We last glimpsed Mrs Jordan briefly when as Dorothy Francis, a young actress at the Smock Alley theatre in Dublin, she had been seduced by the manager James Daly. She was twenty at the time, the daughter of an actress, Grace Phillips, and the stage-struck son of a family of Irish gentry, Francis Bland, who, having promised marriage and fathered several children by her, had finally been induced by his family to cast her off. He had subsequently married an heiress, leaving his former mistress to struggle on as best she could on a meagre allowance, which on his death in 1778 was cancelled altogether. She had maintained a precarious living by acting, appearing in Dublin at various times with Sheridan's father, Thomas Sheridan, and Tate Wilkinson, later the manager of the Yorkshire circuit and an important influence in her daughter's life. After a brief spell as a milliner's assistant Dorothy followed her mother onto the stage, using her father's christian name of Francis for fear of antagonising the Blands, who might still come to their family's aid, by using their name in public. Her freshness, her gaiety, the rollicking good spirits which she brought to comedy and her pathos in tragic or sentimental roles attracted immediate attention. After playing at the Crow Lane

Theatre in Dublin, she gravitated to Smock Alley as a leading lady and here it was not long before she attracted the lecherous and squinting gaze – for Daly, otherwise extremely handsome, was cross-eyed – of the manager. It is not certain how her downfall was accomplished; there was often, as has been said, an element of blackmail in his seductions. Her mother had recently fallen ill, her younger brother and sister looked to her for support. A young girl dependent on his favour for her livelihood, she could have had little defence against a determined assault. There was certainly no liking on her part and when she discovered she was pregnant, though still under contract and in debt, she fled to England with her mother and the younger children. So great was her revulsion that in later days, though normally the most forgiving and generous of women, she would never speak to Daly or have the slightest dealing with him.

Destitute and three months pregnant, Dorothy arrived in England and with her mother made her way to York where, failing any other connection or prospect of employment, her mother hoped to persuade her former acting colleague, Tate Wilkinson, to take on her daughter. Wilkinson's memoirs recall his first meeting with the pair whom he went to call on at the inn where they were staying. Dorothy, shabbily dressed, depressed and silent, showed no signs of the talents her mother fulsomely described and Wilkinson, distrustful, as he said, of actresses' mamas, was at first inclined to refuse her out of hand. But he was a kindly man, with pleasant memories of his acting days in Dublin, and he agreed to return a little later to give her an audition. The transformation which took place when Dorothy, in that melting and entrancing voice to which all her contemporaries paid tribute, recited some lines from a popular tragedy so pleased and surprised him that he parted from her convinced that he had found a treasure.

She made her début with Wilkinson in Rowe's tragedy, *The Fair Penitent*, following the play, at her mother's request, with a song, 'The Greenwood Laddie'. 'She was heard throughout the play', wrote Boaden, 'with the greatest interest and sympathy, and the manager began to tremble at the absurdity, as he reasonably thought it, of Callista arising from the dead, and rushing before an audience in their tears, to sing a ballad in the pastoral style, which nobody called for or cared about. – But on she jumped, with her elastic spring and the smile that nature's own cunning hand had moulded, in a frock and a little mob cap and her curls as she wore them all her life; and she sang her ballad so enchantingly as to fascinate her hearers . . .'[7]

There was soon no doubt that Wilkinson had found a treasure, so much so that, news of her success having reached Dublin, the odious Daly tried to have her arrested for breach of contract, and it was only through the kindness of an elderly theatre-lover in York, who put up the money to release her, that she escaped being imprisoned. Meanwhile, her pregnancy having become obvious, it was necessary to her to find another name in order to save scandal. Declining Tate Wilkinson's advice to take the family name of Bland, she fell in with his suggestion, jokingly put forward, that since she had crossed the water she should take the name of Jordan. She was Mrs Jordan from that day, Tate Wilkinson claiming the honour of being her godfather in her new identity.

Mrs Jordan never forgot the miseries of her first confinement; so great was her sympathy for others in the same condition that when she became famous she kept supplies of baby linen and necessities to be sent to those in need. Nor did she escape the spite of her fellow actresses, who, jealous of her popularity, attempted to have her hissed off the stage for immorality when she reappeared after her baby, a daughter, had been born. Tate Wilkinson's support and her power to delight her audiences were enough to carry her through a period of temporary embarrassment, and her next three years with Wilkinson were attended by almost continual success though her life of travelling from town to town was often arduous and exhausting. Sentimentally, however, she seems to have met with a check, having fallen in love with Mrs Inchbald's unsatisfactory stepson George, who was also playing in the company. But George at that time thought himself cut out for better things, and the matter went no further.

Tate Wilkinson's company, through which both Kemble and Mrs Siddons had passed, was well known as a forcing ground for talent and in the summer season, when the London theatres were closed, it was not unusual for actors from Covent Garden or Drury Lane, travelling in the provinces, to scout for promising new players there. William Smith, otherwise known as 'Gentleman' Smith, the same that had played Macbeth to Mrs Siddons, had seen Mrs Jordan on a visit to York during race week and been so impressed by her that Wilkinson, not wishing to lose his new-found star, had doubled her salary and bound her to a three-year contract. Consequently, it was not until 1785 that Mrs Jordan, on Smith's enthusiastic recommendation, was free to accept an engagement from the autumn of that year at Drury Lane.

It had at first been understood that she would specialise in tragic roles as a second string to Mrs Siddons. But Mrs Jordan, though all her life she would have a hankering for pathetic roles, had no intention of opening her career by inviting comparisons with the queen of tragedy. In polite comedy, too, her way was blocked. The elegant Miss Farren had created a near monopoly in 'fine lady' parts; no one could equal her, it was said, 'in the flutter of a fan or the agony of the drawing room curtsy'.[8] After some reflection Mrs Jordan decided that her best opening lay with the youthful heroines of Shakespeare's comedies, and in romping hoydenish roles and 'breeches' parts in which her trim figure and perfect legs could be displayed. It was the privilege of new actresses at Drury Lane to choose their opening roles, and following this policy Mrs Jordan chose the part of Peggy, the artless heroine of *The Country Girl*, adapted and pruned of Restoration bawdiness by Garrick from Wycherley's *The Country Wife*.

'She came to London', wrote Mrs Inchbald, describing her début on October 18th, 'with no report in her favour to elevate her above a very moderate salary (four pounds) or to attract more than a very moderate house when she appeared. But here moderation stopped. She at once displayed such consummate art, such bewitching nature – such excellent sense and such innocent simplicity – that her auditors were boundless in their plaudits and so warm in her praises when they left the theatre that their friends at home would not give credit to the extent of their eulogisms.'[9]

Her appearance in masculine attire in the third act excited particular admiration – Sir Joshua Reynolds pronounced her figure the neatest and most perfect he had ever seen. But her fertile invention as an actress, wrote Boaden, was at its height in the letter scene, when Peggy, instructed by her elderly fiancé to write a letter rebuffing a young admirer, gleefully changes her letter, while he is out of the room, to a naive declaration of love. 'The very pen and ink were made to express the rustic petulance of the first epistle and the eager delight that composed that second which was to be despatched instead of it to her lover.'[10]

After the stormy passions of Mrs Siddons, Mrs Jordan burst like sunshine on the London stage. Here at last, it seemed, was a magnet to draw the crowds to comedy as well as tragedy. Smith, who loved Drury Lane, congratulated his protégée wholeheartedly, and Mrs Jordan, returning home after her first night, must have felt with satisfaction, as Boaden put it, that she would not long be rated on the treasurer's books at only £4 a week.

VI

The first performance of *The Country Girl*, as Mrs Inchbald recorded, was only moderately attended; the second and third, as news of Mrs Jordan's talents spread, brought increasing crowds. Mrs Jordan's salary was doubled; young George Inchbald, regretting his former coldness, called unsuccessfully to offer his hand; the critics vied in singing her praises. 'It was not as an actress, but as herself, that she charmed every one', wrote Hazlitt later. 'Nature had formed her in the most prodigal humour: and when nature is in the humour to make a woman all that is delightful she does it most effectually . . . Her face, her tones, her manner, were irresistible. Her smile had the effect of sunshine, and her laugh did one good to hear it. Her voice was eloquence itself: it seemed as if her heart were always at her mouth. She was all gaiety, openness and good-nature. She rioted in her fine animal spirits, and gave more pleasure than any other actress, because she had the greatest spirit of enjoyment in herself.'[1]

For her second role that season Mrs Jordan turned to Viola in *Twelfth Night*, making the transition from farce to poetic comedy with seemingly effortless ease. However much she had studied the part, and she had studied hard during her years with Wilkinson, the outward effect was one of perfect spontaneity. Charles Lamb recalled it in a retrospective essay:

> There is no giving an account of how she delivered the disguised story of her love for Orsino. It was no set speech, that she had foreseen, so as to weave it into an harmonious period, line necessarily following line, to make up the music . . . but, when she had declared her sister's history to be a 'blank', and that she 'never told her love', there was a pause, as if the story had ended – and then the image of the 'worm in the bud' came up as a new suggestion – and the heightened image of 'Patience' still followed after that, as by some growing (and not mechanical) process, thought

springing up after thought, I would almost say, as they were watered by her tears.[2]

Mrs Siddons had not welcomed Mrs Jordan's arrival in London; during the previous summer when she had been playing for Tate Wilkinson in York, she had expressed the opinion that Mrs Jordan would be wiser not to leave the provinces. Now Mrs Jordan's success, which *Twelfth Night* had overwhelmingly confirmed, had the effect of dividing the town into Mrs Siddons' supporters and her own. It was some time before each actress could learn the lesson to stick to her own genre. When Mrs Siddons, who was eight months pregnant and wished for an untaxing role, played with Miss Farren in a comedy, *The Way to Keep Him*, in December, her admirers could only regret it, while Colman described her as 'a frisking gog'. And when Mrs Jordan tried the part of Imogen in *Cymbeline*, she completely failed to carry it off. Much shorter than Mrs Siddons, she lacked both her stature and her majesty. 'She had not the natural dignity of the wife of Posthumus', wrote a critic. 'She could not burst upon the insolent Iachimo in the terrors of offended virtue. She could not wear the lightnings of scorn in her countenance.'[3]

For the rest of the season Mrs Jordan kept to comedy. The absence of Mrs Siddons, who gave birth to a son at the end of December, left the way open for her rival who romped her way from success to success. The line of carriages outside the theatre on Jordan nights, and the throng of people struggling for admittance, now equalled those when Mrs Siddons played. Theatre-going in those days could be a perilous business. Anna Seward, 'the Swan of Lichfield', described fighting her way through 'the terrible, fierce, maddening crowd' for a place on Siddons' nights and Sheridan's, sister Betsy had much the same experience in trying to reach her box for a performance of *The Country Girl*.

'When we got to the House', she wrote in a letter to her sister, 'we found ourselves in such a Croud as I never before encounter'd . . . After we had nearly reach'd the Box Office a cry of Pick-pocket raised a general confusion and those at the top of the Stairs were forcibly push'd down by the pursuers of said Gentleman. At this instant I saw a door open into a sort of lobby, into which I made

Mrs M— enter but found it impossible to accompany her and was by the Croud brought Back to the Street. What made the Croud so intollerable was that I firmly beleive three parts of it were pickpockets, for the Constables Bawl'd themselves Hoarse in telling them the house was full without making the least difference in the number. Again the Torrent push'd me up to the spot where I had left Mrs Morris where we had the pleasure of cooling our heels for half an hour, during which time we heard various lamentations about purses etc. that had been convey'd away. At length we got admittance but the fright and additional cold I had got made me pay dear for the evening's amusement.'4

*   *   *

With two such stars as Mrs Siddons and Mrs Jordan, and with Kemble whose talents, not yet fully realised, promised equal fame, it seemed that the fortunes of Sheridan and Drury Lane were made. It was ten years since at the age of twenty-four Sheridan had taken over Garrick's half of the ownership and patent of Drury Lane, in partnership with his father-in-law, Thomas Linley, and a Dr James Ford, physician to the royal family; and eight years since, with the purchase of the other half share, he had acquired the controlling interest. Of the complications of mortgages, borrowing and interest payments there is no need to speak – for all its burden of debt the theatre, carefully and conscientiously managed, was potentially a paying proposition. Sheridan's term of tenure had started gloriously: the memorable first night of *The School for Scandal* took place on May 8th, 1777. On that evening, recalled the playwright Frederick Reynolds who was passing near the theatre, he heard such a roar from within that, thinking the building was collapsing, he took to his heels. It was the applause that greeted the falling of the screen at the end of the fourth act. So great was Sheridan's elation at his triumph that he was found dead drunk, later that evening, by the watch. *The School for Scandal* had been followed three years later by *The Critic*, and with that ultimate satire on playwriting in general Sheridan's own career as a dramatist virtually came to an end. Henceforth, as he became increasingly absorbed by politics, the theatre took second place in his ambitions though his refusal to delegate, to allow even the lightest decision to be taken without his agreement, made the task of those who attempted to run it from day to day near impossible. King, the stage manager, when he finally gave up the post in frustration, complained in a letter to the press that he had not the authority 'to command the cleaning of a coat, or adding, by way of decoration, a yard of silver lace', both of which, he added sourly, 'were *often much wanted*'. Playwrights might as soon abandon hope as send their plays to Drury Lane. The task of reading plays Sheridan reserved to himself though he had neither the leisure nor the inclination to attend to it. 'Melancholy proofs of this', wrote Boaden, 'appeared in the piles of long forgotten tragedies and comedies which he had promised to consider and never opened. Mr Kemble, whom I one day found sitting in the great man's library, pointed to this funeral pile and added to his action the declaration of his belief that in these morning attendances he had read more of these productions than ever had or would the proprietor.

'Sheridan's habit', continued Boaden, 'was to keep his visitors distributed variously, according to their rank and intimacy with him. Some, like ourselves, penetrated into the library; others tired the chairs in parlours; and tradesmen lost their time in the hall, the butler's room and other scenical divisions of the premises. A door opening above stairs moved all hopes below; but when he came down his hair was drest for the day, and his countenance for the occasion; and so cordial were his manners, his glance so masterly and his address so captivating, that the people, for the most part, seemed to forget what they actually wanted, and went away as if they had only come to look at him.'[5]

However careless Sheridan's attitude to the running of the complex concerns of Drury Lane, there was one question which always commanded his immediate attention. This was the matter of the theatre's patent, the royal charter by which Drury Lane and Covent Garden held the monopoly of legitimate or spoken drama in London. (The Haymarket Theatre, as has been noted, was allowed by special dispensation to play legitimate drama in the summer months.) Any threat to the patents was a threat to the well-being of the two main theatres, and Sheridan, a rival in all else to the manager of Covent Garden, made common cause with him where the monopoly was in question. With the population of London expanding and the demand for entertainment increasing, it was inevitable that a challenge should come and, though it was not until 1843 that the monopoly was finally broken, a long string of skirmishes preceded it.

For Sheridan the first, and certainly the most dramatic, of these was the attempt of John Palmer, one of Drury Lane's leading actors and the first Joseph Surface in *The School for Scandal*, to set up a theatre in Wellclose Square, near the Tower of London, which would bring legitimate drama to the growing population of East London. The foundation stone was laid in 1785, and in a prospectus which did credit to Palmer's nickname of 'Plausible Jack' investors were assured that the enterprise had a legal basis, the details of which would be revealed in due course. It was not until 1787, when the 2,500-seat Royalty Theatre, in which Palmer had invested £18,000 of his own money, was completed that the proprietors of the patent theatres, who had disingenuously lain low during the period when it was being built, rose to challenge him. Palmer's so-called authority proved to be no more than a permission granted, as was the custom with provincial theatres, by the local magistrates, together with a licence from the governor of the Tower of London. Weighed in the balance against an Act of Parliament which in 1737 had forbidden all theatrical performances in London not previously allowed by royal patent or licensed by the Lord Chamberlain, it was virtually worthless. After only one night, at the end of which Palmer was forced to admit he had no valid legal case, the theatre was closed down.

When in 1788 Palmer, defeated but unrepentant, returned to acting at Drury Lane, there was a lively interest among his colleagues as to how his first meeting with Sheridan would turn out. Palmer, it appears, made quite a scene of it:

After a profound bow he approached the author of *The School for Scandal* with an air of penitent humility; his head declined, the whites of his eyes turned upwards, his hands clasped together and his whole air exactly that of Joseph Surface before Sir Peter Teazle.

He began thus:

'My dear Mr Sheridan, if you could but know what I feel at this moment – *here*' (laying one hand upon his heart).

Sheridan, with inimitable readiness, stopped him. 'Why, Jack! You forget I *wrote* it.'[6]

*   *   *

'Plausible Jack's' attack on the privileged position of the patent theatres had failed, but it would have a significant delayed reaction. After three months' closure the Royalty Theatre had been allowed to re-open for entertainments that excluded the spoken word – burlettas (a combination of songs and recitative), pantomimes, tumbling, tightrope dancing and the like; any attempt at spoken dialogue was visited by prosecution. But from the legal quibble which prevented the Royalty and similar theatres from threatening legitimate drama by speaking rather than singing words, a new form of popular entertainment would arise. The burletta, originally purely musical, evolving into a play in doggerel verse, with a piano or orchestral accompaniment, provided a cloak for every variety of theatrical piece, from rewritten classics to blood-and-thunder melodrama; crude, highly coloured, usually spectacularly staged, they eventually presented a greater challenge to the patent theatres than straight drama could ever have done.

But this was in the future. Meanwhile, despite the disorder at the top, things were going well at Drury Lane. Mrs Siddons and Mrs Jordan shone in their respective spheres, Kemble's star was rising fast. In the autumn of 1786 he appeared in Grétry's opera *Richard Coeur de Lion*, an immense success in Paris two years earlier. Two rival translations had been commissioned by Covent Garden and Drury Lane. The Covent Garden version had had little effect, but Drury Lane's, by the soldier dramatist General Burgoyne (best remembered for his surrender to the Americans at Saratoga) was an immediate sensation. Mrs Jordan, fetchingly disguised as a minstrel boy, discovered the captive Richard with a song, and Kemble, 'a noble figure, pacing his melancholy exercise within the walls of his prison', responded gallantly in kind, though neither then nor at any time did he pretend to be a singer. Michael Kelly, the well known tenor who later took the leading role, confessed his amazement when he first

1. Mrs Siddons as Isabella and Henry Siddons as her son in *Isabella*, after the painting by William Hamilton.

2. Above: The pit entrance to Drury
   Lane on Siddons night: Kemble is
   billed as Hamlet for the following
   day.

3. Kemble as Hamlet, 1783—
   Kemble adopted the 'Van Dyck'
   costume shown here in the year
   of his debut at Drury Lane.

4. Richard Brinsley Sheridan, after the painting by Reynolds.

5. Kemble and Mrs Siddons as Mr and Mrs Beverly in *The Gamester*, 1783.

6. Garrick and Mrs Pritchard in *Macbeth*, after the painting by Zoffany.

7. Macbeth and Lady Macbeth after the murder of Duncan, by Fuseli, 1812—
Mrs Siddons is said to have inspired the figure of Lady Macbeth.

8. Kemble and Mrs Siddons in *Macbeth* by Thomas Beach.

9. Mrs Jordan as Euphrosyne in *Comus*.

10. Mrs Jordan as Viola by Hoppner.

11. Above: Priscilla Hopkins (later Mrs John Philip Kemble) as Peggy in *The Country Wife*.

12. Mrs Siddons by Gainsborough.

13. Mrs Siddons as the Tragic Muse by Reynolds.

heard Kemble singing; he recounted too how the conductor, when Kemble was rehearsing the song, had remonstrated from the orchestra, 'Mr Kemble, my dear Mr Kemble, you are murdering time.' 'My dear sir', answered Kemble, coolly taking a pinch of snuff, 'it is better for me to murder time at once than to continually be beating him as you do.'[7]

Events were moving in Kemble's direction. In 1788 William 'Gentleman' Smith left Drury Lane, with a farewell performance of *Macbeth* in which Mrs Siddons played Lady Macbeth and Kemble Macduff. One of the Garrick school, Smith had little liking for Kemble and his sister, and though Kemble hid any impatience for the tragic roles which would fall to him on Smith's departure, there was no doubt that his growing ascendancy at the theatre had hastened Smith's retirement. In February of the same year William Brereton who had taken precedence of Kemble in young romantic leads, as Smith had done in tragic ones, died after a year's confinement in Hoxton Asylum. His death would have more than professional consequences for Kemble; in December 1788 he married his widow, Priscilla.

A host of apocryphal stories sprang up around Kemble's courtship and marriage. One version had it that a daughter of Lord North's had fallen madly in love with him and that Lord North had offered a large sum of money in return for an immediate marriage elsewhere, Mrs Brereton being the first woman that came to hand; it was added that when Kemble, having married her, went to claim his money the nobleman haughtily disclaimed all knowledge of the bargain. (When Kemble, some years later, was shown this story in print, he underlined the offending paragraph and inscribed in the margin: 'A lie!'.) Another account had him approaching the lady of his choice with the remark that she might expect to hear news of a piece of good fortune very soon. This oracular statement, accompanied by a chuck under the chin and the familiar name of 'Pop', was rightly construed as a proposal by the lady's mother, who told her, 'Have him, girl.'

The simplest explanation for Kemble's choice of bride was that, though with his looks and talents he might have married more ambitiously, his chosen profession, to which he was entirely devoted, called for a wife who understood the theatre and accepted its demands. Mrs Brereton had been born to the stage; her father for years had been the prompter at Drury Lane and she herself, though less talented than her former husband, had long been a member of the company. Genest, the theatre historian, described her as 'pretty but not very capable' on stage; off stage, according to her niece Fanny Kemble, who knew her in later life, she was 'quick, keen, clever and shrewd, with the air and address of a finished woman of the world'. With none of the fire and fascination of Mrs Inchbald, she had a more amenable character and a greater willingness to submerge her own interests in her husband's concerns. Kemble's choice, though it excited some derision at the time, was to prove a very happy one.

Mrs Inchbald took Kemble's wedding philosophically. She had long since accepted that he was not for her. 'We think we know', wrote Boaden, 'that Mr Kemble could never have borne with the independent turn of her mind.' Two egoists, they had taken one another's measure. Attraction had mellowed into friendship, and before long Priscilla Kemble, as much as her husband, came to treat her as a valued friend.

*   *   *

1788 saw a domestic change in Kemble's life; it brought another, equally momentous, to his career. The death of Brereton, the temporary defection of Palmer to the Royalty Theatre, and the retirement of Smith left Thomas King without the nucleus of players, inherited from Garrick's day, on whom he had relied. He himself was an actor of the old school who found it as hard to accept the rumbustious bounce of Mrs Jordan as Kemble's grave and studied declamation. His acting, wrote Hazlitt, 'left a taste on the palate, sweet and sharp like a quince; with an old, hard, rough, withered face, like a John-apple, puckered up into a thousand wrinkles; with shrewd hints and tart replies'.[8] He now found himself increasingly isolated and at the same time more than ever at odds with Sheridan.

The reasons were simple. Sheridan had been absorbed in the Warren Hastings trial though 1787. His six-hour speech in Parliament that February, condemning the former governor of Bengal for corruption, oppression and assorted crimes, had been a rhetorical

66

tour de force, its brilliance underpinned, as so often in Sheridan's work, by minutely laborious preparation. In June 1787 Westminster Hall had been crowded to suffocation for a second feat of eloquence, Sheridan's speech as manager of Hastings' trial, delivered over four days before an audience that included the queen and the Prince of Wales. Many of them were moved to tears, Mrs Siddons (who was among them) fainted, and all were swept with emotion as on the fourth day Sheridan moved to the climax of his peroration and col-lapsed into the arms of Burke: 'My lords, I have done'. ('A good actor', remarked Gibbon, who went round to see him next day and found him perfectly well.) The excitement of the trial had been fol-lowed soon after by the illness of George III, who since May 1788 had begun to show signs of madness. For Sheridan, a supporter of the Prince of Wales and his intermediary with Parliament in the dis-cussions that took place concerning a possible regency, this was a hectic time. Small wonder that King, whose duties as a manager had never been defined and who lacked all authority in financial matters, was driven to distraction seeking decisions from Sheridan who, while abandoning none of his powers, was always too busy to deal with things himself. In the summer of 1788, on the eve of the new season, exasperated beyond measure, King announced his retirement from the post and in a statement to the press gave voice to some of his complaints:

> I have been called to account by authors for the non-performance of works I never before heard of; arraigned for rejecting per-formers, with whom I had no power to treat; and censured for the very limited number of pieces produced which it was not part of my province to provide. Should any one ask me what was my post at Drury Lane and add the further question if I was not the Manager, who was? – I should be forced to answer . . . to the first 'I don't know' – and to the last 'I can't tell'.

Sheridan and his fellow proprietors, caught unawares by King's defection, were compelled to replace him at short notice. They turned without hesitation to Kemble, whose talents and experience made him the natural successor. Sheridan's preoccupation with political matters and the urgency of finding a manager before the season began gave Kemble the leverage to demand and be given a far greater degree of authority than King had had and when, following King's letter to the press, a journalist suggested that he had accepted office on degrading terms he was able to refute the suggestion publicly.

'I find myself arraigned', he wrote, 'by an anonymous writer, as having undertaken the management of Drury Lane theatre under *humiliating restrictions*. I do assure the writer and the public that no humiliation degrades my services to those who do me the honour to employ me, and that the power entrusted to me is perfectly satisfactory to my own feelings and entirely adequate to the liberal encouragement of poets, performers, and to the conduct of the whole business of the theatre.'

His appointment was greeted with delight by Mrs Siddons, who before the news came out had written a letter of fluttering excitement announcing the secret to her friend Sir Charles Hotham:

And what do *you think* and you my dear Lady *Dorothy*, aye and *you* Miss Hotham, if you are at charming Dalton where I wish I could fly to tell you this secret with which I am ready to burst, and which fills me with joy and fear and excitement of all sorts and kinds, for God knows, how he will be able to go thro' such a fag as it will be, you are all crying 'the deuce take her what can she mean?' Why then this I mean, John Kemble is Deputy Manager* at Drury Lane – and now the murder's out![9]

For five years Kemble had bided his time. His sister had been able to take the stage by storm; Kemble, lacking her commanding genius, had had no such easy passage. Silently curbing his impatience, he had seen the parts he coveted taken by older actors and watched the affairs of the theatre slip into increasing disorder. His moment had now come. He had prepared for it and waited for it and it must have been with a wealth of inward satisfaction that on September 23rd 1788 he inscribed his laconic first entry in his theatre diary: 'This day I undertook the management of D.L. Theatre.'

* Sheridan retained the title of Manager.

VII

Kemble was thirty-one when he became the manager of Drury Lane. As an actor he was coming into his prime and though he would never be the equal of his sister, of whom he once said that he never acted with her without being conscious of her superiority, it is worth pausing, as he moves into the centre of the stage, to assess the qualities that made him, in the years between Garrick's retirement and the advent of Edmund Kean, the greatest actor of the age.

During the years when he dominated the theatrical scene there were few of his distinguished contemporaries, literary, theatrical or political, who did not record their impressions of Kemble's playing. For Byron he was 'glorious', for Pitt, the noblest of actors, for Hazlitt at times too coldly classical: 'He is the very still life and statuary of the stage . . . an icicle upon the bust of tragedy'.[1] From the wealth of testimony, however, two main characteristics emerge.

The first was his intensity. He was at his best in parts in which one ruling feeling or idea was expressed, seizing upon it and working it up with conscious grandeur and consistency. In characters of more fluctuating nature, Hamlet for instance, he was less successful; he was a 'lordly vessel', as Walter Scott expressed it, 'goodly and magnificent when going large before the wind, but wanting the facility to go "ready about".'[2] In the single-minded roles in which he excelled the intensity was deepened by restraint; by keeping long tracts of a performance in a deliberately low key he made the transition to sudden bursts of passion doubly effective. Describing this technique, the actor Macready wrote of him that 'like a Rembrandt picture his performances were remarkable for the most brilliant effects, worked out with wonderful skill on a sombre ground, which only a great master of his art could have achieved'.[3]

The second distinguishing quality of Kemble's playing was his studied and scholarly approach. Whereas Garrick, more spontaneous and more instinctive, habitually went for the first and most immediate interpretation of a part, infusing it with life and vigour, Kemble pondered long and 'with metaphysical exactness' over the niceties of a text, and if his performances lacked the impact of the broader, bolder style of Garrick, at their best they could surpass his in finesse and subtlety. At their worst, however, they laid him open to the charge of pedantry and it was this excessive deliberation that was most often instanced against him in comparison with his sister. Mrs Siddons devoted much thought to her roles, and her notes on such parts as Lady Macbeth and Constance make fascinating reading, but her imagination and her instinct took her far beyond mere study. The painter Benjamin Haydon once described the difference between the sister and the brother: 'Mrs Siddons could act, as you know, Lady Macbeth twenty nights and vary it each night. This was not from previous thinking. Oh no! But fired by the part as she proceeded, her native faculty flashed out in gleams of power which no previous labour could have given her in cold study. Kemble came into a part with stately dignity as if he disdained to listen to Nature, however she might whisper, until he had weighed and examined the value of her counsel.'[4]

The idea of nature and of truth to nature as a guide to actors was one so often repeated in the theatrical criticism of the period that it calls for some analysis. Kemble, whose style was grand, declamatory and classical, was frequently described as being on distant terms with nature – 'he is in fact', wrote Hazlitt, 'as shy of committing himself with nature as a maid is of committing herself with a lover'[5] – and this is not surprising. What is perhaps surprising is to find that Mrs Siddons, with the emotional whirlwind she generated, the plenitude of her sweeping gestures, the violence of her shrieks of despair, should be described as an actress who took nature as her guide and that she herself should give as her criterion for taking a part that 'it should be in nature'. But what she sought and what the critics described was not truth to the behaviour of everyday life but an emotional validity. The heroic decisions, the conflicts between love and duty which perplexed the heroines of eighteenth-century drama, could not be portrayed realistically: a heightened idiom, bearing the same relation to real life as poetry to prose was necessary, but, as in opera, it was only effective when, however extravagantly, it reflected a genuine emotion. It was a concept which Mrs Siddons kept continually before her, and of which Kemble, through over-preparation, sometimes lost sight.

In one point of comparison with his sister, Kemble stood at a decided disadvantage. Mrs Siddons' voice was not the least of her incomparable assets. Strong and sweet, 'with the melancholy yet shattering tone of a nightingale',[6] it was equal to the most sustained and passionate effects. Kemble's voice was his weakest point: cursed with a habitual cough and in later life with asthma, his need to husband his breathing and soothe his throat often checked the full flow of his declamation. But his slow and measured delivery, never dull because always full of sense and meaning, made a virtue of necessity and became an essential part of his technique. His pauses, pregnant with significance, were famous: Sheridan ridiculing this 'slight degree of tardiness' suggested playing music in the pauses of his Hamlet.

Equally famous as he grew older, and the subject of endless satire, were his oddities of pronunciation. Leigh Hunt proposed a lexicon to be printed on the playbills for those confused by his peculiar 'orthöepy':[7]

beard	– bird		leap	– lep
cheerful	– churful		merchant	– marchant
conscience	– conshince		odious	– ojjus
err	– air		stir	– stare
fierce	– furse		virtue	– varchue
hideous	– hijjus		virgin	– vargin
infirmity	– infaremity		ye	– jee

Kemble's most notorious departures from the norm however were dictated by antiquarian zeal: 'magot-pie' for 'magpie' and 'aitches' for 'aches'. It was doubtless true, as he maintained, that in the lines from *Macbeth*:

Augurs and understood relations have
By magot-pies and choughs and rooks brought forth
The secret'st man of blood –

the blank verse halted without the extra syllable in 'magot-pie'; similarly when Prospero menaced Caliban:

For this tonight thou shalt have aches –

71

it could be argued that Shakespeare had intended 'aches' to have two syllables. Whether it was worth insisting, as he sometimes did, on these same 'aitches' to howls of dissent from the pit is another matter, but Kemble had made his judgment and above all where Shakespeare was concerned was prepared to hazard all in his defence of what he thought to be the proper reading.

*   *   *

'Huzza! Shakespeare for ever!', wrote Kemble in a letter to the Shakespearean scholar, Edmond Malone, at the end of his first season. He had given ample expression to his enthusiasm in the course of it, with no less than eight productions of Shakespeare's plays, the most notable being *Henry VIII* and *Coriolanus*, put on with all the pageantry at his command. In *Henry VIII*, the part of Wolsey belonging by precedence to an older actor, Thomas Bensley, Kemble combined the two lesser parts of Griffith and Cromwell. With little to do on stage he was able to give his full attention to the production, elaborately mounted, with a splendid procession in the final act. Mrs Siddons was Katharine of Aragon, majestic in the scorn with which she confronted Wolsey, awful in the solemnity with which she delivered the rebuke to his instrument, the surveyor who was bringing false witness against Buckingham:

> If I know you well,
> You were the Duke's surveyor, and lost your office
> On the complaint o' the tenants: take good heed
> And charge not in your spleen a noble person,
> And spoil your nobler soul, I say, take heed!

A fellow actor once met the said surveyor coming off stage in a state of perspiring agitation. On being asked what was the matter, 'The matter!' he replied. 'That woman plays as if the thing were in earnest. She looked on me so through and through with her black eyes, that I would not for the world meet her on the stage again.'[8]

Kemble's *Coriolanus* was based on a version compiled by Thomas Sheridan amalgamating Shakespeare's tragedy with one on the same subject by the poet James Thomson. Whatever its literary defects, which were considerable, it was immensely successful as a piece of theatre. Its climax was a spectacular stage procession with banners, music and a skilfully handled crowd of extras on the occasion of Coriolanus' triumphant return from battle. Mrs Siddons, as Volumnia, took part in the procession. 'I remember her', wrote the actor Charles Young, 'coming down the stage . . . marching and beating time to the music; rolling (if that be not too strong a term to describe her motion) from side to side, swelling with the triumph of her son.'[9] Kemble, in the character of Coriolanus,* a role he would perfect and deepen over the years, gave the performance by which, perhaps more than any other, he is remembered in theatrical history. His stately physique, his classical features, the brilliance of his dark eyes have been captured in Lawrence's famous portrait. Statuesque in repose, he was equally striking in sudden, almost pantomimic movement; Walter Scott describes the screams from the audience when the Volscian assassins, approaching him from behind, seemed to pass their swords through him: 'There was no precaution, no support; in the midst of the exclamation against Tullus Aufidius he dropped as dead and as flat as if their swords had already met in his body.'[10]

* * *

In these first productions of *Henry VIII* and *Coriolanus* were summed up Kemble's guiding principles in conducting the theatre which he now, at least in theory, controlled. Both as an actor and a manager he looked to Shakespeare as the mainstay of his repertoire. Farces, melodramas and musical pieces he must have, with new authors and composers to catch the changing moods of the day, but elsewhere he distrusted novelty. His own talents were best displayed in classic roles; rather than waste time and money on untried works he preferred to devote his resources to improving the production and act-

---

* Like his sister, Kemble could strike awe into his fellow players. Tom Moore recounts how once, during a performance of *Coriolanus*, a young actor, losing his head in the speech where he accuses Coriolanus,

> For that he has . . .
> Envied against the people, seeking means
> To pluck away their power

looked fiercely at Kemble and added, 'And that he is always seen going about the streets making every one uncomfortable.' At the end of the play the unfortunate fellow went round to apologise, but the great actor merely looked bitterly at him and said, 'Beast!'[11]

ing of established plays. In this attitude he was supported by Sheridan whose own opinion of modern drama, from pieces sampled from the vast pile of manuscripts sent for his approval, was not high. He saw besides that though Kemble might demand more money for the restaging of standard pieces, the financial risks were less than those of gambling on something new.

Kemble's antiquarian approach to the theatre, combined with a natural love of splendour, was sometimes pedantic. In preparing the procession for a pantomime, for instance, he could give such instructions as these:

> The banners *Anglo Saxon, Dane, Saxon Line restored* and *Norman* should be very large; and the words upon them silver, as that they will be seen better, I think, than gold – these banners I call *generical*. The banners Rollo, Plantagenet, York, Tudor, Stuart and Brunswick should be smaller; these banners I call *specific*, and let them all be of beautiful form and very richly ornamented . . . The banners on which are inscribed the names of the kings, as 'Alfred the Great, Founder of the British Monarchy, 872–901', 'Edward the Elder' & c. should all be of one shape; let it be round, the ground black, the inscriptions gold, with rich borders & c. . . . You will observe that there are no arms borne in England before Richard I, and then I give every king his arms and motto on shields of shapes proper to the times.[12]

On the whole, however, his search for historical fitness did not go beyond an attempt to give a general impression of authenticity. In costume, though he ransacked ancient books of prints, illuminated manuscripts and the like in his pursuit of information, he was well aware that he could not apply his researches too rigorously. *King Lear*, for instance, was set in ancient Britain at a period when people were probably tattooed or painted with woad, but it was possible to indicate the remoteness of the time without going to such lengths; nor was it likely that anything of the sort had been in Shakespeare's mind. But even had Kemble wished, the expense of replanning the theatre's wardrobes on lines of strict historical accuracy was too great for anything but gradual reform. On his assumption of the management there was almost everything to do in this department.

Though some actors tried to dress in character – and leading actors were usually responsible for the choice of their costumes – others followed the policy inaugurated at the court of Charles II that players, being considered as in the presence of their sovereign, should wear the dress of the court drawing-room.

In scenery the same anachronisms prevailed. The charming sets of de Loutherbourg lent enchantment to some forest scene or represented an exact view of Tilbury fort as a background to the sleeping sentinels in Sheridan's *The Critic*, but there was nothing exact or enchanting about the sets of dirty flats that were commonly hurried together to represent some scene and repeated as backgrounds to several plays in turn. The old stock of scenery was too vast for any wholesale condemnation, but from the first Kemble made it his aim to replace it as far as finances would allow.

With his aim of bringing greater authenticity to the scenery and costumes went a desire to improve the acting of his lesser players. Some years later, on a visit to France, he was taken behind scenes at the Théâtre Français, and seeing an actor earnestly rehearsing his part in varying tones and attitudes, enquired what weighty role he was preparing. He was told that he had only five words to say: 'Madam, your coach is ready.' It was an attitude Kemble found hard to instil at Drury Lane, for in England, as he said, the theatres were 'like eastern regions, where all must be half deified sultans, viziers and bashaws, or depressed and sullen slaves'.[13] The actor who represented Laertes or Horatio considered himself a degraded man because he was not the Hamlet of the evening and from carelessness or resentment gave a poor supporting performance. Kemble, who had always taken the parts assigned to him, often to the detriment of his own reputation (it was not beneath his dignity, even after he had arrived at Drury Lane, to play in pantomime), felt that his leading actors should show the same helpful spirit in accepting subordinate roles and that his lesser actors should throw their whole heart into their work. He spent much time in drilling the extras in crowd scenes and processions and was forced to give more than he wished to cajoling or forcing his best players into complying with his plans. He had most trouble with his actresses. Already, in his first season, such entries as these appear in his journal:

December 17th. Great Quarrel with Miss Farren about her dress; she acted at last however for I would not change the play for her Humour.

December 22nd. Mrs Jordan again fancied herself ill. I spent above two hours coaxing her to act. NB. She was as well as ever she was in her life and stayed when she had done her part to see the Pantomime.

With Sheridan, during his first season, he had less difficulty than he might have expected. Great as was his admiration for Sheridan – and he reverenced him as a writer, wrote Boaden, only less than Shakespeare – he had assumed his post with few illusions as to his reliability as a man of business. But he had set out his terms quite forcibly in taking on the management and Sheridan, for the time being, showed every sign of humouring him. 'Keep as punctual with Kemble as you can', he warned Peake, the treasurer of Drury Lane; it was an injunction that would lose its force in later years when Kemble's demands for his arrears of salary, sometimes polite, sometimes peremptory, but almost always unsuccessful, became too numerous to count. Meanwhile he took pleasure in his relationship with Sheridan. Sharing with him an almost limitless capacity for wine which he used, according to Walter Scott, to 'swallow by pailfuls', he would drink deep with him, sometimes in his own home, sometimes at that of the Irish tenor, Michael Kelly, who had joined the company at Drury Lane that year and who with his beautiful mistress, the singer Mrs Crouch, kept open house after the theatre. At such gatherings, Sheridan, arriving from the House of Commons, and Kemble from Drury Lane, would settle more points in a few minutes than in hours spent seeking a decision in the morning.

Sheridan's political hopes, which had been at their height that autumn, had now been dashed, together with those of the Whigs, by the news of the king's recovery from madness. In February 1789 he was declared completely cured, and the news was the signal for festivities of every kind at both theatres. The queen and the royal princesses signalled their disapproval of Sheridan's role in the negotiations for setting up a regency by making their first public appearance at Covent Garden and ostentatiously ignoring Drury

Lane. But Sheridan, not to be outdone in showing loyalty, had been the moving spirit behind a splendid gala evening, with a concert, supper and a ball, given by Brooks's Club, the stronghold of the Whigs, at the King's Theatre in the Haymarket. Mrs Siddons, dressed as Britannia, declaimed an ode composed for the occasion and at the end of it sat down, to great applause, in the exact position of the figure on a penny piece.

*   *   *

Early in 1788, wishing to consolidate his hold on Drury Lane, Sheridan had purchased the share of the property belonging to his partner, Dr Ford, who had originally combined with his father-in-law and himself when he had bought up Garrick's half share of the theatre in 1776. Ford had never been more than a sleeping partner and he was happy enough to resign his holding for £18,000, which Sheridan, by mysterious means, once more contrived to raise. In the words of his biographer, Thomas Moore, 'That happy art – in which the people of this country are such adepts – of putting the future in pawn for the supply of the present must have been the chief resort of Mr Sheridan in all these later purchases.'

But though Dr Ford had never taken an active part in the theatre – it was unlikely that Sheridan would have permitted him to do so – his connection with Drury Lane had opened doors for his son Richard Ford, an amiable, rather colourless young man who used to frequent the green-room and not long after her arrival had fallen in love with Dorothy Jordan, who with unassailed success was continuing to enchant her audiences – displaying her excellent legs as the young Sir Harry Wildair in *The Constant Couple*, or dressed in a pinafore, bib and tucker as the bouncing Miss Hoyden of Sheridan's *A Trip to Scarborough*. 'To see her when thus attired', wrote Leigh Hunt of her Miss Hoyden, 'shed blubbering tears for some disappointment and eat all the while a great thick slice of bread and butter, weeping and moaning and munching, and eyeing at every bite the part she meant to bite next, was a lesson against will and appetite worth a hundred sermons . . .'[14]

Richard Ford was entranced by Mrs Jordan and she, though not perhaps so strongly drawn, saw in his courtship the possibility of marriage, which in his first approaches to her he seems to have promised. But Dr Ford, like the father of Francis Bland, had no desire to see his son throw himself away on an actress, and since it was he who controlled the purse strings Richard Ford, whilst he swore his intentions were honourable, begged Mrs Jordan to accept a postponement of their wedding till his father could be brought round. On these terms Mrs Jordan accepted him and for five years, until 1791, lived with him as his wife, calling herself by his surname and bearing him three children. The arrangement did not go unnoticed by the press, which marked each birth in disrespectful terms, sometimes including Mrs Siddons, that other prolific mother, in a single paragraph. Thus we read, after the birth of a child to Mrs Jordan, under the heading *Theatricals*: 'Homeward Bound: The Jordan from Edinburgh – a small sprightly vessel – went out of London harbour laden – dropt her cargo in Edinburgh. The Siddons, been to refit – said to be damaged in the upper works &c.'

The rivalry between Mrs Jordan and Mrs Siddons, though still latent, had now somewhat subsided. Mrs Siddons had her brother as manager, but it was not his way to extend particular favours to any one, so much so that at the end of his first season she withdrew from the theatre for a year partly for reasons of health but also, it was rumoured, because of differences between them. Wisely, Kemble and his predecessor King had seldom allowed the two actresses to appear on the same evening. Mrs Jordan had no inclination, as she said, 'to fill the house and let Mrs Siddons run away with the reputation for it',15 and Mrs Siddons presumably felt the same.

With Kemble Mrs Jordan was in frequent conflict. Though she drew as great a crowd as Mrs Siddons her salary, when Kemble took over, was only £12 weekly as against Mrs Siddons' £30. To strengthen her demands for more she resorted to the only weapon at her command – the withdrawal of her labour on the plea of illness, sometimes indeed genuine, for her frequent pregnancies took their toll of even her abundant vitality. Kemble, caught between Mrs Jordan and the procrastinating Sheridan, whose reluctance to part with money was the most consistent element of his management, and faced with the displeasure of the public when their favourite did not appear, held his ground as best he could. It was only when Mrs Jordan, flaunting a rival offer from Covent Garden, went over his head to Sheridan that her demands were met. On the subject of Mrs Jordan's salary, Kemble had had no authority; but he asserted it elsewhere by refusing to accept her brother George Bland, whom she hoped to introduce at Drury Lane, and by fining the door-keeper five shillings for allowing him to appear behind scenes. His resolution had been sufficiently sapped by the following year, however, for him to find a place for Bland within the company – 'though I had no use for him', he noted – making the most of the family resemblance to cast him as Sebastian to Mrs Jordan's Viola. It was always Kemble's policy to humour if he could his leading actresses, and despite continuing skirmishes in his capacity as manager, as an actor he admired her greatly. Though their paths seldom crossed on the stage, Kemble's qualities not lending themselves to a romp, when they played together some years later in Wycherley's comedy *The Plain Dealer*, he confessed himself quite subdued by her charm: 'It may seem ridiculous to a torpid heart – I could have taken her into my arms and cherished her, though it was in the open street, without blushing.'[16]

VIII

'I am very sorry my luck was to commence Manager this year', wrote Kemble in his journal at the end of his first season, 1788-9. 'The Theatre laboured under great disadvantages from frequent indispositions of the Performers, from the uncommon severity of the winter, from the concern all People took in his Majesty's indisposition and from their loyal Joy for his Recovery. Long may he live!' But the season had been a financial success, the most profitable for several years, and he himself, surviving numerous challenges to his authority, had laid the foundations of an ascendancy on which he would build over the next few seasons. From the first his reign was characterised by close and careful attention to detail. 'It is a *literal* and *positive* fact', asserted the *Morning Post* soon after he took over, 'that not a *Lady's petticoat* is *trimmed* without first consulting Mr Kemble.' Sometimes his anxiety made him too busy; he was apt to be drilling his players even during the performance, a mode of combining the duties of manager and actor which spread confusion among the inexperienced. 'Who can forget', wrote Walter Scott 'how Mrs Siddons in her noviciate was appalled, almost annihilated by the aside frown of Garrick? We ourselves remember to have seen a very pleasing-looking young person much disturbed by Kemble's directions about lifting and lowering the sword in the scene betwixt the princess Anne and Richard.'[1]

With older players Kemble ruled by a mixture of tact and firmness, and though he gained a reputation for 'uncommon asperity' behind the scenes there were few who doubted his integrity or his devotion to the theatre as a whole. He curtailed the actors' right to issue orders for free places. 'Mr Bensley and Mr Baddeley were for making a Riot but I quieted them', he noted; and a few days later, 'I hear no more objections and now exercise the Right of forbidding orders peaceably. This comes of Resolution.' Pursuing his policy of persuading them to work together as a company, he reformed the listing of the players' names on the playbills, displaying them in the order of their social rank in the play rather than in accordance with their importance as actors – a system which lasted for the next forty years. On one tricky point he met with some trouble. This was the so called 'conjunction copulative', the *and* with which a star player's name was preceded on the playbill after the other players had been listed. Thus:

And
The Romp by Mrs Jordan.

It was with Mrs Jordan, before she had been billed in this way, that one such argument arose:

'It is not in the bond', said Kemble, producing Mrs Jordan's articles, 'I cannot see it in the bond.'

'Bond me no bond', answered little Jordan. 'No bond could ever bond me. Mrs Siddons has been indulged with it, Mrs Crouch has been indulged with it and I'll be indulged with it.'[2]

Kemble gave in, at least when Mrs Jordan played her best known roles, for as he noted sagely in his journal: 'Always keep well with the leading Performers, particularly with the Women, though they should be ever so unreasonably troublesome – By humouring half a dozen you uncontrolably command three score.'

*　　*　　*

The absence of Mrs Siddons during Kemble's second season left a void in tragedy which no other actress could hope to fill. Sheridan made light of her absence which his failure to pay her arrears in salary had helped to precipitate. The public, he said, had had enough of lugubrious dramas; it would do no harm to have a rest from them. Mrs Jordan, expecting to be confined with her third child by Richard Ford, was away most of the autumn; she returned to the stage in *The Country Girl* in February 1790, 'somewhat increased in Bulk', said a paper, 'though from late accounts we should rather incline to read diminished'.[3] But even her absence, thanks to Kemble's skilful management, was not felt too greatly. His own favourite project for the season was a revival of *Henry V*, he himself appearing in the leading role. 'I do not think even his Coriolanus exceeded his "royal Hal" ', wrote Boaden; 'as a *coup de théâtre* his starting up from prayer at the sound of the trumpet was one of the most spirited excitements ever displayed on the stage.'

Another great attraction was an opera, *The Haunted Tower*, with music by the young composer Stephen Storace. Storace had been a friend of Mozart's in Vienna and his sister, Nancy Storace, had sung the role of Susanna in the first ever performance of *The Marriage of Figaro*. Now, at Drury Lane, she sang in *The Haunted Tower* with the Irish tenor Michael Kelly, who like her had known Mozart and taken part in that memorable first performance, doubling the parts of Don Basilio and Don Curzio. Trained in the opera houses of Italy and Vienna, Kelly and Nancy Storace would raise the vocal standards of Drury Lane to new heights, Kelly in particular making history as the first playhouse tenor *not* to sing his high notes *falsetto*, while Storace's operas, with their Mozartian echoes, brought a new distinction to the theatre's music. Kelly, genial, convivial, with an Irishman's ready wit, was an especial favourite with Sheridan, who delighted in telling jokes at his expense, while even Kemble, habitually grave, unbent at Kelly's cheerful board. 'Come Kemble', he would call down the supper table, ' "open thy ponderous and marble jaws" and give us your opinion.'[4] For many years, according to his memoirs, Kelly lived on terms of 'strictest intimacy' with the great actor, and if Kemble sometimes complained that the 'musical junto' was favoured by Sheridan, who spent more money on operatic spectacle than on his productions of Shakespeare, it never prevented him from enjoying Kelly's company or sharing his potations.

The Haunted Tower ran for fifty nights to crowded houses. Its success, together with that of *Henry V*, and a lavish musical version of *The Tempest*, was more than enough to offset the season's occasional failures, a revival of *The Two Gentlemen of Verona*, for instance. 'A very ineffectual piece and I am sorry I ever took the Trouble to revive it', noted Kemble. 'NB It was very ill acted into the bargain.'

The sudden illness of his younger brother, whom he had sent to his old college at Douay, took Kemble briefly from the affairs of the theatre. 'This day I set off to Flanders to see my brother Charles', he wrote in his journal for January 19th 1789, and on January 22nd, 'Met my brother on the way.' The meeting had been appropriately theatrical. The two brothers had been travelling by coach, Charles, recovered, on his way back to England, Kemble towards Douay, when Kemble looking up from the book he was reading saw his brother's coach approaching and with an exclamation of 'Charles!' jumped down to greet him.

Charles, like his brother, had been intended for a less precarious career than the theatre, and on his return to England a place was found for him in the Post Office. But no more than his elders could he be diverted from the stage, and four years later he began a career, scarcely less distinguished than theirs, under his brother's aegis at Drury Lane.

*   *   *

In December 1790, half way through Kemble's third season, Mrs Siddons returned at last to Drury Lane. Any misunderstandings with her brother had been righted. Sheridan, who for all his blusterings had found he could not do without her, had settled her arrears in salary. Her first appearance, in the part of Isabella, filled the house to suffocation and she was greeted at the end by five minutes of sustained applause. Her benefit performance, as her husband wrote with satisfaction to their friend Dr Whalley, was 'a golden letter day', with the highest takings in the theatre's history. But despite her gratifying reception she made only eight appearances that season. Her health was still not good and she had spent much of the previous year in an effort to recover from the effects of nervous and physical exhaustion. 'Charming Siddons has spent some weeks with me', wrote Mrs Piozzi (formerly Dr Johnson's beloved Mrs Thrale) in her journal for May 1790. '. . . The Physicians have mistaken her Case & have under a silly notion of Scorbutic Humours – dosed that poor Dear with Mercurial Medicines, till they have torn the fine Vessells to pieces and shattered all the nerves that her Profession had not ruined before.' 'Poor pretty Siddons', she added, 'a warm Heart and a cold Husband are sad things to contend with . . .'[5]

Neither ill health nor marital coldness, however, had kept Mrs Siddons altogether from the stage. During the period of her absence she had reaped a rewarding harvest from engagements in the provinces where her salary, if not always so high as at Drury Lane, at least was certain to be punctually paid. Provincial audiences though, she found, were less inspiring than those in London. 'Acting Isabella for instance out of London', she told Tate Wilkinson, 'is double the fatigue. There the loud and long applause, at the great points and striking situations, invigorated the system – the time it occupied recruited the breath and nerve. A cold respectful audience chills and deadens the actress and throws her back upon herself; whereas the warmth of approbation confirms her in the character and she kindles with the enthusiasm she feels around her.'[6]

Sometimes the audience was not respectful. In Leeds, familiarly known as the Botany Bay of actors, a voice from the gallery bawled out, 'That's right . . . Soop it oop, ma lass!' as she prepared to drain the poisoned cup. On another occasion, when it was very hot and Mrs Siddons very thirsty, her dresser sent a boy in haste to fetch her some beer between acts. He returned when she had already gone on stage and in the midst of the sleep-walking scene from *Macbeth* came up and offered her the foaming mug. In vain she grandly waved him away; he persisted in presenting it for several minutes before the frantic gestures of the stage hands from the wings at last persuaded him to go away. Slopping beer as he went, he hurried off, leaving the audience in such fits of laughter that all Mrs Siddons' powers could not restore the illusion. It was no wonder that after the curtain fell on her final night in Leeds she clasped her hands and exclaimed, 'Farewell, ye brutes!' Proud and indignant, she lacked the aplomb of her brother in dealing with vulgar interruptions. Tom Moore recounts how once, when the squalling of a child in the audience was ruining his performance, Kemble walked forward and announced in tragic tones: 'Ladies and gentlemen, unless the play is stopped, the child cannot possibly go on.'[7]

*   *   *

For some time the structure of Drury Lane had been in a dangerous state. Built by Wren, immortalised by Garrick, it had now reached the stage when alterations and repairs could no longer hold it together and architects pronounced its doom. Sheridan, undisturbed by regrets for departed glories, was meditating a new and grandiose scheme, that of erecting an entirely new theatre, capable of accommodating twice the numbers of the previous one. The proposition had much to commend it in commercial terms: the value of the theatre's monopoly was growing steadily as London's population and its demand for entertainment expanded, and it made financial, if not always artistic, sense to exploit it to the utmost. The same idea had occurred to the proprietors of Covent Garden, who were commissioning the architect Henry Holland to remodel the interior and to increase its seating capacity. Sheridan, going further, commissioned Holland to design a vast new playhouse; new land to accommodate the extra space was acquired and £150,000 worth of debentures was issued and taken up by the public. On June 4th 1791, at the end of Kemble's third season as manager, the old Drury Lane closed down for ever with a performance of *The Country Girl* and a musical afterpiece, Storace's *No Song, No Supper*. Jack Palmer, the 'Plausible Jack', whose own theatre-building plans had come to naught at the Royalty Theatre, delivered the farewell address, and a pleasant epitaph by Colman, the Haymarket manager, in the papers next day, commemorated its final hours:

> On Saturday night, of a gradual decay, and in the 117th year of her age, died *Old Madam Drury*, who existed through six reigns, and saw many generations pass in review before her. She remembered Betterton in his declining age; lived in intimacy with Wilks, Booth and Cibber; and knew old Macklin when he was a stripling . . . She had a rout of near two thousand people at her house the very night of her death; and the old lady found herself in such high spirits, that she said she would give them 'No Supper' without a 'Song'; which being complied with she fell gently back in her chair and expired without a groan. Dr Palmer (one of her family physicians) attended her in her last moments and announced her dissolution to the company.

While the rebuilding of the theatre was going on the company found temporary homes, first at the King's Theatre in the Haymarket, where the vast stage, intended for displays of ballet as well as opera, dwarfed the scenery transferred from Drury Lane, and then at the smaller Haymarket Theatre, till then only permitted to play straight drama in the summer months. Two seasons were to pass before the new theatre was ready, during which time Kemble carried on his management harassed by considerable inconveniences and increasingly restive under the difficulties of dealing with Sheridan. Though the terms of his contract had been clear enough, to implement them was something else again. Had indolence and inattention been his only complaints he could have carried on the business in Sheridan's absence; but Sheridan allowed nothing to be done without his permission, and could seldom be pinned down long enough to give it. He would make appointments and not keep them, or arrive in a hurry to postpone them to another day. A typical letter from Kemble describes himself as waiting from one o'clock in the afternoon till one in the morning to see him; on another occasion, having arranged to meet him at the house of Peake, the treasurer, at teatime, he waited for him all through the night, drinking deep with Peake and a friend and boasting, as he never did when sober, of his achievements as an actor. As for Sheridan, he would turn up in the green-room of the theatre drunk, and asking the name of some well-known actor, declare he should never play at Drury Lane again; his enormous charm and humour were seldom displayed for the benefit of his players though he could use them to such effect when he wished that even Mrs Siddons, hard bargainer though she was, let herself be deceived again and again. Once, for instance, she had gone to his house determined not to leave it without the large sum of money he owed her. She came out after some time, reported a friend who was waiting for her, looking 'quite *rayonnante*'.

'Well', said he, 'I hope you have succeeded.'

'Yes, indeed I have.'

'Well, and how was it?'

'Why, you see, we had a great deal of conversation together – he showed me that he is under great difficulties; however, he has positively undertaken to pay me the whole debt next month, provided in the meantime I advance him £50. This I have done, so you see I have obtained my object.'[8]

No one was more under Sheridan's charm than Kemble. Sheridan's own private opinion of Kemble was that, acting apart, he was a dull dog, industrious and excellent in his way but 'very limited in his genius'. Kemble, on the other hand, till disillusion finally set in, was one of his greatest admirers, though from time to time, smarting under some exceptional grievance, he would throw aside his allegiance and denounce him. 'I know him thoroughly', he would say, 'all his sophistry, all his petty artifices – but I will become a member of his own society, *the Friends of the People,** and when he rises to speak I'LL PUT HIM DOWN.'[9] But these were only temporary outbursts, soon to be drowned in drink and forgotten under Sheridan's blandishments, though once however, when the prospects of the new Drury Lane and Kemble's authority had been more than usually undermined, he announced his fixed determination to resign. The scene took place in Kelly's house where Kemble, expecting Sheridan's arrival after the House of Commons had risen, had repaired, and where, knowing Sheridan's persuasive powers, he set about fortifying his resolution with claret. 'At length', wrote Boaden, who witnessed it, 'Sheridan arrived, took his place next to Mrs Crouch at the table, looked at Kemble with kindness, but the kindness was neither returned nor acknowledged. The great actor now looked unutterable things, and occasionally emitted a *humming* sound like that of a bee, and groaned in spirit inwardly . . . A considerable time elapsed and frequent repetitions of the sound before mentioned occurred; when at last, "like a pillar of state", slowly uprose Kemble, and in these words addressed the astonished proprietor: "I am an EAGLE, whose wings have been bound down by frosts and snows; but now I shake my pinions and cleave into the general air, into which I am born." He then deliberately resumed his seat and looked as if he had relieved himself from unsupportable thralldom.'

But Sheridan, continued Boaden, 'knew the complacency of the man under the notion of a fine figure, and saw that his eagle was not absolutely irreclaimable; he rose, took a chair next to the great actor; in two minutes resumed his old ascendancy. The tragedian soon softened into his usual forgiving temper; and I am ashamed to say how late it was when, cordial as brothers, I took one arm of Kemble and Sheridan the other, and resolutions were formed "that melted as breath into the passing wind".'

* A society advocating electoral reform of which Sheridan was a leading member.

IX

Since 1789 the successive shock waves of the French Revolution had been felt in London as elsewhere and the stage, which in Johnson's words 'but echoes back the public voice', had greeted its first manifestations with spectacles that celebrated the fall of the Bastille and the dawn of liberty across the Channel.* Meanwhile Burke, in his *Reflections on the French Revolution*, recalled 'the tears that Garrick formerly and Siddons not long since, have extorted from me' as he deplored the real tragedy unfolding.

With the events of the Terror the mood changed – at a performance of *Cymon*, an elaborate musical extravaganza, the appearance of a French banner in the procession was greeted with hisses and cries of 'Off, off!' from the audience. And it was at the end of this very piece, on January 24th 1793, that Kemble announced the closure of the theatre on the following night as a sign of mourning for the death of Louis XVI. Sheridan, who had been away when the announcement was made, berated him later for allowing foreign politics to interfere with his receipts.

The trial for treason, in the following year, of leading radical figures, members of the London Corresponding Society accused of conspiring to overthrow the government, provoked intense public interest in an atmosphere grown increasingly repressive since France's declaration of war. 'NB', noted Kemble, to whom everything related to his profession, 'the trial of Messrs Hardy, Horne Took & c. hurt the Theatre very much.'

Among those on trial was the playwright Thomas Holcroft, whose melodrama, *The Road to Ruin*, first played at Covent Garden three years before, was one of the great successes of the day. The threat of execution hung over him and his fellow prisoners, together with the

* Though the Lord Chamberlain banned an entertainment, *The Bastille*, at Covent Garden, the subject flourished at the 'unofficial' theatres; within a month of the fall of the Bastille, Sadlers Wells, the Royal Grove and the Royal Circus, had put on their versions of the event.

certainty that should they be found guilty a far greater number of prosecutions would follow. Against this background it is pleasing to learn that Mrs Inchbald, as soon as she heard of his arrest, went to visit him in prison and this despite the fact that only a few months previously she had broken off all relations with him. Holcroft, long a colleague at Covent Garden, had recently discovered a violent passion for her, and when it was not reciprocated had been equally violent in his pique.

Mrs Inchbald's connection with Holcroft was not her only link with the treason trials or with radical circles, for William Godwin, whose famous *Cursory Strictures* condemning the trials almost certainly swung the balance of public opinion which led to all the prisoners being acquitted, had become not only a friend but 'conscious', as he said, 'of some tenderness towards her'. He it was who had read and recommended to her publisher her novel *A Simple Story*, whose appearance in 1791 had made her one of the best known novelists of the day, and whose portrait of Kemble, haughty, forbidding, yet glowing with inward sensibility, was an acknowledged influence on Charlotte Brontë in creating Mr Rochester.

Kemble had read the early part of the novel as far back as 1778. The pulse of their mutual attraction beats strongly through its pages though its happy ending with the marriage of Dorriforth, now through his inheritance of a title, Lord Elmwood, to Miss Milner is already shadowed with ill omen. 'After the sacred ceremony was over Miss Milner felt an excruciating shock when, on looking on the ring Lord Elmwood had put on her finger, she perceived it was – a mourning ring!' The second part of the book takes place seventeen years later. Lord Elmwood and his wife are separated. 'The beautiful, the beloved Miss Milner is no longer beautiful – no longer beloved – no longer – tremble while you read it! – no longer – *virtuous*', while Lord Elmwood, whom she has betrayed, has become an implacable misogynist. When his wife dies, reconciled with God but not with him, he refuses to set eyes upon their only daughter; her sufferings, and the series of dramatic incidents which bring father and daughter together, are the theme of the story.

Whether Kemble recognised himself in this second half, its hero drawn more from his roles in gothic dramas like *The Count of*

Narbonne than from real life, is not clear but he certainly rejoiced in his friend's success. Through her he was introduced to Godwin and Mary Wollstonecraft whose feelings about Mrs Inchbald, 'Mrs Perfection' as she called her, were always tinged with jealousy. Mrs Siddons too met Godwin in her company, and her son Henry, then aged fourteen, was so overcome at meeting the great writer that he knelt and kissed the chair on which he had been sitting.

To all the Kemble family Mrs Inchbald remained a valued friend, borne with them on their upward journey through the world. Mrs Siddons, who had taken up sculpture as a pastime, presented her with one of her first busts; Mrs Kemble took her with her on visits to great country houses; from Kemble himself, who called her his 'dear Muse', came stately invitations to dine: 'Mr Kemble has the pleasure of Mr Twiss's company to-day at dinner and will be infinitely charmed to find the tenth Muse at his table also. Mr Kemble would not willingly appear ceremonious, so he does not send cards to the nine sisters, as he observes the tenth never visits without them.'[1]

A Simple Story had taken its toll of Mrs Inchbald's health and spirits. 'I was ten months incessantly finishing my novel', she told Godwin later when he urged her to undertake more fiction. In the little room in Frith Street which was her lodging, she had sat with her shutters closed to avoid all distraction and had paid for her concentration with devastating nervous headaches.

Dramatic composition cost her no such pains. She could earn as much, she declared, in ten days' playwriting as she had made by her novel, and the year that followed its publication saw her engaged, with a lighter heart, on a comedy, *The Wedding Day*, for Mrs Jordan at Drury Lane.

It was Mrs Inchbald's first play for that theatre, still, thanks to Sheridan's fame, the more prestigious of the patent houses. For all his admiration for his Muse Kemble had never used his influence to obtain her a commission there. The 'treasures of our ancient authors' in his view provided comedies enough; it was only at the insistence of Mrs Jordan, who had long been clamouring for a new vehicle for her talents and denouncing Kemble for his reluctance to provide one, that Mrs Inchbald was at last invited to write for Drury Lane.

A gay little piece, with Mrs Jordan as a young country bride, betrothed to a crotchety widower and rescued in the nick of time by the unexpected reappearance of his first wife, her comedy delighted Mrs Jordan and her audiences. It gave her too a favourite song, 'In the Dead of the Night' a line from which, 'Cupid knock'd at my window disturbing my rest', swept through the town and was heard on every mouth, wrote an admirer, 'like the natural notes of some sweet melody which drops from it whether it will or no – nothing but Cupid, Cupid! The whole city, like the heart of one man, opened itself to Love.'[2]

*   *   *

The public which was enchanted by Mrs Jordan in *The Wedding Day* was taking great pleasure too in following her life off stage. Items of theatrical gossip were always plentiful in the daily press and the affairs of leading actors such as Kemble and Mrs Siddons were followed with close attention. But with Mrs Jordan the papers had a field day when towards the summer of 1791 there came the news that she was being courted by no less a personage than the Duke of Clarence, and with it a flurry of speculation as to her reception of his suit. 'Had the illustrious youth crossed the Ford', as one paper maintained in July, or had he been unsuccessful, as another asserted in August, finding 'the Ford too dangerous to cross the Jordan?'. Whatever the answer to these important questions there was no doubt that the Duke was deeply enamoured and, though prevented by the terms of the Royal Marriage Act from making her his wife, was eager to replace Richard Ford as her protector.

The Duke of Clarence was the third son of George III. Born in 1765 he had been sent to sea as a midshipman at the age of fourteen and had spent nine of his eleven years in the navy on active service, retiring with the honorary rank of rear-admiral in 1789. Tradition has it that he first began to take an interest in Mrs Jordan in the following year when he saw her in the part of Little Pickle, in an otherwise undistinguished farce *The Spoil'd Child*. The pranks of Little Pickle, a naughty schoolboy, were interspersed with songs, and for the royal sailor watching from his box there was, it seems, a special charm in one where Mrs Jordan, half wistful, half comic, played a homesick sailor boy:

What girl but loves the merry Tar?
We o'er the ocean roam, sir.
In ev'ry clime we find a port,
In ev'ry port a home, sir . . .

The courtship of Little Pickle by the merry tar caused great amusement in the press and gave material for numerous unflattering cartoons. But despite his royal birth and the ardour of his suit the Duke's success in the matter was by no means a *fait accompli*. Had Richard Ford kept his promise to marry her, Mrs Jordan would have undoubtedly stuck to him. Of her three children by him, two were living, and she had her daughter by Daly to provide for. Her own experience of being an illegitimate child and the memory of her mother's struggles had left her determined that her children should not suffer the same fate. But Richard Ford, even when faced with the challenge of an illustrious rival, lacked the courage to make her his wife, though he was content to go on introducing her in company, as he had done for some years, as Mrs Ford.

The Duke, on the other hand, though he could not offer marriage, was prepared to make a legal settlement which besides providing for any future children would settle an annuity on her for life. These inducements, coupled with her disillusion with Ford, went far to soften Mrs Jordan's resistance. The Duke's admiration could not but be flattering; four years younger than herself, bluff, breezy and good-natured, he was moreover far from unattractive. When at last Mrs Jordan, despairing of marriage, broke with Ford and became his mistress, she was soon whole-heartedly attached to him.

It took some months before the financial arrangements regarding this new relationship were settled. Mrs Jordan, wrote the Duke to his brother the Prince of Wales, behaved throughout like an angel. The care of her children was her first concern; on her two children by Ford she settled all her savings, together with half her future income from the theatre, while the Duke himself made provision for her eldest daughter, Fanny Daly. These three were to live with Mrs Jordan's sister, who had already looked after them for her while she was acting or on tour. Mrs Jordan herself was to receive a yearly allowance of eight hundred guineas from the Duke.

It was not to be expected that these arrangements would not be misreported or criticised. Richard Ford, though he had been relieved of all financial responsibility for his children, which he was in no position to discharge, was cast by the press as an injured man and Mrs Jordan as an unnatural mother who had abandoned her children from ambition. The malicious tongue of the rival actress Mrs Crouch, who was enjoying a brief liaison with the Prince of Wales, was thought to be behind these charges. They could not be sustained, however, when Mrs Jordan, having induced Ford to write two letters exonerating her, sent copies of them to the papers. 'Lest any insinuations be circulated to the prejudice of Mrs Jordan', he had written, 'in respect of her having behaved improperly towards her children in regard to pecuniary matters, I hereby declare that her conduct in these matters has been as laudable, generous, and as like a fond mother as it was possible to be.' A second letter, written 'in gratitude for the care Mrs Jordan has ever bestowed on my children', gave his consent for her to visit them freely whenever she wished.

The publication of the letters did not stop Mrs Jordan's annoyances from the press. The lovers were criticised for their too demonstrative behaviour in public; one paper took exception to their 'playful gambols' in the royal box, another announced that 'the conduct of a certain pair, in their journey to and from the neighbourhood of *Richmond* [where the Duke had a house] is the *daily* occasion of a blush in everything on that road except the *milestones*';[3] cartoonists, taking up the theme, made much of the fact that 'jordan' was another word for chamberpot. Mrs Jordan's health suffered under these and other attacks, and her cancellations of performances on the plea of illness drew further criticisms. It was suggested that her head had been turned and that she was neglecting her professional obligations; more than once when she did appear there were hisses from the audience.

Finally, after unsuccessfully appealing to the public in an open letter to the papers, she confronted her critics in person. In the midst of a performance, when a growing undercurrent of hisses was making itself heard through the applause of her supporters and those experienced in the theatre began to fear a riot, she broke off her part and walked forward to the front of the stage.

'Ladies and gentlemen', she began, 'I should conceive myself utterly unworthy of your favour, if the slightest mark of public disapprobation did not affect me very sensibly. Since I have had the honour and the happiness to strive here to please you, it has been my constant endeavour, by unremitting assiduity, to merit your approbation. I beg leave to assure you, upon my *honour*, that I have never absented myself one minute from the duties of my profession but from *real* indisposition. Thus having invariably acted, I *do* consider myself under the public protection.'

'This was exactly the way to treat them', wrote Boaden, who was present. 'The manner was extremely good; the little *hardship* that sat upon her brow, and like a cloud, kept back the comic smile that but waited their cheer, to burst forth – the graceful *obeisance*, that followed her complete triumph (for it was complete) . . .'[3] From then on the evening went entirely Mrs Jordan's way. She returned home on the arm of the Duke, who had been anxiously watching from the wings, satisfied that she had won back her audience's heart. 'Mrs Jordan's first appearance since the 26th of November', noted Kemble in his journal. 'A great Riot on her entrance but she addressed the Audience in a very elegant sensible way and all was well again.'

*   *   *

While Mrs Jordan's affairs were being blazoned abroad for the pleasure of a scandal-loving public, Mrs Siddons was having her own private troubles. Her health was still not good. 'My spirits are absolutely worn out with fatigue, the springs of my poor machine have been overstrained, and I must have complete rest of body and mind to restore them to their natural tone again',[4] she wrote to a friend and elsewhere spoke of a tormenting complaint, possibly a nervous skin disease, for which she was hoping to take the waters. In the autumn of 1791 she had a miscarriage and did not return to the London stage till the beginning of 1792, and then for only a limited number of performances. The summer saw her hurrying off to Edinburgh to play for her brother Stephen Kemble, who had just become the manager of the Theatre Royal there. But though by late September her daughter Sally was writing to a family friend that 'my belov'd mother is at length cur'd of her complaint, and quite an

94

alt'red woman',[5] Mrs Piozzi, whose letters and journals are full of references to Mrs Siddons, had another tale to recount that autumn. 'And so poor Mrs Siddons' disorder that we have all been at such a stand about', she wrote, 'turns upon close Examination to be neither more nor less than the P— given her by her husband. What a world it is!'[6]

'Poor Siddons pities my very soul to see her', she wrote to a friend soon after. 'An indignant melancholy sits on her fine face and care corrodes her very vitals. God only can comfort her, and his grace alone support her for she is all resentment . . . I am sincerely afflicted for her suffering virtue, never did I see a purer mind, but it is now sullied by the thoughts that she has washed her hands in innocence in vain! How shall I endure the sight of her odious husband?'[7]

Whether or not William Siddons was guilty of passing on a venereal infection to his wife, it seems clear that dissension between them was a cause of Mrs Siddons' ill health. Mrs Piozzi had already noted Siddons' coldness towards her. 'I know not the cause', she wrote in her journal, 'but five thousand women are better liked by their families.'[8] Handsome, good-mannered, with a pleasant talent for light verse, William Siddons might have shone in the less demanding sphere of a provincial theatre; as it was, dissatisfied with himself he took out his dissatisfaction on his wife, and was guilty, if Mrs Piozzi was right, of other lapses too. There was no dramatic break between them and the following year must have seen some kind of reconciliation between them, for Mrs Siddons was once more pregnant by the end of 1793, but there was no doubt that she often suffered from her husband's attitude. Blameless though she was, it is possible to feel a certain sympathy for William Siddons too. He put his finger on the problem when Kemble, who always got on well with him, expressed his wonder that he and Mrs Siddons did not suit each other better. What could he possibly object to, he asked, for his wife had 'beauty, virtue, talents'? 'True', replied Siddons sadly, 'but all insufficient for happiness. She is too Grand a thing for me.'[9]

X

On March 12th 1794, after long delays, the new Drury Lane was opened to the public for the first time with a concert of sacred music to mark the beginning of Lent. A board from the stage of the old Drury Lane which Sheridan, as a gesture of sentiment, had included in that of the new, was all that remained of the former theatre, and the orchestra on this opening night was banked up against the background of a gothic chapel with fretted roof and illuminated stained-glass windows. This splendid spectacle, after Kemble's own heart, was one of a series of new scenes by the artist William Capon, who like Kemble brought an antiquarian's zeal to the theatre and whose reconstructions of gothic architecture would be used as a background to many of Kemble's Shakespearean productions.

The dramatic inauguration of the theatre was planned for Easter Monday, April 21st. Kemble and Mrs Siddons were to appear in a new production of *Macbeth*, Mrs Siddons undeterred by the fact that she was six months pregnant. 'I suppose', said one wit, 'she means to carry all before her.'[1] Making his début on this occasion was Kemble's younger brother Charles, in the part of Malcolm. 'You will see shortly two young men in the profession in whom I take an interest', said Kemble to Boaden. 'One of them is my brother Charles; *he* will make an actor.' Avoiding the false kindness of pushing him forward too soon, he would bring Charles slowly through the gradations of his art, providing him with a grounding as thorough as his own.

The new production of *Macbeth* was Kemble's most ambitious yet. 'I am told that the banquet scene is a thing to go and see of itself', wrote Mrs Siddons to her friend Lady Harcourt. 'The scenes and dresses are as superb and characteristic as it is possible to make them. You cannot conceive what I feel at the prospect of playing there. I daresay I shall be so nervous as scarcely to be able to make myself heard in the first scene.'[2]

For once, Sheridan had not stinted Kemble on expenses. No less than seven scene painters, Capon among them, had been commissioned to provide some sixteen changes of scene, new costumes had been designed, Kemble himself was magnificent in highland dress and a bonnet adorned with tall black ostrich feathers. The performance was notable for its 'new readings'. In the banquet scene, for instance, the ghost of Banquo, commonly played, as one reviewer observed, 'like a man turned out of a meal sack', was omitted altogether, leaving the guilty fancy of Macbeth and the imagination of the audience to fill the vacant chair. In the scene with the witches in the fourth act, on the other hand, Kemble gave body to the invocation,

> Black spirits and white,
> Blue spirits and grey,

by introducing four bands of children as imps, among whom, as Kemble recalled later, a black-eyed urchin named Edmund Kean caused such confusion by egging on his comrades to every kind of mischief that Kemble, after one performance, dismissed them from the stage.

Kemble's Macbeth, studied and perfected over the years, had reached a stage where it matched and complemented his sister's inimitable Lady Macbeth. He had played it once, for his benefit, in 1785, returning to it in his first season as manager. His interpretation would not stay static; and on this evening apparently, after the exertions of preparing for the opening, he showed signs of fatigue. But at his best, wrote Walter Scott, he was unapproachable in the part, 'nor can we conceive that the bold and effective manner of Garrick, touching on the broad points of the character with a hand however vigorous, could at all compare with Kemble's exquisitely and minutely elaborate delineation of guilty ambition, drawn on from crime to crime, while the avenging furies at once scourge him for further guilt, and urge him to further enormities. We can never forget the rueful horror of his look, which by strong exertion he endeavours to conceal, when on the morning succeeding the murder he receives Lennox and Macduff in the ante-chamber of Duncan. His efforts to appear composed, his endeavours to assume the attitude and appearance of one listening to Lennox's account of the external

97

terrors of the night, while in fact he is expecting the alarm to rise within the royal apartment, formed a most astonishing piece of playing. Kemble's countenance seemed altered by the sense of internal horror, and had a cast of that of Count Ugolino in the dungeon, as painted by Reynolds. When Macbeth felt himself obliged to turn towards Lennox and reply to what he had been saying, you saw him, like a man awaking from a fit of absence, endeavour to recollect at least the general tenor of what had been said and it was some time ere he could bring out the general reply, "'Twas a rough night." Those who have had the good fortune to see Kemble and Mrs Siddons in Macbeth and his lady, may be satisfied they have witnessed the highest perfection of the dramatic art. There cannot have been, and we fear never will be, anything to compare to it.'[3]

*   *   *

A prologue, extolling Shakespeare and dedicating the new theatre to his fame, had preceded the opening performance of *Macbeth*. Kemble, who delivered it, had received his text only the day before. He had picked it up on his way to dine with Michael Kelly, where Sheridan too was expected, and in the hour and a half before Sheridan's arrival had got its fifty lines word-perfect. Like his sister Kemble was an exceptionally 'quick study'. 'I have often heard him say', wrote Kelly, 'that he would make a bet that in four days he would repeat every line in a newspaper, advertisements and all, verbatim, in their regular order, without misplacing or missing a single word.'[4]

The epilogue for the evening was given by Miss Farren, who in the guise of housekeeper to a noble lord showed off the new building to the audience. In obedience to her wand an iron safety curtain interposed itself between stage and audience and, on being raised again, revealed an artificial lake and a cascade of water from a tank above. The destruction by fire of two theatres, the King's Theatre, Haymarket, and the Pantheon,* had left the public very much alive to the dangers of a conflagration. But though these elaborate precautions were reassuring, Miss Farren's boastful challenge to the powers of fire could be seen as tempting fate:

* The Pantheon, originally a centre for balls and masquerades, was used in place of the King's Theatre when the latter burnt down in 1789, and burnt down itself in 1792.

The very ravages of fire we scout,
For we have herewithal to put it out:
In ample reservoirs our firm reliance
Whose streams set conflagrations at defiance.

Fifteen years later, before the exterior of the building was completed, the theatre was burnt to the ground.

Meanwhile, though the outside remained unfinished for lack of funds, the splendour of the interior delighted the audience. Surprisingly light and airy for its vast size, it was likened to a giant bird-cage from the way the lines dividing the boxes converged in the centre of the ceiling. The decorations were in the neo-classical manner; a multiplicity of cut-glass candelabra lighted the interior as brightly, said one bedazzled spectator, as the sun at noon. A wider proscenium arch, with far greater depth behind the stage, made possible scenic effects well beyond the scope of the former theatre. The auditorium itself held 3,611 spectators, some 2,000 more than previously, and the actors' voices had to project a hundred feet rather than sixty as before. The difference was all-important. With so much distance to command it was inevitable that much of the intimacy between actor and audience would be lost. Henceforward, wrote the playwright Richard Cumberland, there were 'theatres for spectators rather than playhouses for hearers . . . The splendour of the scenes and the ingenuity of the machinist and the rich display of dresses aided by the captivating clamours of music now in a great degree superseded the labours of the poet . . . On the stage of the old Drury in the days of Garrick the moving brow and penetrating eye of that marvellous actor came home to the spectator. As the passions shifted, and were by turns reflected in the mirror of his expressive countenance, nothing was lost; upon the scale of modern Drury many of the finest touches of his art might necessarily fall short.'[5]

Mrs Siddons, for all her initial enthusiasm, soon sensed how much had been lost by the change of scale which forced on her a bolder, larger style. 'I am glad you are come to Drury Lane', she wrote to the actor William Dowton when he made his début in 1796, 'but you are come to a wilderness of a place, and God knows, if I had not made my reputation in a small theatre I should never have made it.'[6]

The effect on the actors was not the only consequence of the theatre's greatly increased size. The rush for seats and the frequent overcrowding in the old Drury Lane had had the effect of stimulating the public's appetite; the ease of access and the cheerless look of the vast new theatre when it was half empty were correspondingly discouraging. To gather some three and a half thousand people together new and spectacular attractions must continually be sought. It was to Kemble's credit that, thanks to his own and his sister's acting and the splendour of the productions, the popularity of Shakespeare continued unabated; his cuts and additions, however reprehensible, must be seen in the context of the audience he wished to please. But increasingly as time went by Drury Lane and the newly enlarged Covent Garden edged towards the repertoire of the non-patent theatres (whose right to perform legitimate drama they consistently denied) in their efforts to attract a wider public. Pantomimes, processions, dashing melodramas played an increasing role; performing animals, horses, dogs, even elephants were brought on to the stage. 'Why do they take my horses?' asked the proprietor of Astley's Amphitheatre plaintively. 'I never tried to engage Mrs Siddons.'[7]

For Sheridan personally the construction of the new Drury Lane, on which he had embarked with such hopes, was an eventual disaster. Disputes as to the ownership of the theatre's patent had cost him some £20,000 before he could obtain the clear title demanded by his shareholders and had delayed the commencement of the building; the move to the King's Theatre and then the Haymarket had involved him in a considerable loss; the cost of rebuilding the theatre had overrun the original estimate by £70,000. Whatever the difficulties caused by his carelessness in running the old Drury Lane, the theatre had always been potentially viable. Now, with greatly increased running costs and encumbrances far heavier than he had foreseen, he was entangled in such a confusion of mortgages and liabilities that it seemed impossible that he could ever extricate himself. A small but interesting detail in the design of the new theatre was a portent of the future. In the old Drury Lane the treasurer, Richard Peake, had had an office inside the theatre from which, when the actors came to claim their unpaid salaries, there was no escape; he had sometimes been kept prisoner there for hours, not daring to unbar the door. In the new theatre matters were more conveniently arranged: the window of the treasury opened onto the street outside, allowing the besieged cashier to make himself scarce on Saturday paydays when the exchequer was bare.

For the moment, however, all was optimism and Kemble, descending from the Shakespearean heights, applied himself with enthusiasm to providing lighter entertainments. Turning author himself, he translated and adapted a musical French romance *Lodoiska*. Set in Poland, with a cast of wicked baron, captured princess and gallant rescuer, its high spot was the storming of a blazing castle by a band of Tartars – a spectacular scene that nearly ended in disaster on the opening night when the wind blew the flames the wrong way and Mrs Crouch, the heroine in the tower, was in imminent danger of being burnt. Michael Kelly, who played the hero, seeing her danger, was rushing up the bridge which led to her tower when a carpenter inadvertently removed a support and he fell to the ground. A moment later, the blazing tower, with Mrs Crouch still inside it, collapsed with a violent crash. Mrs Crouch screamed with terror but Kelly, luckily unhurt, was just in time to catch her in his arms and carry her, amid 'loud and continued applause', to the forefront of the stage.

After the accident, recalled Kelly in his memoirs, 'Mr Sheridan came to sup with me and I told him I was lucky in not having broken my neck. He left us earlier than usual to go to the Duchess of Devonshire's. The Duchess, who had been at the theatre, asked if I had been much hurt; to which (with his usual good nature in making blunders for me) he replied: "Not in the least; I have just left him very well and in good spirits; but he has been putting a very puzzling question to me which was – Suppose Mr Sheridan, I had been killed by my fall, who would have *maintained* me for the rest of my life?" '

*   *   *

Lodoiska, the first of a line of such battling melodramas as *Timour the Tartar* and *The Miller and his Men*, was the money-spinner of the season and Kelly's fortuitous rescue so popular that it was repeated, with less danger, at each succeeding performance. The critics might complain that such trumpery spectacles were a form of prostitution, but there was no doubt that they brought in the crowds. On July 12th, when the theatre closed for the summer, it had grossed some £20,000. Whatever troubles lay ahead, the new Drury Lane had got off to a flying start and Kemble could bask in its reflected glory.

Stage matters apart, he was becoming an important personage. His Shakespearean revivals had won him the respect of literary circles. The great Shakespearean scholar, Edmond Malone, though he cannot have approved the actor's editorial liberties, admired him as 'a man of education and gentlemanly manners',[8] with whom he was always happy to dine and to discuss English drama, past and present. Kemble's library, with its collection of plays and theatrical history, became, as he grew more affluent through the 1790s, the leading collection of its kind, and he was always ready to open it to scholars or provide learned information to enquirers. In his later years, when he became a friend of Walter Scott, it was his 'love of black-letter learning, especially of dramatic antiquities',[9] that formed the first bond of fellowship between them; and Scott recalled with pride how, in the interests of historical accuracy, he once removed the great bunches of plumes, 'resembling an undertaker's hearse', from the highland bonnet which Kemble was wearing in preparation for going on as Macbeth, and replaced them by a more authentic eagle's feather. This innovation, Kemble told him, was worth three distinct rounds of applause.

The fashionable world threw open its doors to Kemble as it had done to his sister. He was invited to the houses of the great – to dine with Lady Holland or the Duchess of Devonshire, to stay with Lord Abercorn or the stage-struck Earl of Guildford, in their country houses. His journal was scattered with aristocratic names. 'Dined at the Duke of Leinster's', we read in his diary for an Irish tour; on another day, 'Passed this morning delightfully with the venerable Earl of Charlmont', and on yet another, 'The Earl of Milltown supp'd with me after the Play tonight – my wine was very bad, and he sent me some excellent Port and Claret next day.' Priscilla Kemble aided and abetted him in his upward progress and Kemble saw to it that she was not left out. When the playwright Robert Jephson invited him to dinner without her, Kemble made her call for him about nine o'clock 'that they might recollect I had a wife'.

The Prince of Wales and the royal dukes were frequent visitors to Drury Lane. It was not to be expected that Kemble would be a favourite with the Duke of Clarence, who had too often heard Mrs Jordan's complaints against the 'Kemble coterie'. But the Prince of Wales was a devoted admirer. He frequently summoned Kemble to his box at the theatre. 'He was very gracious indeed', noted Kemble on one such occasion. 'There was nobody in his Box – he kept me till the end of the first Act of the Farce.' He even – not at all to Sheridan's liking, for Sheridan had no wish to share his social successes with his actors – invited him to dine at Carlton House. 'I liked Kemble very much', he told the actor Charles Mathews years later, when he was king. 'He was one of my earliest friends. I remember once he was talking and found himself out of snuff. I offered him my box. He declined taking any – he, a poor actor, would not put his fingers into a royal box. I said, "Take some, pray, you will *obleege* me." Upon which Kemble replied, "It would become your royal mouth better to say *oblige* me",[10] and took a pinch.' Kemble's views on pronunciation were unyielding. 'He would correct any body, at any time and in any place', wrote Coleridge, who always professed 'a great liking – I may say a sort of nondescript reverence'[11] for him.

If Garrick had transformed the position of the actor in society, it was Kemble who consolidated it. Unlike Garrick, who in mixing with the great, noted Walter Scott, 'was desirous to procure their notice more than a man of his commanding genius ought perhaps to have been',[12] Kemble never used his actor's gifts to court attention. He took a ready and agreeable part in general conversation but no more. He would never, like Garrick, 'oblige with imitations'; and though he always referred to himself as a player, and was ready when the occasion arose naturally to talk of theatrical matters, he would never discuss his own conception of a role. Those who asked him to do so received the answer, rather coldly given, 'You must come and see me do it.'

Kemble's grave and formal manners, shading into *hauteur* with those he did not know, were a byword. He lived, as it were, with the cloak of the 'noble Roman' round him, or as someone put it crossly when he turned up late, with a drawled perfunctory excuse, for a breakfast appointment, as though he had eaten a 'poached curtain rod'. His wit was stately rather than spontaneous, seldom exceeding what Boaden called a 'grave Cervantic humour', and a later biographer, less flatteringly, a 'grim and forced jocularity'. The sobriety of Kemble's bearing, which went so well with his classical appearance, was thrown into strong relief, however, by his disorderly and ungovernable behaviour when, as often happened, he was drunk. It was an age of drunkenness. Sheridan's addiction to the bottle was notorious, but so too was that of Pitt, Fox and other leading figures of the day. Amidst these great drinkers Kemble kept pace, though, mindful perhaps of Garrick's celebrated advice to an aspiring young actor – to keep off the bottle and always be word-perfect – he was seldom the worse for wear on stage.

Kemble drank, as he moved, in the best circles. He drank with Sheridan, 'waxing majestic' as he grew more tipsy, though once forgetting himself so far as to fling a decanter at his unreliable employer's head. He drank with Walter Scott – he was the only man, said the novelist, who seduced him into very deep potations in his middle years. 'When we have heard Kemble pour forth the treasures of his critical knowledge over a bottle', he wrote, 'we were irresistibly reminded of the author of Epicene giving law at the Mermaid or the Apollo.'[13] He drank at the Beefsteak Club, inspiring the respect of even such veteran topers as the Duke of Norfolk (who was regularly carried out insensible). He drank at dinner parties. Sydney Owenson, later Lady Morgan, recalled her first meeting with him at Lady Cork's, when Kemble, half tipsy, fixed a glassy look at her short and fashionably windswept hair. At last, leaning over, and doubtless thinking of some Roman hairstyle, he 'actually stuck his claws in my locks and addressing me in the deepest sepulchral tones, asked, "Little girl, where did you get your wig?" '[14] On another occasion, having become drunk at dinner he refused to leave with the other guests, on the sensible grounds that since it was the last time he would be invited to that house he might as well make the most of it. And so he stayed till the next day, 'the whole time lauding the classical drama, and attacking modern comedy'.[15]

Kemble's drinking, as time went by, became as much a part of his legend as his theatrical achievements. It in no way detracted from his popularity. John Taylor, in his memoirs, recalls one delightful occasion when, having drunk late and long at Deptford with Fanny Burney's brother Charles, he took a lift back to London on a fishmonger's cart and got on so well with the driver on the way that he asked to be taken to Billingsgate. Here a crowd soon gathered to see the famous actor, and he was taken on a ceremonial tour of the market, delighting his audience with his 'humourous sallies'. He finally left, having been presented with a turbot for Mrs Kemble, amidst the cheers of the assembled crowd.

Though frequently drunk and disorderly, Kemble was usually high-minded and chivalrous when it came to women. During the first years after his arrival at Drury Lane he had been almost wholly absorbed in furthering his career. Once married to Priscilla Kemble – his 'Pop' as he called her – he showed few signs of straying, and only once, to the delight of a scandal-loving public, was he openly caught out.

The episode took place one evening in the January of 1795, when Kemble, very drunk, burst in on an attractive young singer, Fanny De Camp, and tried to assault her in her dressing-room. Miss De Camp resisted forcibly, the actor was repulsed, and a few days later, in an attempt to make amends, the following notice was published in the papers:

> I, John Philip Kemble, of the Theatre Royal Drury Lane, do adopt this method of publicly apologising to Miss De Camp, for the very improper and unjustifiable behaviour I was lately guilty of towards her, which I do further declare her conduct and character had in no wise authorised; but on the contrary, I do know and believe both to be irreproachable.

'Kemble's advertisement, so like that of a penitent Hackney coachman under the threatened Lash of a sharp prosecution, excites much notice, I understand', wrote Mrs Piozzi to a friend; 'but am shocked to find his offence, tho' actionable, considered by the fashionists more as a jest than an enormity.'[16]

Mrs Kemble's reaction is not recorded, but there seem to have been no further lapses, and eventually, though not till the last years of his life, she managed to wean her husband from the bottle too.

She became quite fierce with those who tried to tempt him back to his old ways. When John Taylor dined with him not long before his retirement and remarked in a jovial mood, 'Come, Johnny, we have not drunk a glass of wine together', he met a sharp reaction. 'I am Johnny', said Mrs Kemble firmly. 'Mr Kemble does not drink wine and I am ready for you.'[17]

XI

If Kemble's attempted assault on Miss De Camp had left his dignity impaired, embarrassment was swallowed up in triumph one month later when on February 28th, 1795 he made his first appearance in Richard Cumberland's *The Wheel of Fortune*. 'There is a part in it that will do something for me', he told Michael Kelly when he first read the play; 'at least I feel I can do something for *it*.'[1] In the role of Penruddock, a stern but noble misanthrope, much wronged yet refusing revenge on the rival who had ruined him, he gave one of his most memorable performances. 'I believe it to be a perfect one', wrote Leigh Hunt. '. . . The very defect which hurts his general style of acting, that studious and important preciseness, which is affectation in all his other characters, contributes to the strength, to the nature of Penruddock.'[2]

It was Kemble's habit, according to Boaden, 'by intense meditation' to work himself into a part he felt to be important, and during the weeks before his first performance he saw him gradually assume the character he was to play. 'I saw in his walk and occasionally in his countenance, the image of that noble wreck of *treachery* and *love*, which was shortly to command the tears of a whole people.' Years later, an habitué of the Garrick Club recalled the general 'gulping' sound, 'mingled with sobbing and blowing of noses',[3] which invariably accompanied his performance.

Penruddock was a triumph, but Kemble when acting, as Boaden put it, could be either 'a worm or a god'; unlike his sister, who never fell below a consistently high level, his playing was frequently uneven: 'He dozed or walked through a part; or sublimed it with energy and grace.' In Penruddock he had sublimed it; the following season an eagerly awaited melodrama, *The Iron Chest*, displayed him in the opposite capacity.

The Iron Chest, adapted from William Godwin's best-selling novel *Caleb Williams*, was the work of George Colman the younger, who had recently taken over the management of the Haymarket Theatre from his father, and who like his father was a successful playwright. Stephen Storace had composed the accompanying songs and music and Kemble, as the remorse-stricken Sir Edward Mortimer, the secret of whose crime is hidden in the iron chest, was to play the leading part. Matters went badly from the start. Kemble was out of humour with the play;* its preparations too seemed doomed to go awry. Stephen Storace, who had insisted on struggling to the first rehearsal after a severe bout of fever, caught a fatal chill on the cold stage, and returned home to his bed, never to leave it again. Kemble, who had a bad cold, was too ill to attend rehearsals till three days before the performance, and the rehearsals themselves, thanks to illness and disorder among the players, were scarcely deserving of the name. 'They yclep it a rehearsal, I conjecture', wrote the angry author, 'because they do NOT rehearse . . . The ragged master of a theatrical Barn might have blush'd for the want of discipline in the pompous Director of his Majesty's servants at the vast and astonishing new-erected Theatre Royal, in Drury Lane.'[4]

The first night confirmed the author's worst misgivings. He found Kemble, still unwell, swallowing opium pills in his dressing room before the performance. The curtain rose to discover Sir Edward Mortimer in his library. 'Gloom and desolation sat upon his brow; and he was habited, from the wig to the shoe string, with the most studied exactness . . . The picture could not have looked better . . . but in justice to the picture it must also be added that, the picture could scarcely have acted worse.'[5] Either from dislike of the play or from genuine illness Kemble did no more than walk through a part which called for violent exertion. His sing-song tone of solemn declamation, varied only by his stifled fits of coughing, soon had the

* The fault, thought Walter Scott, was partly Colman's. He had originally called his hero Philip, Kemble's second name, and in a pointed passage seemed to mock the actor's antiquarian interests:

> Philip is all deep learning and black letter;
> He shows it in his very chin . . . His brain
> Is crammed with mouldy volume, cramp and useless
> Like a librarian's lumber room.

Sir Philip was changed to Sir Edward, but Colman's first choice of name, if intentional, had been unwise.

audience half asleep. 'Frogs in a marsh, flies in a bottle, wind in a crevice, a preacher in field, the drone of a bagpipe, all, all yield to the inimitable, and soporific monotony of Mr Kemble', wrote Colman, who in a furious preface when his play was published vented some of his spleen on the actor who had ruined it. At the end of the first act, when it was clear which way things were going, he had begged him to explain he was unwell, but his request was haughtily refused. His illness was quite evident to the house, said Kemble; 'he had coughed very much upon the stage and an apology would *only make him look like a fool*'.[6] The play dragged on: Kemble 'groaned, he lag'd, he coughed, he winced, he wheezed',[7] the audience growing so restive that at last, on Sheridan's insistence, he was forced to excuse himself – his apology, however, said Colman, had the effect of bringing discredit on the author rather than the actor. At the end of the evening he drew up the balance of his account with Kemble:

> For his illness, – Compassion,
> For his conduct under it, – Censure,
> For his refusing to make an apology, – A Smile!
> For his making an apology, – A Sneer,
> For his mismanagement, – A Groan,
> For his acting – A Hiss[8]

Colman's angry preface to *The Iron Chest* caused a furore when six months after Kemble's first performance – which was followed by another, equally disastrous – he published his play. The controversy it aroused, and his attacks on the 'miserable mummer', as he called Kemble, stirred up great interest in his own production, this time successful, of *The Iron Chest*, at the Haymarket. Relations between the author and the actor remained the worst possible for many years, though in a second edition of the play the intemperate preface was withdrawn – the first in consequence is a collector's piece. They were finally reconciled over a bottle of wine, Kemble putting down Colman's attacks to an author's natural touchiness. He had in truth much to answer for. He had the art, as Charles Lamb put it, 'of diffusing a complacent equable dulness (which you knew not where to quarrel with) over a piece which he did not like beyond any of his contemporaries', and in an amusing essay he describes his like treatment of a tragedy by William Godwin. Once again Kemble had a cold, once again, regardless of the action of the play, he had 'wound himself up to an even tenor of stately declamation from which no exigence of dialogue or person could make him swerve for an instant'. When finally, at the close of the fifth act, with an irrelevance that seemed to stagger the heroine herself, he whipped out a poignard and stabbed her to the heart, the effect, wrote Lamb, was as if a murder had been committed in cold blood. 'The whole house rose in clamourous indignation, demanding justice. The feeling rose far above hisses. I believe at that instant if they could have got him they would have torn the unfortunate author to pieces.'[9]

*   *   *

Kemble's comments on *The Iron Chest*, after its disastrous first night, were laconic. The play, he noted in his journal, was 'very bad indeed'. He was far more distressed by the news of Stephen Storace's death, three days after the performance. 'Poor Stephen Storace died this morning only in his thirty fourth year!', he wrote in his journal, and a week later, 'This day I followed Stephen Storace to his Grave – I shuddered to hear the Earth and pebbles rattle on his Coffin! – I hope never to go into Marylebone Church again – I will endeavour to live better – He was only thirty four! – One may die tonight.'

Storace's death was an enormous loss to Drury Lane where his operas, incidental music and adaptations of other works had been immensely popular. It was a tragedy for English music too. His career had promised much; his friendship with Mozart had been reflected in the music of his operas, most of all in his last and most successful work, *The Pirates*, four years earlier. *The Iron Chest* had proved to be his downfall, though his music had been the only thing that pleased on that ill-fated evening. One final work of his remained, an opera, *Mahmoud*, with words by the popular writer Prince Hoare, and this, at Hoare's request, was to be performed for the benefit of Storace's widow and children.

'All the performers', wrote Michael Kelly, 'took the greatest pains to do justice to the posthumous work of the composer. Kemble's acting, as the hero of the piece, was a masterly performance.'[10] Amidst so much good will it is distressing to learn that the profits destined for Storace's widow never reached her, for Sheridan, who had given the theatre for the benefit, swept up all the takings from the doorkeepers, leaving not a shilling for the widow or her family. This high-handed action, which Haydon, who had it from Prince Hoare, recorded in his diary, shows the darker side of Sheridan's management. It was not an isolated incident and Fanny Kemble, whose mother Miss De Camp, some years after her brush with Kemble, married his younger brother Charles, recalls the dismal Saturdays a year or two later when, after prolonged periods of non-payment of their salary, 'the poorer members of the company, and all the unfortunate work people, carpenters, painters, scene-shifters, understrappers of all sorts and plebs in general of the great dramatic concern, thronging the passages and staircases, would assail Sheridan on his way to the treasury with pitiful invocations: "For God's sake, Mr Sheridan, pay us our salaries!" and his plausible reply of "Certainly, certainly, my good people, you shall be attended to directly." Then he would go into the treasury, sweep it clean of the whole week's receipts (the salaries of the principal actors whom he dared not offend, and could not dispense with, being, if not wholly, partially paid), and going out of the building another way, leave the poor people who had cried to him for their arrears of wages baffled and cheated of the price of their labour for another week. The picture was not a pleasant one.'[11]

Already the optimism with which the new Drury Lane had been opened was giving way to something approaching desperation. Despite a number of successful spectacles the burden of debts incurred in building the theatre and the expenses of running it was proving impossible to carry; Sheridan's borrowings for his personal expenses drained it further. For Kemble, strictly honest and straightforward, 'a child even in business matters', the strains of his position were proving intolerable. Tradesmen, doubting their chances of replayment from the treasurer, took to demanding pledges from him before they would supply goods; actors and workmen, with equal trust in his good faith, would do the same. Kemble's good nature and his devotion to the theatre led him to sign a number of such guarantees, which for a time were honoured by the treasury. But when one day he found himself arrested for debt, his indignation was extreme.

It was the last in a series of exasperations, and at the end of April 1796, only two years after the re-opening, he resigned his post as manager, defeated just as King had been. Before this, however, he had been involved in a theatrical fiasco still more resounding than *The Iron Chest* – and one for which, this time deliberately, he was in part responsible.

*   *   *

For some months before the performance of *The Iron Chest*, the learned and theatrical world had been humming with the news of a hitherto undiscovered play by Shakespeare, and Sheridan, despite rival offers from Harris at Covent Garden, had obtained the right to perform it at Drury Lane. The play was *Vortigern and Rowena*, the work of the celebrated Shakespearean forger, William Henry Ireland.

William Henry Ireland, at that time a boy of seventeen, was the son of Samuel Ireland, a dealer in prints and curiosities who had made a speciality of acquiring relics of Shakespeare and whose admiration for all things connected with the bard had a powerful influence on his son. William Henry, who felt himself neglected by his father, and who had brooded long on the example of Chatterton's medieval forgeries, had gained all the attention he could wish when he announced his discovery of a cache of Shakespearean documents in a trunk in the attic of a friend. The friend, like the rest of the story, was a figment of his imagination, but the imposture satisfied not only his father but half the learned world as well. Scholars and celebrities flocked to Samuel Ireland's house, where he presided on a chair that was once Anne Hathaway's, to see the previous manuscripts which William Henry, using scraps of old vellum and watered-down brown ink, produced as fast as he was able. Among the visitors was Boswell, who, having examined them, called for brandy and exclaimed, 'Well, I shall die now contented that I have lived to see the present day', then kneeling down in front of them, continued, 'I now kiss the invaluable relics of our bard; and thanks to God that I have lived to see them.'[12]

Mrs Jordan and the Duke of Clarence were callers too and professed themselves equally convinced, and when, after the announcement of its discovery, *Vortigern* was accepted blind at Drury Lane,

Mrs Jordan agreed to play one of the leading female roles. The task of forging as well as composing five acts of a play was too great for even William Henry's powers; he contented himself with producing a 'transcript' of the supposed original on which he laboured for two months of frantic composition. Even as he did so there were signs of growing scepticism. Edmond Malone, who had never been convinced by the earlier documents, was preparing a pamphlet unmasking them as forgeries. Kemble, who was to play the leading role, showed himself increasingly dubious, and being obliged by Sheridan to go ahead with the play, chose April 1st as the date for its production.

Samuel Ireland, who was in charge of negotiating with the theatre, soon learnt the pitfalls of dealing with Sheridan. A series of letters, now in the British Museum, tells a plaintive tale of appointments missed, of alluring promises unfulfilled. 'Your conduct' writes Ireland, after months of confusion, 'is so very different from that which your Conversation on the subject seem'd to imply that I am really at a loss to know what is intended.'

At last the text of *Vortigern* was completed and delivered. 'There are certainly some bold ideas', observed Sheridan when he read it. 'It is very odd; one would be led to think that Shakespeare must have been very young when he wrote it.'[13] Meanwhile the forces of the unbelievers were gathering strength. Mrs Siddons, who was to have played one of the two heroines, announced that her health was unequal to the part. 'All sensible persons are convinced that Vortigern is a most audacious impostor', she wrote to Mrs Piozzi.[14] Kemble had come to the same conclusion, and though Sheridan foiled his attempt to give the play on April Fool's day, made sure by his casting of the lesser roles that it could not be taken seriously. Sheridan, cheerfully cynical, at least felt certain that the controversy would fill the theatre for 'you know', he told Kemble, 'every Englishman considers himself as good a judge of Shakespeare as his pint of porter.'[15]

The first night of *Vortigern* took place on April 2nd 1796. Every seat in the boxes had been taken days before and the crowds at the pit door were so great that those determined to get a place paid box prices, and finding no room, dropped down from the lower tier of boxes into the pit. Two days before Malone's pamphlet, totally damning to the Irelands, had been published. The play now took on the status of a test case. The prologue set it out:

> No common cause your verdict now demands:
> Before the court immortal Shakespeare stands.

The first two acts went fairly well. Mrs Jordan, who played Vortigern's daughter Flavia, kind-heartedly reassured the nervous author. By the third act, however, the audience was beginning to show signs of impatience, finding 'its taste insulted by the bloated terms . . . its reason puzzled by discordant images, false ornaments and abortive efforts to elevate and astonish'.[16] The piping voice of a minor actor, Mr Dignum, who called for trumpeters to 'bellow on', had the house in fits of laughter, but worse was to follow in the fourth act with the death of the Saxon general Horsus, played by Mr Phillimore 'of large nosed memory'. Stricken by the fatal blow, he 'so placed his unfortunate carcass that on the falling of the drop-curtain he was literally divided between the audience and his brethren of the sock and buskin'. Groaning beneath the weight, he struggled to extricate himself, 'which for a dead man', wrote William Henry, 'was something in the style of Mr Bannister jun. in The Critic, who tells Mr Puff that he "cannot stay there dying all day".'[17]

From then on *Vortigern* was doomed. Kemble, abandoning the attempt to play it seriously, dealt it the *coup de grâce* when in the final act, in 'the most sepulchral tone of voice possible', he uttered the words:

> 'And when this solemn mockery is o'er . . .'

laying such peculiar stress upon the line as to make it the cue for a howl of execration from the pit. The clamour continued for ten minutes, till Kemble, calling for silence, stepped forward and 'with even more solemn grimace' repeated the offending line.

It was no wonder that Samuel Ireland, like Colman, felt Kemble had completely damned his play – or rather, as he persisted in believing, Shakespeare's – and for long after its *débâcle* he denounced him for his treachery. The controversy, though pamphlets on both sides appeared for several months, had been virtually decided by

Vortigern's fate on stage. Sheridan, who had hoped that continuing uncertainty would ensure a lengthy run, was much displeased with Kemble. His deliberate undermining of its chances had involved the theatre in a considerable loss, both of the money expended on the scenery and that paid to the Irelands. As the manager Kemble might have deplored this; as a lover of Shakespeare who had been forced to undertake the play against his will, he was unrepentant. In any case his patience with Sheridan and the affairs of Drury Lane was rapidly coming to an end. In a dispute with Mrs Jordan soon after the *Vortigern* fiasco, angered by Sheridan's bias in her favour, he had threatened to resign.* His arrest for debt was the final indignity, and this time he carried out his threat in earnest.

* Both Mrs Jordan and Kemble wanted *Hamlet* for their benefit, and since both refused to give way, Sheridan decided that neither of them should have the play – a decision really in Mrs Jordan's favour since Hamlet was one of Kemble's most popular roles.

XII

Mrs Siddons, like her brother, was having trouble at Drury Lane. In May 1796, just off on a summer's provincial tour, she was writing to a friend:

> Here I am, sitting close in a little dark room, in a little wretched inn, in a little poking village called Newport Pagnell. I am on my way to Manchester, where I am to act for a fortnight; from thence I am to be whirled to Liverpool, there to do the same. From thence I skim away to York and Leeds: and then, when Drury Lane opens – who can tell? for it depends on Mr Sheridan who is uncertainty personified. *I have got no money from him yet*; and all my last benefit, a very great one, was swept into his treasury; nor have I seen a shilling of it. Mr Siddons has made an appointment to meet him today at Hammersleys [the bankers]. As I came away very early, I don't know the result of the conference; but, unless things are settled to Mr Siddons' satisfaction, he is determined to put the affair into his lawyer's hands.[1]

For the last two years Mrs Siddons had had a gruelling time. Her seventh child, Cecilia (the last of her five surviving children), was born in July 1794, just after her fortieth birthday, but it was not long before she left home again to take to the road on behalf of her family. In the spring of 1795, she stayed briefly with Mrs Piozzi. 'Dear! charming! excellent! admirable Mrs Siddons remains indeed', she wrote to a friend, ' – but ever on the wing – to serve some Brother or save some Sister, or satisfy cravings from her own hungry Family – or something calls her into Distant Regions – Scotland or Ireland – one week in the Year (now she is got well) – is all I can obtain of her Company.'[2] William Siddons meanwhile, suffering from gout and rheumatism, was forced to stay at home.

At Drury Lane, during the last two seasons, Mrs Siddons had acted in a series of indifferent new roles. 'How I do wish that Somebody would write two or three good tragedies some wet afternoon',[3] she wrote with feeling. The worst had been in Fanny d'Arblay's play *Edwy and Elgiva*, in 1795, when all her art had not been sufficient to prevent her death scene taking place to general laughter. Her biographer, Thomas Campbell, describes the occasion:

Miss Burney [Madame d'Arblay] was peculiarly unfortunate in bringing bishops into her tragedy. At that time there was a liquor much in popular use, called Bishop: it was a sort of negus or punch, I believe, though the origin of its name I must leave more learned antiquaries to determine. But be that as it may, when jolly fellows met at a tavern, the first order to the waiter was, *to bring in the Bishop*. Unacquainted with the language of the taverns, Miss Burney made her King exclaim, in an early scene, '*Bring in the Bishop!*' and the summons filled the audience with as much hilarity as if they had drunk the exhilarating liquor. They continued in the best possible humour throughout the piece. The dying scene made them still more jocose, when a passing stranger proposed, in a tragic tone, to carry the expiring heroine to the other side of a hedge. This hedge, though supposed to be situated remotely from any dwelling, nevertheless proved to be a very accommodating retreat; for, in a few minutes afterwards, the wounded lady was brought from behind it on an elegant couch, and, after dying in the presence of her husband, was removed once more to the back of the hedge. The solemn accents of the Siddons herself were not a match for this ludicrous circumstance, and she was carried off amidst roars of mirth.[4]

'Oh there never was so wretched a thing as Mrs D-arblaye's tragedy', wrote Mrs Siddons. '. . . I was grieved that a woman of so much merit must be so much mortified. The Audience were quite angelic and only laughed when it was *impossible* to avoid it.'[5]

William Siddons had evidently been placated by Sheridan, for the autumn of 1796 saw Mrs Siddons back again at Drury Lane. 'I am, as you may observe, acting again', she wrote in November; 'but how much difficulty to get my money! Sheridan is certainly the greatest phenomenon that Nature has produced for centuries. Our theatre is going on, to the astonishment of everybody. Very few of the actors are paid, and all are vowing to withdraw themselves: yet still we go on. Sheridan is certainly omnipotent.'[6]

It needed all Sheridan's blandishments to keep Mrs Siddons. When all else failed he used to call at her house in his carriage, and swearing on his honour that she would be paid, persuade her to go with him to Drury Lane to perform. After performances he was sometimes the worse for wear, and it may have been about this time that a curious episode, which she later recounted to Samuel Rogers, took place. She was returning home after the theatre in her carriage when Sheridan suddenly leaped in beside her. Sheridan's reputation as a womaniser was well known. 'Mr Sheridan', said she, 'I trust you will behave with all propriety: if you do not, I shall immediately let down the glass, and desire the servant to show you out.' Sheridan did behave with all propriety, 'but', continued Mrs Siddons, 'as soon as we had reached my house in Marlborough Street and the footman had opened the carriage door – only think! the provoking wretch bolted out in the greatest haste, as if anxious to escape unseen.'[7] The footman, presumably, was left to draw the worst conclusions.

Since Kemble flatly refused to return to Drury Lane as manager, though after some hard bargaining he returned as an actor, a lesser player, Richard Wroughton, took on the job that autumn. With neither the ambition nor the ability of Kemble he was content to take the line of least resistance. 'The distracted state of the concern was obvious from the very playbills', wrote Boaden; 'and Wroughton was, perhaps, as little the object of envy, as manager ever was.'[8] The end of the season too saw the loss of one of the theatre's most valued actresses, the beautiful and accomplished Miss Farren, who after years of playing heroines of rank and fashion was now to become one in reality. Her marriage to the Earl of Derby, six weeks after the death of his previous wife, was the culmination of a long established relationship. Her farewell performance in April brought the largest house on a night not devoted to a benefit that the theatre had ever known, and a valedictory address, hastily composed by Sheridan in the course of the performance, lamented her loss to comedy. The Countess elect, too overcome to reply, came forward to curtsy left, right, and to the front, as was the custom on occasions of high stage ceremonial, but left it to Wroughton to offer her adieus.

The departure of Miss Farren left Mrs Jordan in sole command of the comic scene. She had not often appeared with Miss Farren, each preferring to shine alone, but when she had the combination had been irresistible. Together in the previous year they had appeared in Richard Cumberland's play *First Love*, and the grateful author had written afterwards: 'When two such *exquisite* actresses conspired to support me, I will not be so vain as to presume I could have stood without their help.'[9]

After the first storms of publicity had died down Mrs Jordan had settled to a relatively peaceful domestic life with the Duke of Clarence. A model husband in all but name, he proved himself an affectionate father – Mrs Jordan eventually bore him ten children. Her notes to him, during the early years of their relationship are full of charming family touches. 'I desired George [their son, aged three] to put a kiss in this note', she ended one letter, ' – he immediately spit in it.'[10] Boaden, who first met her at the end of the 1790s, describes calling at her London house to discuss a play: 'She was in charming spirits . . . and occasionally ran over the strings of her guitar. Her young family were playing about us, and the present Colonel George Fitzclarence, then a child, amused me much, with his spirit and strength; he attacked me as, his mother told me, his fine tempered father was accustomed to permit him to do himself. He certainly was an infant Hercules.'[11]

Though Mrs Jordan, like all the other players at Drury Lane, found difficulty in obtaining her salary, she was probably, thanks to the Duke, better off than the rest. He was 'a powerful friend who would not allow her to be trifled with'.[12] His interventions on her behalf frequently infuriated Kemble, who, it was said, always manifested a steady aversion to the very sound of his name. But Mrs Jordan's earnings were of more than academic interest to the Duke, who was always chronically in debt. As one wit put it, early in their relationship:

> As Jordan's high and mighty squire
> Her play-house profits deigns to skim;
> Some folks audaciously enquire,
> If *he* keeps *her* or *she* keeps *him*![13]

The season of 1796–7 had been a melancholy one for Drury₁ Lane.
The one that followed, to everyone's surprise, brought three
sensational successes, the first of which, *The Castle Spectre*, provided Mrs Jordan with one of her most striking scenes. The
author was Matthew or 'Monk' Lewis – his gothic best seller,
The Monk, had appeared two years before – and the scene in
question the appearance of her mother's ghost to Angela, the
imprisoned heroine.

> The secret of the spectre [wrote Boaden] was exceedingly well
> kept; the bill of the day gave not a glimpse beyond the mere title;
> and the actors in the piece answered to all kind enquirers as to who
> the spectre was, or by whom represented – 'You'll see'. The set
> scene in this theatre had an oratory with a perforated door of pure
> Gothic, over which was a window of rich tracery, and Mrs Jordan,
> who played Angela, being on the stage, a brilliant illumination
> suddenly took place, and the floors of the oratory opened – the
> light was perfectly celestial, and a majestic and lovely but melan-
> choly image stood before us; at this moment, in a low but thrilling
> harmony the band played the strain of Jomelli's *Chaconne* in his
> celebrated overture . . . And the figure began slowly to advance;
> it was the spirit of Angela's mother, Mrs Powell, in all her beauty,
> with long sweeping envelopements of muslin attached to the
> wrist . . . Mrs Jordan cowered down motionless with terror, and
> Mrs Powell bent over her prostrate duty in maternal benediction:
> in a few minutes she entered the oratory again, the doors closed,
> and darkness once more enveloped the scene.[14]

The part of Percy, the hero, a kind of pantomime Harlequin to
Mrs Jordan's Columbine, was played by Kemble. It was one of his
sympathetic characteristics that, once uninvolved with management,
he would 'do anything' on stage. He never forgot his strolling years
and with all his high ideals of acting would express his dissatisfaction
when a performance fell short of them with the homely phrase: 'I
acted tonight thirty shillings a week.' The spectacle of Kemble, the
grave tragedian, climbing from a sofa to a gothic window to rescue

his Angela, and then, alarmed by the stirring of his black guards,* falling back from the height 'as though he had been shot', delighted the audience, though such acrobatics, said a critic, were more suited to a barn than a theatre.

The Castle Spectre ran a record forty-seven nights in its first season. 'It is a vile thing', noted Kemble in his journal, 'but the audience applauded very much.' Sheridan shared his low opinion; and when, in the course of an argument with Lewis, the author offered to bet him all the play had made for Drury Lane, he replied that he could not afford it. 'But I'll tell you what', he added, 'I'll bet you all it is worth.'[15]

The season's second success, still more elaborately got up, was a musical version of *Blue Beard*. The stage directions called for a procession, with elephants, through a mountain pass, and a thrilling glimpse of Blue Beard's secret chamber. The key of the door of his outer apartment, charmingly decorated with scenes of love, is turned by the intrepid hero:

> *The door instantly sinks, with a tremendous crash, and the Blue Chamber appears streaked with vivid streams of Blood. The figures in the picture, over the door, change their position, and ABOMELIQUE is represented in the action of beheading the Beauty he was, before, supplicating. The Pictures and Devices of Love change to subjects of Horror and Death. The interior apartment (which the sinking of the door discovers) exhibits various Tombs, in a sepulchral building; – in the midst of which ghastly and supernatural forms are seen; – some in motion – some fixed – in the centre, is a large skeleton, seated on a Tomb (with a Dart in his hand) and, over his head, in characters of Blood, is written*

'THE PUNISHMENT OF CURIOSITY.'

*   *   *

The Castle Spectre and *Blue Beard*, with their ghosts and tombs and gloomy dungeons, reflected one aspect of the transition to roman-

---

* Monk Lewis, cheerfully cynical, was unrepentant about introducing black guards in a castle supposedly set in Wales. 'I thought it would give a pleasing variety to the characters and dresses, if I made my servants black', he wrote, 'and could I have produced the same effect by making by heroine *blue*, *blue* I should have made her.'

ticism which in the theatre, as in every other branch of the arts, was beginning to take place. 'Monk' Lewis, in his introduction to *The Castle Spectre*, directly invoked the romantic spirit:

> Oft, with glimmering lamp,
> Near graves new open'd, or midst dungeons damp,
> Drear forests, ruin'd aisles, and haunted towers,
> Forlorn she roves, and raves away the hours!

Another very different aspect of the same gradual movement was represented in the third great success of the season, Kotzebue's play *The Stranger*.

'The eager fancy for German sentiment, which was then steadily increasing', writes the Kembles' Victorian biographer Percy Fitzgerald, 'might seem to us almost incomprehensible. The sickly perversion of all moral relations which pervaded it ought to have been foreign to British tastes.' Incomprehensible or not, there was a growing fashion for German drama, and the works of Kotzebue, translated by various hands, became immensely popular; between 1796 and 1801 twenty of his plays were published in England. Mrs Inchbald wrote a translation of his *Lover's Vows*, for ever celebrated as the play whose proposed performance so shocked Sir Thomas Bertram in *Mansfield Park*. By the standards of the time the same suggestion of immorality could have been levelled at *The Stranger* – Victorian prudery was already foreshadowed in the late eighteenth century, and though the morals of fashionable society continued to be free and easy, on stage and in books strict standards were maintained.

The plot of *The Stranger*, in which an erring wife, who has deserted her husband and children for a lover, is reconciled at last with her husband, was therefore considered highly shocking. Adultery was being condoned. It would not be long, complained one critic, before 'not a child in England will have its head patted by its legitimate father'. Nonetheless the play, with Mrs Siddons as Mrs Haller, the repentant wife, and Kemble as the Stranger, her husband, who has arrived incognito to take up lodgings at the gate of the castle where she is now working as a housekeeper, stirred emotions untouched by English writers of the day. Romantic sensibility ran riot in the ending of the final scene:

Mrs Haller: Forget a wretch who never will forget you – . And when my penance shall have broken my heart – when we again meet in a better world –
Stranger: There, Adelaide, you shall be mine again.
They part, weeping, but as they are going, she encounters the Boy and he the Girl.
Children: Dear father! Dear mother! *They press the children in their arms with speechless affection; then tear themselves away – gaze at each other – spread their arms and rush into an embrace. The children run and cling round their parents. The curtain falls.*

Kemble, relieved of the cares and toils of management, was able to give his all to the part of the Stranger. Friends who visited him while he was studying it found him deep in 'gloomy abstraction' and displaying an unusual carelessness in his dress. 'He brooded over the recollection of disappointed hope till it became part of himself', wrote Hazlitt. '. . . His person was moulded to the character. The weight of sentiment which oppressed him was never suspended: the spring at his heart was never lightened – it seemed as if his whole life had been a suppressed sigh!'[16] The subtlety and pathos of Kemble's performance were matched by the restrained melancholy of Mrs Siddons. She played the part till the very end with 'touching but tearless self command', wrote Campbell, which by contrast 'made the effect of her agitation in the last scene indescribable'. She herself was deeply affected by the role. 'My Mother crys so much at it that she is always ill when she comes home',[17] wrote her daughter Sally to a friend.

'Those who know the play of The Stranger', wrote Thackeray in *Pendennis*, 'are aware that the remarks made by the various characters are not valuable in themselves, either for their sound sense, their novelty of observation, or their poetic fancy. Nobody ever talked so. If we meet idiots in life, as will happen, it is a great mercy that they do not use such absurdly fine words. The Stranger's talk is sham, like the book he reads, and the hair he wears, and the bank he sits on, and the diamond ring he makes play with – but, in the midst of the balderdash, there runs that reality of love, children, and forgiveness of wrong, which will be listened to wherever it is preached, and sets the whole world sympathising.'

123

Sheridan, who had taken a close interest in the play,* had written
a song for it, which the Duchess of Devonshire set to music:

> I have a silent sorrow here,
> A grief I'll ne'er impart.
> It breathes no sigh, it sheds no tear,
> But it consumes my heart.
> This cherished woe, this loved despair,
> My lot for ever be,
> So my soul's lord, the pangs I bear
> Be never known by thee.

Green-room gossips had it that during rehearsal Sheridan pointed
to his pocket and was heard to mutter, 'I have a silent *bottle* here.'

With such outstanding successes as *The Stranger, Castle Spectre* and
Blue Beard, it might have been thought that the fortunes of Drury
Lane would revive. In fact, though the house was repeatedly sold out
for performances of the three, the expenses involved in putting them
on, particularly *Blue Beard*, absorbed all the season's profits. At the
end of the season the theatre was nearly £1,000 in deficit and its
prospects seemed more dubious than ever. Kemble, with his triumph
in *The Stranger* behind him, and with leisure to roam the bookstalls
and to visit his distinguished friends, must have felt himself well rid
of its anxieties.

* Ostensibly a translation, he claimed to have rewritten most of it.

XIII

Mrs Siddons, weeping nightly as Mrs Haller in *The Stranger*, may have found in her tears some relief for her own overburdened emotions at home. Through the season of 1797–8, a family drama no less poignant was unfolding, its leading figures her eldest daughters and the painter Thomas Lawrence. Unlike Kotzebue's play, however, it held no promise of a happy ending.

Lawrence's portrait of Mrs Siddons, supposedly in the role of Mrs Haller, was exhibited at the Royal Academy in 1797; it was accompanied by another of her brother John Philip Kemble. A third more ambitious painting, 'Satan Summoning up his Legions', showed brother and sister in heroic guise. The head of Satan was that of Kemble; in the pit at his feet the face of an angel (which Lawrence later painted out) was that of Sarah Siddons. For Lawrence, already highly successful as a portrait painter the picture was his supreme attempt at a composition in the grand manner, but though he regarded it as his masterpiece, the critics handled it severely, one likening his rebel angel to 'a mad German sugar baker dancing naked in a conflagration of his own treacle'.[1]

The paintings were the outward sign of Lawrence's abiding fascination with the Kemble family. Over the years he drew or painted Kemble in some of his most famous characters, and his portraits of Mrs Siddons were still more numerous – the first of them, as Zara in Congreve's *The Mourning Bride*, was done when he was only thirteen. But Lawrence's fascination did not stop short with the actress and her brother. From 1797 onwards, when Mrs Siddons was forty-two and Lawrence twenty-eight, he was deeply involved in the lives of her daughters Sally and Maria, and the centre of a complex family tragedy.

In 1797 Sally and Maria Siddons were twenty-two and eighteen respectively. They had been educated for some years in France, till the outbreak of war in 1793 made it necessary for them to return, and were now living in their parents' house in London. Both were delicate. Sally suffered from asthma and Maria already showed signs of consumption. Both had inherited a share of their mother's beauty, and Lawrence, whose admiration for Mrs Siddons was always mixed with something deeper, was inevitably drawn towards them. It was Sally who had first attracted him. Not so pretty as her sister, she had, according to Campbell, 'a remarkable mixture of frankness and sweetness in her physiognomy'. Lawrence himself was brilliantly good-looking, with a charming manner, soft spoken and '*douceureux*', that had endeared him to the fashionable sitters, both male and female, who from his first arrival in London had forwarded his success. Some time in 1796 the two had come to a secret understanding, though Mrs Siddons, who was in their confidence, was reluctant to consent to a formal engagement. Lawrence, despite his fame as a painter, had considerable financial embarrassments; Mrs Siddons as the bread-winner of the family had decided views about money. She was worried too about Sally's health and may, moreover, have had subconscious reasons for wishing to defer the match. Before matters came to a head, however, a new situation arose. Maria, hitherto too young to be taken seriously, was now emerging as a beauty. There was a feverish brilliance about her looks that owed something to her incipient disease, but though shallower and more selfish than Sally, she had a vivid and more sensual appeal. When in the course of 1797 Sally fell seriously ill and was confined to the house during a long convalescence, Maria with few scruples about her sister's happiness began gradually to take her place in Lawrence's affections. The intrigue was conducted in conditions of great secrecy, an affair of notes of assignation and snatched meetings in the park or Lawrence's studio. By the time Sally was better, her illness probably lengthened by her distress over Lawrence's defection, it was Maria, not she, who was engaged to him.

The first attachment, between Sally and Lawrence, had not been revealed to William Siddons, but to this second one he gave his reluctant consent, agreeing to pay off Lawrence's debts as a marriage settlement. Maria's health was giving cause for alarm; he feared that thwarting her might make her worse or even precipitate an elopement. Though Mrs Siddons' niece, Fanny Kemble, in her memoirs years later says that there were stormy scenes between Mrs Siddons and Lawrence over the transference of his affections, it seems likely that Sally, always self-effacing, had determined to make no protest once she realised his feelings were beginning to cool.

The formal ratification of Maria's engagement did nothing to bring about the hoped for improvement in her health. Confined to the house, as her sister had been the previous year, the excitement of a secret intrigue over, she began to reveal herself in the less attractive guise of a possessive and demanding invalid. Sally Siddons meanwhile, hiding any signs of resentment, greeted Lawrence when he came to the house with the placid goodwill of a prospective sister-in-law; tactfully leaving Lawrence to Maria, she would move to some other part of the room to talk to her young uncle Charles Kemble and his friends. Lawrence became dejected, restless and moody as he began to realise that his short but violent passion for Maria had been a mistake and it was really the gentler Sally that he loved.

The engagement was broken off. In a letter dated March 5th, 1798, unconsciously revealing, Sally gave the news to a friend, Sarah Bird:

A great, great change has taken place in our house; when you write to Maria, avoid, if possible, mentioning Mr Lawrence, at least for the present; all that affair is *at an end*. Are you astonish'd? Had you been present for some weeks past you would not be so much surpris'd. Maria bears her disappointment as I would have her, in short like a person *whose heart could never have been deeply engag'd* . . . It is now near a fortnight since this complete breaking off, and Maria is in good spirits, talks and thinks of dress, and company and beauty, as usual. Is this not fortunate? Had she *lov'd him*, I think this event would almost have broken her heart; I rejoice that she did not.[2]

A month later, unbeknownst to Maria, Sally was writing to Lawrence; he had evidently declared his love, and she, half willing, stood on the brink of renewing hers. 'Oh then, judge me not by others', she wrote, in obvious reference to Maria, 'think not that when you have won my heart you may abandon me and I shall soon recover. I tell you now, before you proceed any further, that *if I love you again* I shall love more than ever, and in that case *disappointment* would be *death*.'[3]

This time it was Lawrence's love that stayed fixed and Sally's, under the combined influence of her mother and her sister, that wavered. Maria was getting no better. Mrs Piozzi, who visited the family that spring, deplored the treatment she was getting. 'Shutting a young half-consumptive girl up in *one unchanged air* for 3 or 4 months would make *any* of them ill, and ill humoured too, I should think. But 'tis *the new way* to make them breathe their own infected breath over and over again now, in defiance of old books, old experience and good old common sense.'[4]

In June 1798, in an effort to restore Maria's spirits if not her health, it was arranged that the two sisters should go to stay at Bristol Wells, under the care of Mrs Pennington, a friend of Mrs Siddons and a member of the literary coterie which included Mrs Piozzi, and Dr Johnson's friend Anna Seward. Mrs Pennington was a gushing lady. 'Her incessant talk is rather fatiguing', wrote Sally to Sarah Bird, 'and the beauties of Nature call forth such a *torrent of eloquence* that there is no possibility of enjoying them in her company. It seems to me quite impossible she can feel the sensations she finds such fine language to explain.'[5] But she was kindly and reliable, and having no children herself was prepared to take a maternal interest in the fate of poor Maria – flattered too, perhaps, to help so celebrated a figure as Mrs Siddons.

Sally, after a month's stay in Bristol, left with her mother on her usual summer tour of the provinces. Mrs Siddons was now in her confidence regarding Lawrence but both had agreed, in order not to distress Maria, to keep the whole affair from her (and from William Siddons too). A renewed attack of Sally's illness revived all her mother's fears for her daughter, together with misgivings at the prospect of her marrying. 'Will a husband's tenderness keep pace with and compensate for the loss of a mother's', she wrote to Mrs Pennington. '. . . Dr Johnson says a man must be almost a prodigy of virtue who is not soon tir'd of an ailing wife; and sad experience has taught even *me*, who might have hop'd to have assured that attention which *common gratitude* for a life of labour in the service of my family shou'd have offered, that illness, often repeated, or long continued, soon tires a man.'[6]

Her mother's persuasions, her own ill health and the violent reaction of Maria, who had got wind of her attachment on her return to Bristol in September, were too much for Sally. She agreed to cease all communication with Lawrence, whom Maria, as her illness gathered momentum, had come to blame for her decline. Lawrence, to whom Mrs Siddons imparted her daughter's decision in a highly emotional scene, was beside himself. 'I pray God his phrenzy may not impell him to some *desperate action!*'[7] she wrote to Mrs Pennington. She herself was overwrought. Maria's illness was making terrifying strides; there was scarcely any hope of her recovery. Poor Sally's position, as she tended her dying sister, was almost impossible.

Unable to see Sally, self-command thrown aside, Lawrence hastened to Bristol where, staying in a hotel under an assumed name, he began a hectic exchange of letters with Mrs Pennington. Mrs Pennington, flattered and half-fascinated by Lawrence, made the most of her position as a go-between and continued as his confidante when he returned to London. With reason it was Maria's influence, far more than her mother's, that Lawrence feared as the chief obstacle to his marrying Sally. His fears were quickly realised. On October 7th 1798 Maria died, having extorted, almost with her dying words, a promise from her sister never to become Lawrence's wife. 'Sally, sacred, sacred be this promise', she had concluded according to Mrs Pennington. '. . . *Remember me*, and God bless you!'

'And what after this, my friend', wrote Mrs Pennington, 'can you say to *Sally* Siddons? She has entreated me to give you this detail – to say that the impression *is* sacred, *is* indelible – that it cancels all former bonds and engagements – that she entreats you to submit and not to profane this awful season by a murmur.'[8]

Lawrence's reaction to the news of this death-bed promise was that of a man near madness. He saw Mrs Pennington as part of a conspiracy to deprive him of the girl he loved. Mrs Pennington, whom only lately he had called his 'dearest friend', was horrified and hurt to receive, in reply to her account of Maria's death, a letter written in a shaking, near-illegible hand:

It is only my Hand that shakes and not my Mind. I have played deeply for her, and you think she will still escape me. I'll tell you a secret. *It is possible she may. Mark the end.*

You have all played your parts admirably!!!!
If the scene you have so accurately described is mention'd by you to one *Human Being*, I will pursue your name with execration.[9]

'This letter has the stamp of a *dark* and *desperate* character, to which I do not chuse to fix the proper name', wrote Mrs Pennington in a flurry to Mrs Siddons. '. . . It is critical to advise under such circumstances but I am much inclined to think I should at all hazards put the affair at once into the hands of Mr Siddons and trust to his candour and good sense. I should also consult with Mr Kemble . . . *What a wretch!* My nerves and my nature shudder at this man. What will you do to save yourself, and above all dear, dear Sally from him?'[10]

Lawrence's letter only confirmed Mrs Siddons in her view that any marriage between Sally, who had been very ill following Maria's death, and one so unstable would be a disaster. She was still unwilling, though, to confide in her husband. 'I would follow your advice implicitly', she wrote to Mrs Pennington, 'but that Mrs Kemble, with a thousand good qualities, is so fond of talking over other people's concerns, and that so indiscriminately, that it is no exaggeration to say this affair would be known in every Milliner's shop in Town, had she the least intimation of it. The confidence between Mr S. and my brother is unbounded, and I fear, were I to acquaint my Husband of it, there is no doubt of the forenam'd consequences. Mr S., too, is unhappily, so cold and repelling, that instead of tender sympathy I shou'd expect harsh words, "unkind reproof, and looks that stab with coldness". Yet all this I wou'd and will boldly encounter the very moment that I see occasion.'[11]

In the midst of her grief and her anxiety at Lawrence's distracted state, Mrs Siddons could not bring herself wholly to blame him, and a subconscious desire to protect him may have lain behind her wish to keep the matter from her husband. She was convinced that Sally would be wretched with Lawrence, but she herself had felt his fascination. Any idea of a love affair between them, in view of the rigid respectability that was the understructure of her emotionally demanding public life, was out of the question, but she undoubtedly felt more for him than she had for any other man. Years later, when she was contemplating her own death, she asked that Lawrence should accompany her body to the grave, and Lawrence in his final years seldom spoke of her without emotion. In his pursuit of first one daughter, then the other, he was perhaps pursuing the unattainable ideal of their mother.

Sally, devoted to her mother, shattered by the experience of her sister's death and the solemnity of the oath laid upon her, allowed herself to be persuaded out of love. The violence of Lawrence's letter to Mrs Pennington had horrified her. 'I seriously believe he is at times quite mad', she wrote to her. '. . . I fly with *horror* from such a passion.'[12] But a little later, though still insisting that her attachment was wholly over, she wrote pathetically: 'I do not shut my eyes to conviction; *I see him as he is*. Yet, oh pardon me if I sometimes cast over him that brilliant veil of enchantment which conceal'd his errors from our fascinated eyes.'[13]

Thereafter, as Lawrence's first protests subsided and his letters to her went unanswered, she had the dubious satisfaction of seeing his affections gradually withdrawn. He would bow to her coldly at the theatre; he passed her without speaking in the park, when his glance was like 'an electric shock' to her. Her mother, on whose approval she so depended and whose counsels after her sister's death had most swayed her, did not cease seeing Lawrence, however. 'He is frequently at my Uncle's house', Sally wrote to Sarah Bird, 'and I believe scarcely ever misses a night when my mother performs, when he generally pays her a visit in her dressing room. This I hear not from my mother, for unless I force her to it, she never mentions him.'[14]

In 1804, in answer to growing rumours that Mrs Siddons was carrying on an affair with Lawrence, William Siddons published an advertisement in the papers, offering a reward of £1,000 to any one who could give information as to the source of such 'wicked and unjust slanders'. Slanders they surely were, but there was a hint of estrangement between Sally and Mrs Siddons over Lawrence, and her puzzled resentment at her mother's continuing association with him cast a shadow over Sally's final years. In 1803, a year before the scandal which William Siddons tried to put an end to blew up, she died, a victim of the same illness as her sister.

Kemble, always a loyal brother, had followed the course of his niece's illness with sympathy and distress. He travelled specially to see her. 'Set off for Bristol Wells to see Maria', he noted in his journal for July 12th, and the following day, 'Arrived at the Wells – poor Maria very ill.' With Lawrence, who painted him as Coriolanus that year, he was on close and friendly terms, though not sufficiently intimate to know of the emotional entanglements that had preceded and followed his engagement to Maria. 'Mr Kemble is very much afflicted for Maria', wrote Lawrence to Mrs Pennington, 'and Mrs Kemble equally so; but the former with more delicacy.'[15] He showed great sympathy for Lawrence as it became clear that Maria was dying. 'How I love Mr Kemble for his attention to you at this time', wrote Mrs Pennington, 'but do you not feel it is to the lover of Maria? What do you conceive would be his feelings if he could think it was to that of her Sister?'[16]

During the final weeks of Maria's illness, Mrs Siddons had abandoned all her stage engagements to nurse her; sitting up for nights on end she was at times nearly fainting with exhaustion. It was in this miserable state that Mrs Jordan, unlike her in so many ways, but similar in her devotion to her children, came to her aid and in a generous gesture rose above their long-established rivalry. 'You will be surprised to see me advertised for *Friday*, but I trust not *angry* when I tell you the reason', she wrote to the Duke of Clarence. 'Mrs Siddons had bound herself to play on that night, but since, she is in constant fear of losing her second daughter. Mr Siddons came here to request that I would play, otherwise Mrs Siddons would be oblig'd to quit her child. On so serious an occasion, I thought it would not be either humane or indeed politick to refuse and hope you will agree with me in this opinion; to the *first reason* I am *sure you will assent*.'[17]

Mrs Siddons mourned long for Maria. 'Every hour some trivial circumstance reminds me of her', she wrote, 'and this morning when I saw a gown of hers, well cou'd I say with poor Constance:

> Grief fills the room up of my absent child,
> Stuffs out his vacant garments with his form.'[18]

But there was little let-up in her theatrical commitments, and within a few weeks of her daughter's death she was back on stage once more, choosing Isabella in *Measure for Measure* for her opening part, 'because it is a character that affords as little as possible to open wounds which are but too apt to bleed afresh.'[19]

William Siddons, lacking his wife's creative resources, felt, if possible, the loss of his daughter even more. Maria had always been his favourite child, and during their mother's frequent absences his daughters had become exceptionally close. 'The Father's sensation of loss will not abate so readily as that of our transcendent and now doubly dear Mrs Siddons', wrote Mrs Piozzi to Mrs Pennington. '*She* must return to the duties and cares of life and in them . . . will find a medicine for her grief. But his expectations from a daughter's beauty, his purposed pride in those charms which 'tis now clear she possessed, are blasted in the most incurable manner.'[20]

Towards Lawrence's attachment to Sally, when Mrs Siddons at last unfolded the story to him, William Siddons showed none of the indulgence of his wife. He received the information, Mrs Siddons told Mrs Pennington, 'with that coldness and reserve which has kept him so long ignorant of it, and that want of an agreeing mind (*my* misfortune though not his *fault*) that has always check'd my tongue and chilled my heart in every *occurrence* of importance *thro' our lives.* No, it is not his fault, it is his nature. Nay, he would never have hinted to Sally anything of the matter, had I not earnestly represented to him how strange such a reserve must appear to her; whereupon he testified his total disapprobation, nay, abhorrence, of any further intercourse with Mr L., whom he reprobated with the spirit of a just man *above* the *weaknesses* which are the misfortunes of the race in general.'[21] Poor Sally would have needed a stronger character than she had to resist such an interdiction. For Mrs Siddons her husband's want of an 'agreeing mind', and his lack of understanding at this crisis in her life, would have dangerous consequences.

XIV

The griefs and emotions of 1798 had done nothing to diminish Mrs Siddons' powers as an actress. If anything they had deepened the impact of her playing. 'Do you not remember', wrote Mrs Piozzi to Mrs Pennington some years later, 'dear Siddons saying she never acted so well as once when her heart was heavy concerning the loss of a child?'[1] No longer as dazzlingly beautiful as in her early years, when her loveliness, according to Boaden, was the only obstacle to belief in her Lady Macbeth, and lacking the 'nymph-like figure' that had once been hers, she was still dramatically good-looking. Pathos and imaginative intensity remained the hallmarks of her playing, but the tenderness of earlier performances had given place to greater majesty and force. 'Were a wild Indian to ask me What was like a queen? I would have bade him look at Mrs Siddons',[2] wrote Tate Wilkinson, and a wag, in speaking of her role as Mrs Haller, expressed wonder that any seducer should have dared take liberties with her. She could reduce her audiences to terror as well as to tears. The actor Bartley, who played Edward IV opposite her Margaret of Anjou, recalled years afterwards the electrifying impression when, as the guards who preceded her stood aside, 'the giantess burst into view', framed in the centre of an arch. 'Her head was erect, and the fire of her brilliant eyes darted directly upon mine. Her wrists were bound with chains . . . nor had she, on her entrance, used any action beyond her *rapid walk* and *sudden stop*, within the extensive archway, which she really *seemed to fill*. This, with the flashing eye, and fine smile of appalling triumph, which overspread her magnificent features, constituted all the effort.'[3] When, as Agnes in Lillo's *Fatal Curiosity*, hinting to Old Wilmot at the murder of their unknown son, 'she crouched and slid up to Wilmot, with an expression in her face that made the flesh of the spectator creep', the diarist Crabb Robinson, losing all command of himself, broke into a shriek of laughter and would have been ejected from the theatre, had not a neighbour realised that he was in a fit of strong hysterics.[4]

By the turn of the century most of Mrs Siddons' great parts were already behind her; for the rest of her career she kept chiefly to established roles. But the year that followed Maria's death saw the creation of one of her most popular parts, though it was one she privately regarded with distaste – Elvira, the camp follower from Sheridan's bombastic tragedy *Pizarro*, an adaptation of Kotzebue's play *Die Spanier in Peru*.

Kotzebue, as *The Stranger* had already shown, had the gift of wringing the hearts of his contemporaries. The combination of heavy German sentiment, inflated language and what someone called 'slop morality' was something that Sheridan could have mocked as brilliantly as he had heroic tragedy in *The Critic*. But times were different: Britain was at war with France and in her embattled state the patriotism of the Peruvian prince Rolla, rallying his people against the cruel and plundering Pizarro, had an emotional appeal to which even the satirical Sheridan could not fail to respond. Seen in the perspective of nearly two hundred years, the play seems absurd: in the context of the time it was a sensational success.

Since *The Critic* Sheridan had written nothing substantial for the theatre though he had often spoken of writing a new comedy.

'Not you', said Michael Kelly to him once, 'you will never write again; you are afraid to write.'

'He fixed his penetrating eye on me', wrote Kelly, 'and said, "Of whom am I afraid?"'

'"You are afraid", said I, "of the author of *The School for Scandal*".'[5]

Pizarro, rewritten by Sheridan from an English translation of Kotzebue's play, was virtually a new work – it was even translated back into German. Sheridan, always dilatory – witness the famous occasion when his father-in-law and Tom King had locked him into the prompter's room to finish *The Critic* – had not completed the fourth act by the time the play was advertised and every box already taken. Kelly, who was composing the music, was in despair. Not one line of poetry for the songs had been written, and his daily applications to the author were met with the promise, always unfulfilled, that he would have his text the following day. Finally, one evening, when Kelly was in the midst of entertaining friends, Sheridan appeared to carry him off to Drury Lane, where the painters and scene-builders were preparing the set for the Temple of the Sun. Settling down on a bench in the empty pit, with a bowl of negus before him, he invited him to admire the scene where the principal choruses would take place and promised him the words next day. 'My dear Mick', he said, 'you know you can depend on me and I know that I can depend on you; but these bunglers of carpenters need looking after.'⁶

To Kelly's surprise he turned up next day as promised, and after dinner they set to work. 'I sang two or three bars of music to him', wrote Kelly, 'which I thought corresponded with what he wished and marked them down. He then made a sort of rumbling noise with his voice (for he had not the slightest idea of turning a tune) resembling a deep gruff bow, wow, wow; but though there was not the slightest resemblance of an air in the noise he made, yet so clear were his ideas of effect that I perfectly understood his meaning though conveyed through the medium of a bow, wow, wow.'⁷ This was almost all Kelly had to work with, for though Sheridan explained the various situations in which music would be needed, the words for only two songs ever materialised, and Kelly, perceiving that 'it was perfectly ridiculous to expect the poetry of the choruses from the author of the play', found an impoverished writer to provide them.

Kelly's situation was nothing to that of the actors, for, according to his memoirs, while the house was filling for the first performance the fifth act had still not been completed, and Sheridan, upstairs in the prompter's room, was writing the last part of the play while the rest was being acted. Not till the end of the fourth act did Mrs Siddons, Charles Kemble and Barrymore receive their speeches for the fifth. But Sheridan, said Kelly, was 'careful in his carelessness'. He was quite aware of his power over his actors and the veneration in which they held his talents; moreover he knew that these three were quicker in study than any other performers concerned, and that he could trust them to be word-perfect, even at half an hour's notice.*

* They had the words of the literal translation of Kotzebue to fall back on should Sheridan fail to complete his version in time.

The play was an immediate triumph. With one *coup*, it seemed, Sheridan had retrieved his crumbling fortunes and those of the theatre. Kemble, as the heroic Rolla – a role in which he is immortalised by Lawrence's painting of him, sword in one hand, the child he is rescuing from a raging torrent in the other – won more popular as opposed to critical acclaim than in any other part. His speech to the Peruvian soldiers on the eve of battle, easily applicable to the contemporary situation, brought patriotic cheers as he compared the Spaniards' motives to their own: '*They*, by a strange frenzy driven, fight for power, for plunder and extended rule – *we* for our country, our altars and our homes. – They follow an adventurer whom they fear and obey a power which they hate. We serve a Monarch whom we love – a God whom we adore.'

William Pitt described Kemble in the role as the noblest actor he had ever seen. He was less impressed by the play. 'If you mean what Sheridan has written', he remarked, 'there is nothing new in it, for I heard it long ago at Hastings' trial.'[8] Sheridan's friend and ally Fox went further: Congreve's *Mourning Bride*, he told Samuel Rogers, was execrable, but *Pizarro* was the worst thing ever.

Sheridan, however, was delighted both with Kemble and the play. He had been intensely nervous about the casting. He was confident of Kemble from the first, but he had had grave doubts whether Mrs Siddons as Elvira, the revengeful mistress of Pizarro, would 'fall into the part'. As to Mrs Jordan, who was to play Cora, the Peruvian heroine, had it not been for the drawing power of her name he would never have chosen her. He had no opinion of her powers in tragedy, and her manner, always natural and spontaneous, was ill suited to the declamatory cadences of the play.

The first night saw him too busy behind the scenes to give his full attention to the stage, but a friend who watched it from his box on the third described his anxious solicitude: 'He repeated every syllable after each performer, counting poetically the measure on his fingers, and sounding his voice like a music master, with a degree of earnestness beyond my power to describe. He was in the utmost ill-humour, shocked, almost stamping with anger at everything Mrs Jordan said. With everything Kemble uttered he was invariably delighted; clapping his hands with pleasure like a child. With some passages by Mrs

Siddons he was charmed; at others he was shocked, frequently stating to Richardson and me that "*This* was the way the passage should be spoken" and then repeating it in his own way. Upon his sometimes referring to Mrs Siddons, Richardson said to him, with his Newcastle burr, "Well, well, Sheridan, you should not be so impatient! You know Kemble told you, that after some time she would fall into it."'[9]

Mrs Siddons, once accustomed to the part, did indeed fall into it. Decked out in a plumed Amazonian helmet, she made a proud and passionate Elvira, and Kemble, when praised for his playing of Rolla, claimed the greater glory for his sister. 'Nay, nay, I have everything to aid me; it is a noble character. Carry your wonder to Mrs Siddons; she has made a heroine of a soldier's trull.'[10]

*   *   *

The success of *Pizarro* was phenomenal. It ran for thirty-one nights (excluding Sundays) in succession, an unprecedented run for a tragedy. By the end of the season it had brought some £15,000 to the beleaguered treasury. Thirty thousand copies of the play were sold, and thousands of people, who had never thought of the matter before, plunged deep into Peruvian history. A cartoon by Gillray, entitled 'Pizarro contemplating the product of his new Peruvian gold mine' showed Sheridan exulting over his new-found riches. The Tories, not pleased at having their patriotic thunder stolen by a former supporter of the French Revolution, ascribed his success to Kemble's acting: a caricature in the *Anti-Jacobin Review* showed Sheridan as Pizarro, borne aloft on Kemble's head.

In *Pizarro* Sheridan could claim to have rallied the nation; a dramatic incident at Drury Lane the following year gave him another apt occasion to demonstrate his patriotic zeal. George III, on a rare visit to Drury Lane (for he still detested Sheridan's politics) had just stepped into his box for the playing of 'God Save the King' when a madman from the audience fired at him. At the sound of the report the king stepped back, then with great sangfroid came forward to the front of the box, and putting his glass to his eye, looked calmly round the house. Sheridan, hastening to the back of the box, where the queen and princesses were about to enter, managed to delay them with an excuse; it was only when the would-be assassin had been seized by the performers in the orchestra and dragged into the music-room for questioning that they learnt what had really happened. During the whole of the comedy which followed, the royal ladies were bathed in tears, a focus of far greater interest than the stage. At the end of the play, when 'God Save the King,' at the audience's demand, was being sung again, Mrs Jordan handed Michael Kelly an impromptu verse which Sheridan had written:

> For every latent foe,
> From the assassin's blow,
> God save the King.
> O'er him thine arm extend,
> For Britain's sake defend
> Our father, prince and friend,
> God save the King.

So successful was this extra verse that Kelly repeated it three times amid 'the most rapturous approbation', and the king left the theatre to the loyal shouts of the audience within and the cheers of the crowd who had gathered outside.

*   *   *

The windfall of *Pizarro* had raised the morale of the players at Drury Lane. Kemble, meanwhile, after three years out of office was begin-ning to turn his thoughts once more to the management of the theatre, this time with the understanding that he might buy a share of it. His freedom from responsibilities had released his energies as an actor; in *The Wheel of Fortune, The Stranger* and *Pizarro,* he had reached three peaks of his career. At the turn of the century, like his sister, he was at the zenith of his popularity; Charles Kemble, watch-fully guided, had become an actor second only to his elders, a gentler, more romantic player, but a worthy reinforcement to his family's dominance at Drury Lane. Though Mrs Siddons lamented the loss of her salary in the 'drowning gulf' of the theatre, Kemble, despite considerable arrears, carefully noted in his journal, had amassed a substantial fortune over the years. On this fortune, safely invested in Consols, Sheridan had fixed his eye. *Pizarro* had gained a respite for the theatre, but it had not solved its problems. There was an urgent need for further capital.

Why Kemble, financially and professionally secure, and knowing the embarrassments which beset it, allowed himself to be tempted by the offer of becoming part proprietor is a question not to be answered in merely worldly terms. He was, in the words of Walter Scott, a sworn votary to the drama, and this devotion was the overriding passion of his life. Moreover, he had always maintained that Drury Lane, properly managed, could be a viable concern; if Sheridan could be controlled or eventually dispossessed, there was no reason why it should not thrive, as it had done under Garrick's rule.

Sheridan, however, had no intention of letting go his hold of Drury Lane. Too proud to accept political sinecures, he looked to the theatre as his sole source of income; his invitation stemmed chiefly from a wish for ready money. But his proposals were seductive; in a long and skilfully worded letter, buoyant as ever with financial optimism, he set forward the advantages of taking a share in the theatre, and the dangers, if Kemble did not do so, of its falling into 'vulgar or illiberal hands' which would not respect his talents or ideals. Kemble, for all his long experience of Sheridan's methods, was attracted; in the autumn of 1800, pending negotiations, he reassumed the post of manager.

It soon became clear that nothing had changed, or if so only for the worse, since Kemble had left in dudgeon four years before. The autumn programme, which began with his own appearance in *Hamlet*, was dogged from the first by difficulties. Poor Peake, the treasurer, was besieged from day to day with such notes as the following:

My dear Peake,
    Let me remind you that you are to send the fifty pounds for Mrs Siddons today, or we shall have no King John on Saturday.
    If you possibly can, send me a Draft for the fifty pounds (which you promised to have given me last Monday sen'night) for the Authour of Deaf and Dumb.
    They are standing still in Greenwood's Room for Want of a

little Canvas – Unless you can help us there, we can have no Cymbeline, nor no Pantomime this Christmas.[11]

My dear Peake,
    We are all at a Stand for want of Colours – If you will help us, you shall have Cymbeline and full houses – Otherwise, we must go on with the West Indian, & c.[12]

My dear Peake,
    It is now two days since my necessity made me send to you for sixty pounds. My request has been treated with a disregard, that I am at a loss how to account for.
    I shall certainly go, and act my part tonight – but, unless you send me a hundred pounds before Thursday, I will not act on Thursday – and if you make me come a-begging again, it will be for two hundred pounds before I set my foot in the theatre.[13]

Kemble's negotiations with Sheridan, under these circumstances, hung fire. For two seasons he struggled on, achieving amid difficulties two notable new Shakespearean productions, the *Cymbeline* referred to above and *A Winter's Tale*. Mrs Siddons played Hermione in this and narrowly escaped with her life one evening when in the statue scene her muslin drapery flew over the lamps behind the pedestal and caught fire; she was saved by a stage hand who extinguished it. *Pizarro* continued to draw crowded houses, but its takings, along with the rest of the receipts, more often found their way into Sheridan's pockets than the treasury.
    In 1802 Sheridan's creditors closed in, and Messrs Hammersley, the bankers, applied to the Lord Chancellor on their behalf for first call on the theatre's takings. In the law-case that followed Sheridan pleaded eloquently, if disingenuously, on behalf of the performers; if they were not paid first, he said, the theatre must close down and the creditors lose all chance of repayment. The Chancellor, though he accepted his arguments, did not refrain from censuring him, quoting the famous closing lines from Johnson's *Life of Savage*: 'Negligence and irregularity, long continued, make knowledge useless, wit ridiculous and genius contemptible.'

Sheridan's friends and admirers, despite this, were loud in their congratulations, and even Kemble, who, exasperated beyond endurance by the persistent non-payment of his salary, had determined to leave the theatre, allowed himself to be seduced once more. 'He has now', wrote Mrs Inchbald describing Sheridan's conduct at the trial, 'with only one short speech . . . so infatuated all the Court of Chancery and the whole town along with them, that every one is raging against poor Hammersley, the banker, and compassionating Sheridan; *all*, except his most intimate friends who know all the particulars: *they* shake their heads and sigh! Kemble, unable to get even five hundred out of four thousand pounds, packed up his boxes, made a parting supper to his friends and ordered his chaise at seven o'clock the next morning. As they were sitting down to supper, "Pop! he comes like the catastrophe". Mr Sheridan was announced. – Kemble and he withdrew to the study; and the next thing I heard *all was settled*.'[14]

The reconciliation was only temporary. Kemble's attorney, unable to establish Sheridan's clear title to Drury Lane, advised him strongly against investing in it. Mrs Inchbald meanwhile had been negotiating on Kemble's behalf with Harris, the proprietor of Covent Garden, with a view to his becoming manager and part proprietor there. At the end of the summer season of 1802, bearing Mrs Siddons with him, Kemble bade farewell to Drury Lane, the theatre which had seen him come to fame and which he had graced for nearly twenty years.

XV

Kemble was tired when he left Drury Lane, tired of his struggles with the proprietor, tired of the uphill work of running a near-bankrupt theatre. Exhaustion, as well as the politic desire to leave a breathing space between his departure from Drury Lane and his appearance as manager and part proprietor at Covent Garden, may have influenced his decision to retire from the stage for a year and to travel extensively abroad. Garrick, in the midst of his career, had left London for France and had returned to find his popularity enhanced. Kemble may have hoped that absence would do the same for him.

Having put his negotiations with Covent Garden in hand, he left their completion in the charge of Mrs Inchbald, who as a former member of the company, and the author of numerous plays for that theatre, was well placed to deal with Harris, the proprietor. His social interests he left with equal confidence in the hands of his wife, and a number of letters from her to Mrs Inchbald in his absence show how assiduously she kept his name before the world. From Bentley Priory, where she had helped arrange an evening of amateur theatricals for her host, the Marquis of Abercorn, she wrote delightedly:

> Our Friday evening was most splendid, and to me in every way triumphant – We had to dine and sleep in the house about forty persons – the Prince of Wales, Duke and Duchess of Devonshire, Lady Melbourne and family, the Castlereaghs, Mr and Mrs Sheridan – Lady Westmorland and the Lady Fanes, Lady Ely & c. – The audience consisted of about seventy persons – a large party from the Earl of Essex's, another from Prince Castelcicala; and everybody sup'd. Nothing could be more brilliant – the whole theatricals under my direction, and, I do assure you, most excellently acted. Lady Cahir admirable in *Lady Contest*, and she was a blaze of diamonds! During dinner, the Prince inquired much after Mr Kemble of the Marchioness, went into the most unbounded

panegyric upon him . . . An epilogue was spoken by the Hon. Mr Lamb, in which was a towering compliment to Mr Kemble – warmly received – and after it was over and supper over the Prince came and sat down by me, he would not allow me to stand, and talked in the most familiar manner and the most friendly for an hour: all this in presence of my friend *Sheridan* . . .

I wish you had come, as I do believe there never was a thing of the kind went better, the Billiard Room was the theatre and we had very pretty scenes, a band of music, and the organ struck up God Save the King as soon as the Prince was seated. Lord and Lady A. treated me with the most marked attention; and I dare say Sheridan wished me at the d – l – all the grandees talking of Mr. K's return and the desire they had to see him again – Sheridan is little minded enough to be vexed at seeing any of his Performers admitted with the society he lives with.[1]

While Priscilla Kemble revelled in such flattering attentions, Kemble, in company with Heathcote, his banker, had made his way to Paris. Peace had been declared in April 1802. When he arrived in July – having stopped on the way at his old college of Douay, which he discovered in ruins, after its closure during the Revolution – he found himself warmly received, both by the newspapers and the city's leading actors. His ability to speak good French immediately recommended him, though some found his manner too reserved and ceremonious. But he struck up an interesting friendship with Talma, the greatest French actor of the day, who did the honours of the Théâtre Français. Kemble, regarded as a classicist in his own country, found French classicism too remote from nature for his liking, but admired the finish of the performances and the disciplined dedication which even the humblest players brought to their parts. He promised to send Talma a copy of *Pizarro*, discussed a joint production of Shakespeare with him, and after he left kept up an intermittent correspondence.

From Paris, where he had been liberally entertained by such English visitors as Lords Holland and Egremont as well as the French theatrical world, Kemble left for Spain where he hoped to study the Spanish theatre, to which end he had been diligently learn-

144

ing Spanish. His journey was dramatic. 'He says the grandeur of the country he has been through is not to be described', wrote his wife to Mrs Inchbald; 'that our Welsh mountains are mole-hills to Mount Ossuna – then such torrents – woods – mouldering towers, and broken arches of bridges, as made it delightful, and amply repaid him for the risques he has run in victory; for he says he has often been in great danger.'[2] Madrid he found 'a village to any one who has lived in London', and his lodgings cold and draughty, but he was much taken with the town, its people and its two main theatres.

A letter from his brother Charles, in December, sent him news of the death of his father, Roger Kemble, at the age of eighty-two. 'How in vain have I delighted myself in thousands of inconveniences on this journey, with the thought of contemplating my father's cautious incredulity while I related them to him', he wrote back to Charles. 'Millions of things, uninteresting may be to anybody else, I had treasured up for his surprise and scrutiny!' His natural distress – 'a dejected swelling at my heart that keeps me in a flood of tears for him' – was compounded by his sorrow at being away at such a time. 'You have had much to undergo, Charles; much of grief and much of trouble. I wish I had been at home to partake them with you, and to be of some use to you.'[3] Kemble, as the eldest son, had always taken his responsibilities as head of the family seriously.

In such a state, he told his brother, he had little inclination to think about the arrangements going ahead with Covent Garden, but he had been curiously insouciant about the matter from the first. Considering its importance to him, writes his biographer Percy Fitzgerald, his 'careless postponement of business' while he travelled abroad might seem a little strange, 'but it must be said, he never showed that concern about worldly interests which it was the fashion – and so unjustly – to lay to the charge of his sister. He was later to dispose of his share in the concern with almost the same indifference that he had taken it up.'

Mrs Inchbald, in any case, had looked after his interests well, and when he returned to London in 1803 arrangements with Harris at Covent Garden were all but concluded. Kemble was to take a sixth share of the concern for a price of £22,000, of which he was to put up £10,000, relying on future profits to supply the rest. The Harris family kept control, with seven-twelfths of the theatre and its patent in their hands, but Kemble was to have the option to purchase their share on Harris' death; the majority ownership of one of the two great London theatres, as in the case of Drury Lane, was the goal which lured him on. Meanwhile he was to be manager at a salary of £200 a year, with £37.16s for three appearances a week as an actor. By April, the speculations which had filled the papers since his return were stilled. Kemble, with his sister and his brother Charles, were engaged for the autumn season at Covent Garden. The first family of the English stage had transferred its allegiance.

*   *   *

While her brother passed his time agreeably in foreign travel, Mrs Siddons had been hard at work. Kemble, childless, with his money safely invested, could afford to pause in his career; she had her family to provide for. Unfortunate speculations by William Siddons had depleted her savings, and there seemed little hope of recovering the sums that Sheridan owed her. Her second son George, with a letter of recommendation from the Prince of Wales, was setting off to serve in India, and the cost of equipping him would be heavy. It was essential that she should earn what she could, and in May 1802, with a heavy heart, she left for a protracted tour of Ireland. William Siddons, increasingly crippled with rheumatism, was unable to travel with her, her daughter Sally was not strong enough, and her last child Cecilia, aged eight, too young to accompany her. She took instead the young Patty Wilkinson, daughter of Tate Wilkinson, her old employer on the Yorkshire circuit; Patty, who had come to stay with the family through the last months of Maria's illness, had become almost an adopted daughter to her, and would remain a lifelong companion.

Her daughter Sally, when she left, was seemingly in good spirits, well enough to enjoy parties and the admiration of the young Charles Moore, brother of Sir John Moore, the future hero of Corunna. She left her with no premonitions of disaster; it was her father, old Roger Kemble, on whom her thoughts dwelt most sadly. 'Farewell, my beloved friend!', she wrote to Mrs Piozzi, 'a long, long farewell! O, such a day as this has been! to leave all that is dear to me. I have been surrounded by my family, and my eyes have dwelt with a foreboding tenderness, too painful, on the venerable face of my dear father, that tells me I shall look on it no more.'[4]

The journey to Ireland, otherwise uneventful, provided one Siddonian moment, when, passing through the dramatic landscape of Penmaen-Mawr in Wales, they alighted from their carriage to look at the view. 'A lady, within hearing of us', wrote Patty Wilkinson, 'was in such ecstacies, that she exclaimed, "This awful scenery makes me feel as if I were only a worm, or a grain of dust, on the face of the earth." Mrs Siddons turned round and said, "I feel very differently." '[5]

Her reception in Ireland, first in Dublin, then in Cork and Belfast, was all that she could wish; and when at the beginning of the autumn William Siddons wrote to her urging the necessity to go on working, she decided to stay on rather than return, as he had suggested, to perform in Liverpool. The prospects of profit in Ireland were good but there were other motives behind her decision. At the age of forty-seven, after nearly thirty years of exemplary married life, she had formed an indiscreet attachment which would later involve her in much scandal and distress.

Mrs Siddons had long been starved of affection in her marriage. In the confused and emotionally shattering months leading up to Maria's death her husband had given her little comfort and support: his coldness and lack of 'an agreeing mind' had left her rebuffed in every important crisis of her life. Now, though Sally showed no signs of illness, she was resentful of the necessity, largely due to his mismanagement, that had forced her to leave her family. At a low ebb on her arrival in Dublin, she had fallen in with a young actress, Catherine Galindo, and her husband, variously described as an actor and a fencing master. A hothouse friendship had sprung up among the three, but Mrs Galindo, according to her own account, soon found herself excluded while her husband took the great actress on lengthy carriage expeditions or gave her private fencing lessons – she was planning to appear as Hamlet. Mrs Siddons seems to have become extravagantly fond of Galindo; he was gay, he knew, as she put it, how to keep her 'up, up, up'; he was much younger than she, and his admiration was intensely flattering.

For the time being Mrs Galindo showed no resentment. She regarded the relationship, she wrote later, as no more than the ridiculous passion of an older woman for a man young enough to be her son. Mrs Siddons' influence meanwhile could help her career; she was negotiating to obtain Mrs Galindo a position at Covent Garden where it was already agreed that she herself was to go the following season. An engagement was arranged with Harris during Kemble's absence abroad, but Kemble's anger on hearing of the appointment was extreme. He stormed round to see Mrs Inchbald. 'When Kemble returned from Spain (1803)', she wrote, 'he came to me like a madman, – said Mrs Siddons had been imposed on by persons, whom it was a disgrace to her to *know*; and he begged me to explain it so to her. He requested Harris to withdraw his promise . . . Yet such was his tenderness to his sister's sensibility, that he would not undeceive her himself. Mr Kemble blamed *me*: and I blamed *him* for his reserve; and we have never been so cordial since. Nor have I ever admired Mrs Siddons so much since; for though I can *pity* a dupe, I must also *despise* one. Even to be familiar with such people was a lack of virtue, though not of chastity.'[6]

There was trouble ahead over the Galindos. But meanwhile the pleasant sentimental interlude which had lasted through the summer and autumn of 1802 had been brought to an end by outside events. In December Mrs Siddons heard the news of her father's death, and fresh from her bereavement had to face a furore similar to the one which had taken place over the benefits for Digges and Brereton seventeen years before. She was accused – unfairly, for she had never been asked to do so – of refusing to perform for the benefit of the Dublin Lying-in Hospital, and the old charges of avarice and lack of charity were raised against her, till a letter from the Trustees put an end to them. There was a grain of truth perhaps in the public's accusation: she had not refused to play for charity, but she had made no effort to suggest it.

In February 1803, her son George, on the eve of his departure for India, came to take his leave of her and stayed for a fortnight in Dublin. 'It was gratifying', wrote Patty Wilkinson, 'to see them fondly trying to make all the happiness they could out of the last days of their domestication, though their mutual smiles were more affecting than any tears.'[7] Mrs Siddons' distress when it came to the last moment was so great that he left without a formal goodbye, for fear of over-agitating her.

The pain of parting with George was nothing to what lay ahead. A letter from Sally, at the beginning of February, had declared her well and in good spirits, but at the beginning of March a letter from William Siddons to Patty Wilkinson told a different story. Sally was very unwell, he wrote, but he felt it better that Mrs Siddons should not be told. Patty Wilkinson, however, immediately showed the letter to Mrs Siddons, who would have set off instantly to England, had the onset of equinoctial gales not prevented any ships from leaving harbour. Two days later a second letter from William Siddons, this time to his wife, told her that Sally was much better, and that she should proceed to Cork, where she had made an engagement to play. From Cork, in a state of miserable anxiety she wrote to a friend, Mrs Fitzhugh, who had kept in constant touch with the family:

How shall I sufficiently thank you for all your kindness to me? You know my heart, and I may spare my words; for, God knows, my mind is in so distracted a state, that I can hardly write or speak rationally. Oh! why did not Mr Siddons tell me when she was first taken so ill? I should then have got clear of this engagement, and what a world of wretchedness and anxiety would have been spared to me! And yet, good God! how should I have crossed the sea? For a fortnight past it has been so dangerous that nothing but wherries have ventured to the Holy Head; but, yet, I think I should have put myself into one of them, if I could have known that my poor dear girl was so ill. Oh! tell me all about her. I am almost broken hearted . . . Will you believe that I must play tonight, and can you imagine any wretchedness like it in this terrible state of mind? For a moment I comfort myself by reflecting on the strength of the dear creature's constitution, which has so often rallied, to the astonishment of us all, under similar serious attacks. Then again, when I think of the frail tenure of human existence my heart fails, and sinks into dejection. God bless you! The suspense that distance keeps me in, you may imagine, but it cannot be described.[8]

149

Continued storms, delaying the mail from England, wound up Mrs Siddons' suspense to such a pitch that when, at the end of the week, she received news that Sally was still ill, though not desperately so, she determined to throw up her engagement in Cork and return to England. She travelled with Patty Wilkinson from Dublin, as the crossing to England was held to be safer from there, embarking in a state of miserable uncertainty, since storms had held up her letters and news was still being sent to her at Cork. From Holyhead she made her way as quickly as she could to Shrewsbury, and there found a letter from William Siddons, written ten days earlier, telling her that Sally was now dangerously ill. Only an hour or two after the letter was written Sally had died suddenly. Mrs Siddons was still reading the letter when a messenger arrived and, calling Patty Wilkinson out of the room, told her the news. Patty Wilkinson tried to break the news gradually, but her face betrayed her. Mrs Siddons, she wrote in her diary, sank into 'speechless despondency' and lay for a day at Shrewsbury, 'cold and torpid as a stone'.

A letter of condolence from her brother John met her at Oxford on her way back to London; her brother Charles came to meet her just outside the town and take her back to see her widowed mother. Worn out with travel and emotion, she fell ill, and in an effort to recover her health and nerves spent the summer in the country, at a farm near Cheltenham. From here she kept in touch with the Galindos, to whom she had written two days after hearing the news of Sally's death:

What can I say to you? And why should I write to you, since the dark cloud that hangs over my destiny will not, cannot, be dispersed, *and every ray of sunshine departed from it at the time I left you, never to return!* If I am to write or to speak to those I love, I must speak and write from genuine feeling, and why distress you with my overwhelming sorrows? God knows the portion of each individual is sufficient for himself to bear. I make the attempt to tell you many things that press upon my aching memory, but I feel myself unequal to it. I hope a little time will restore my tranquillity, at present my head is so confused, it is not without difficulty I have said thus much; though I should write volumes,

I could never describe what I have lost in you, my beloved friends, and the sweet angel that is gone for ever. Good God, what a deprivation in a few days!

Adieu! Adieu![9]

In a calmer, though still deeply saddened mood, she wrote to them of the proposed arrangement for Mrs Galindo to join Covent Garden. She confessed that the matter had cost her 'much and various and very bitter contention' but that she had won the day and had obtained an engagement at £5 a week for Mrs Galindo, beginning the season after next. She hoped that they would be satisfied with these modest terms, 'for to live in a state of contention with a brother I so tenderly love, and a husband with whom I am to spend what remains of life, would be more than my subdued spirit and almost broken heart would be able to endure.'[10]

In the event the arrangement never materialised, and Kemble, when he visited Dublin for a summer engagement the following year, discouraged Mrs Galindo from coming with what she considered deliberate rudeness. Meanwhile her attitude to Mrs Siddons had completely changed; her husband had gone over to England before her, in theory to prepare the way for her engagement at Covent Garden, but, according to Mrs Galindo, deliberately lured by Mrs Siddons. In a venomous pamphlet, published much later, in 1809, she accused the great actress of carrying on an affair with Galindo, of ruining her career and her marriage. She published Mrs Siddons' letters, but affectionate and emotional though they were, they lent no substance to the picture of her as a seductress, though they showed her to have been indiscreet, and at one point openly at odds with her husband. 'I have been in such an agitated state of mind from domestic sorrows and cares that I *could* not write', she wrote to Galindo in the autumn of 1803; 'the present cloud is dispersed but how soon it may gather again I fear to think: at all events this I am resolved upon; the *next* storm *shall be the last*: I beg you will divulge this only to Mrs G; be kind and gentle to her if you value my regard and esteem. Oh! I have suffered too much from a husband's unkindness not to detest the man who treats a creature ill who depends on her husband for all her comforts.'[11]

The relationship with the Galindos foundered eventually on money. Mrs Siddons had lent Galindo £1,000, keeping the matter secret from her husband; Galindo failed to repay it, there were scenes and recriminations, matters becoming so bad that in the end Mrs Siddons refused to see him or to answer his letters.

Mrs Galindo's pamphlet, which glossed over the subject of the loan, was a tissue of accusations motivated chiefly, it would seem, by jealousy and a desire for notoriety. Apart from her central theme, that Mrs Siddons had seduced her husband, she accused her of failing to give up her stage engagements to return to the death-bed of her daughter, and hinted unpleasantly at one source of her resentment against William Siddons – his passing on of a venereal infection. The pamphlet, published at five shillings, was widely circulated and certainly actionable, but Mrs Siddons refused to prosecute. 'It is the opinion, I do assure you upon my honour, of all my friends', she wrote to her nephew Horace Twiss, 'that it would be lowering myself, to enter the lists with persons, the indecency of whose characters is become so notorious . . . They have already cost me too much money, and what's more important, too much tranquility to renew a subject so shoking.'[12]

So ended an attachment, impulsively entered into and soon soured, which cost Mrs Siddons much distress and certainly did nothing to improve her relations with her husband. They never separated formally, but in the spring of 1804 William Siddons, now compelled to walk on sticks, moved permanently to Bath for the sake of his health, while Mrs Siddons, for professional reasons, stayed mainly in London and at a cottage she had taken at Westbourne, near Paddington. 'Mrs Siddons and *her* Husband not living at *all* together. Mercy on us!',[13] wrote Mrs Piozzi the following year. In fact the two, though they had grown apart over the years, were never altogether out of sympathy. They visited each other fairly frequently, Mrs Siddons staying with her husband in Bath, and he in his turn coming to see her at her cottage. A pleasing set of verses, written by him after one such visit, gives a glimpse of the affection that still subsisted between them, and of the poetic talent, lightweight but agreeable, which might have flourished in less challenging conditions:

Would you I'd Westbourne Farm describe,
I'll do it then, and free from gall,
For sure it would be sin to gibe
A thing so pretty and so small.

The poplar walk, if you have strength,
Would take a minute's time to step it;
Nay, certes, 'tis of such a length,
'Twould almost tire a frog to leap it.

But when the pleasure-ground is seen,
Then what a burst comes on the view!
Its level walk, its shaven green,
For which a razor's stroke would do . . .

The mansion, cottage, house or hut,
Call't what you will, has room within
To lodge the king of Lilliput,
But not his court, nor yet his queen.

The kitchen-garden, true to keeping,
Has length and breath and width so plenty,
A snail if fairly set a-creeping
Could scarce go round while you told twenty.

Perhaps you'll cry, on hearing this,
What! everything so very small?
No: she that made it what it is,
Hath greatness that makes up for all.[14]

XVI

Kemble made his début at Covent Garden, as he had at Drury Lane, in the role of Hamlet. Twenty years had elapsed since that first performance and it is interesting to read Hazlitt, who saw him only in this latter part of his career, on his mature interpretation. 'There he was', he wrote in the year of Kemble's death, 'the sweet, the graceful, the gentlemanly Hamlet. The scholar's eye shone in him with learned beauty, the soldier's spirit decorated his person . . . The beauty of his performance was its retrospective air: its intensity and abstraction. His youth seemed delivered to sorrow . . . Later actors have played the part with more energy, walked more in the sun – dashed more at effects, piqued themselves more on the girth of a foil; but Kemble's sensible lonely Hamlet has not been surpassed.'

Elsewhere Hazlitt would judge Kemble's Hamlet more harshly, describing him, in a famous phrase, as playing it 'like a man in armour, with determined inveteracy of purpose, in one undeviating straight line'.[2] But even here he was referring not to any physical stiffness – Kemble was the most graceful of actors – but to his conception of the character as following, with deepening intensity, a single line of development. The rapid shifts and transitions of feeling for which Garrick, and later Kean, were famous, were out of keeping with the classical consistency of Kemble's approach to tragedy.

Kemble brought his passion for Shakespeare to Covent Garden. During his years there, working with a freer hand than he had ever had with Sheridan, he was able to give full expression to his ideas on production, mounting no less than twenty-four of Shakespeare's plays with a splendour, pomp and dignity unknown until then. His achievements left their mark on his own age and cast their shadow well beyond. In two important respects – in his search for greater authenticity in costumes and settings, and his attempt, however incomplete, to free Shakespeare's text from the excrescences of later 'improvers' – Kemble laid the foundations for the achievements of the great nineteenth-century actor-managers who succeeded him.

Where costumes and settings were concerned, Kemble followed the lines he had already pursued at Drury Lane. That his efforts were appreciated is shown by a criticism printed in his first year as manager at Covent Garden:

> *King John* has been revived at this theatre. It seems the purpose of the Manager at this house to bring out all the noble productions of our great writers, with every advantage of the mimic art, and certainly no expense in dress or decorations is spared . . . The theatrical stock is extremely rich; their wardrobe is curious, extensive and well assorted; their armour is polished and plentiful and their scenery descriptive of everything remarkable on land or water. We are much pleased, however, with the care Mr Kemble extends to the upholstery of this house. A ricketty chair, a tattered sopha, or a broken table, seldom occur . . . Macbeth and King Harry do not sit upon the same throne. Juliet has her own bier, and her plumes are as decent as though just out of an undertaker's shop, while Desdemona has her own bed and damask curtains.[3]

This is not to say that, even in Kemble's heyday as manager at Covent Garden, anachronisms did not continue to occur. He is described towards the end of his career 'learned and judicious as he was, marching to the fatal field and fighting the battle of Bosworth as King Richard the Third, arrayed in spotless silk stockings and long-quartered dancing shoes, adorned with the Rose of York; or rushing forth as mad Lear or the murderous Macbeth with a flowered satin night gown, which might have been, and possibly was, the lounging robe of one of Louis XV's coxcomb courtiers'.[4] Kemble's scholarship, in any case, was relative; theatrical effect was always his first concern. When, for instance, a historian pointed out that the arches and columns used for such Roman plays as *Coriolanus* and *Julius Caesar* were taken from the buildings of the Emperors rather than from earlier republican architecture and suggested that they should be 'reformed all together', Kemble refused with something like horror: 'Why, if I did, sir, they would call me an antiquary!'[5]

The elaboration of Kemble's Shakespearean productions was not always well received. There were many who thought that his love of display took him too far; that processions, battles and Roman triumphs were given more importance than the text, which was frequently cut to accommodate them. But Kemble was catering for his age. At a time when the rage for melodrama and German sentiment was sweeping away the balanced repertoire which Garrick had brought before the public, and when the large stages of the two patent houses encouraged the taste for spectacle, music and pantomime, Kemble's carefully mounted productions, built round the lofty acting of his sister and himself, kept Shakespeare's popularity as high as it had ever been.

With Kemble's editing of Shakespeare's plays for the stage, his second contribution to the history of Shakespearean production, we are on more dubious ground. Ever since 1789, when he had first put on *Henry V* at Drury Lane, he had been in the habit of publishing his acting versions; his collected Shakespeare, published in 1815, numbered twenty-seven plays. They enjoyed a considerable run, continuing as the basic acting texts, with greater or lesser alterations, well after his retirement. Later collections of English drama, Oxberry's in 1818–22, and Cumberland's in 1828–30, take their Shakespeare almost unchanged from the versions established by Kemble.

Boaden, writing of Kemble's first production of *Henry V*, describes how he set about preparing the play for the stage. 'Now this, in Mr Kemble's notion of the business, was, not to order the prompter to write out the parts from some old mutilated prompt copy lingering on the shelves; but himself to consider it attentively in the author's genuine book: then to examine what corrections could properly be admitted into his text, not as disputing the judgment of the author, but as suiting the time of representation to the habits of his audience, or a little favouring the power of his actors, in order that the performance might be as uniformly good as it was practicable to make it.'

The process may sound relatively harmless; in fact it allowed any number of aberrations, indefensible on scholarly or literary grounds and justifiable only in the cause of theatrical effectiveness. Kemble did show greater reverence for Shakespeare's text than any of his predecessors had done, but he was content in many instances to leave their additions or 'improvements' unchanged. Thus his *Richard III*, even to the famous line – 'Off with his head! So much for Bucking-ham' – was almost entirely Colley Cibber's, and Edmund Kean too would play the same version. His *Macbeth* included an extra dying speech by Garrick, his *Coriolanus* was a mixture of Shakespeare's play and one on the same theme by the poet James Thomson. Elsewhere he kept more closely to the original though he was always ready to cut extensively, usually in the interest of speeding up the action or, as his detractors complained, to provide space for the processions or triumphs he loved. Much poetry was lost in the process, but the success of the plays on stage and the continued popularity of the Kemble versions proved their effectiveness. Vandalism by present-day standards (though less heinous than his predecessors' manglings), Kemble's reworkings of Shakespeare were hailed by his contem-poraries, who saw him as the high priest of the bard. It was left to such critics as Hazlitt, Leigh Hunt and Lamb to find his editorial methods barbarous and for the next generation gradually to restore Shakespeare's texts in their integrity. By then there were no actors of Kemble's or Mrs Siddons' stature and popularity; and Macready, the first actor-manager to bring back Shakespeare unadulterated, lacked the following to succeed financially.

*　　*　　*

It was not to be supposed that Kemble's enthusiasm for Shakespeare, 'the god of his idolatry', would be met with immediate approval by his new colleagues at Covent Garden, many of whom regarded his advent with suspicion and hostility. The theatre till then had been noted for its strength in comedy, and though it lacked any player with the transcendent talents of Mrs Jordan, it attracted the best comic playwrights of the day. Thomas Harris was the soul of pre-cision and punctuality; his authors, like his actors, could be sure of being paid. William Lewis, the former manager, who had been obliged to step down for Kemble, was the theatre's leading actor in the comic line – 'the gay, fluttering, hair-brained Lewis', Hazlitt called him '. . . all life, and fashion and volubility and whim'.[6] Novelty was the life blood of his art, and he relied for fresh material on the theatre's established playwrights. Kemble's scorn for modern comedy was well known: the old stage classics he considered quite sufficient to supplement the long list of tragedies, Shakespeare's predominating, essential for his sister and himself. One comic author, hearing of his coming, was advised 'to fall in gratitude to his knees, that Heaven had blessed him with only *two* children'.[7] But whatever Kemble's theories, Harris, as principal shareholder, had no intention of abandoning the profitable line of modern comedy, which as well as being popular was relatively inexpensive to put on. Kemble, though indulged where Shakespeare was concerned, did not entirely rule elsewhere.

It was necessary, however, to placate his new colleagues, whose fears of his policy were mixed with alarm at the strength of his family connections – not only Charles Kemble and Mrs Siddons, but her son Henry (a Kemble in looks but not in ability) and his wife were now members of the company, bidding fair, said one critic, 'to monopolise all theatrical emoluments'. Kemble took the first step by inviting all the leading actors at Covent Garden to a dinner at his house before the season opened. His capacity for drink, on this occasion, did much to temper his reputation for austerity, and the evening was highly successful. One would like to know more of it, but Boaden, who was present, is unhelpful: 'I shall by no means remove the veil, which in decent life should always be thrown between the convivial and the calm observer.' On another evening, not long before, Kemble and Harris, as new allies, had invited Sheridan to dine: there were always matters of mutual interest for the proprietors of the patent theatres to discuss. Sheridan grew bitter, as the wine began to flow, at the cordiality which Kemble and Harris displayed to one another, and reproached them sarcastically for their hypocrisy. 'Two fellows', said he, 'that have absolutely hated each other deadly all their lives.' 'False', said Harris cheerfully, 'we have not hated each other these *six* weeks – have we, Kemble?'[8]

Drury Lane, since Kemble left it, had been foundering still further, but the autumn of 1803, when Kemble began his reign at Covent Garden, brought one of those reprieves which had so often come to Sheridan at the eleventh hour. This time his saviour was a performing dog, a Newfoundland called Carlo, who in a musical afterpiece,

The Caravan, plunged into real water to rescue a child. The exploit, accompanied by an audible splash, was received with riotous applause and repeated nightly to enthusiastic crowds. Well might Sheridan, sensing profit, rush into the green-room after the first performance with a cry of 'Where is my preserver?' – dismissing the author when he modestly presented himself with, 'Pooh! I meant the dog!'[9]

Meanwhile at Covent Garden the greatest interest of Kemble's first season, following his opening performance as Hamlet, lay in watching his confrontation with the first potential rival he had known since Henderson, the actor George Frederick Cooke. Cooke had come to Covent Garden two years before. Slightly older than Kemble, he had had a brilliant but chequered career in Dublin and the provinces, but his eccentricity and drunkenness had till then kept him from the two main London theatres. He had made his début in London as Richard III, in Colley Cibber's adaptation of the play, and in that character at least, according to most critics, had proved himself superior to Kemble. He had none of Kemble's grace and dignity, but these qualities, despite Kemble's conception of Richard III as an essentially aristocratic figure, refined even in his cruelty, were almost a disadvantage in the role. 'He could never *look* the part of Richard', wrote Walter Scott, 'and it seemed a jest to hear him, whose countenance and person were so eminently fine, descant on his deformity.'[10] Cooke, ungainly and awkward, with a dark sarcastic countenance and a long hooked nose, was far better suited to the part. His tremendous vigour and harsh roaring voice (he compared Kemble's to 'an emasculated French horn') were powerfully expressive in portraying violent passions; he was at his best in villainous roles. He spoke rapidly, hurrying the audience with him; scorning Kemble's declamatory style, he habitually wrote out his parts in prose in order to avoid the sing-song lilt of blank verse. With the discipline to sustain his talents, he might have proved a powerful rival or even a supplanter of Kemble, but his own intemperance, which brought him close to insanity, eventually proved his downfall; and Kemble's position, though he relinquished his Richard III for a time, was never seriously threatened.

The relationship between the two, now that Kemble was manager of Covent Garden, was a matter of lively interest both to their colleagues and the public. Cooke made no secret of his hostility to Kemble, and would abuse him roundly when he was in his cups. Kemble's attitude was conciliatory; he abandoned the role of Shylock to Cooke, and played the Earl of Richmond to his Richard III. He cast him too as Pizarro in the first Covent Garden performance of Sheridan's *Pizarro* – by publishing the play, Sheridan had made it possible for Kemble to transfer Drury Lane's most profitable tragedy to the rival theatre. All was splendidly prepared for the first night, but Cooke, when the moment came, was so drunk that he could scarcely articulate; his incoherent apology, 'Ladies and gentlemen – my old complaint – my old complaint', made matters even worse, and he fell backwards soon after, 'mute as a turtle', leaving Henry Siddons to read through his part. Drunk or not, he remained extremely popular, and he was received with indulgent applause three days later when he returned to play the role.

There would never be much love lost between Kemble and Cooke, and the papers delighted in comparing the two, often, since Kemble lacked the attraction of novelty, to Kemble's disadvantage. But Cooke recognised Kemble's qualities. Once when some discontented players were abusing Kemble behind the scenes, asserting that he was an indifferent actor, Michael Kelly, who was there, asked Cooke if he agreed with them. 'No Sir', he replied, 'I think him a very great one; and those who say the contrary are envious men, and not worthy as actors, to wipe his shoes.'[11] He enjoyed, too, looking back on his conflicts with Kemble. Washington Irving recounts how Kemble once called Cooke to his room, to rehearse Iago to his Othello, but Cooke refused to go: ' "Let Black Jack" – so he called Kemble – "come to me." So they went on the boards without previous rehearsal. In the scene in which Iago instils his suspicions, Cooke grasped Kemble's left hand with his own, and then fixed his right, like a claw on his shoulder. In this position, drawing himself up to him with his short arm, he breathed his poisonous whispers. Kemble coiled and twisted his hand, writhing to get away – his right hand clasping his brow, and darting his eye back to Iago. It was wonderful.'

'Didn't I play up to Black Jack?' said Cooke to Irving when they

14. Kemble as Coriolanus, by Lawrence.

15. Mrs Siddons in 1797, the year of her first appearance in *The Stranger*, by Lawrence.

16. Above: Kemble as Rolla in *Pizarro*, after the painting by Lawrence.

17. Kemble on stage in *Pizarro*, Covent Garden, 1804.

18. Michael Kelly.

19. William Henry Ireland.

20. Charles Kemble, after a drawing by Lawrence.

21. Above: Master Betty as Young Norval in *Douglas* by Opie.

22. Edmund Kean as Sir Giles Overreach in *A New Way to Pay Old Debts*, attributed to Clint.

23. Mrs Inchbald.

24. Below: The Kembles in *Henry VIII*, Mrs Siddons as Queen Katharine, John Philip Kemble as Wolsey, Charles Kemble as Cromwell, Stephen Kemble as Henry VIII, after the painting by Harlowe.

25. Maria Siddons, after a drawing by Lawrence.

26. Thomas Lawrence, after a self-portrait.

27. William Siddons (detail) by Opie.

28. Sally Siddons, after a drawing by Lawrence.

29. Kemble as Richard III by William Hamilton.

met years later in New York. 'I saw his dark eye sweeping back upon me.'[12]

*   *   *

Cooke, for all his drunken eccentricities, was a worthy and inspiring rival, and Kemble always looked on him as such. But there was nothing worthy or inspiring in the rivalry which arose soon after between the Kembles and the newly discovered idol of the British stage – Master Betty, the Young Roscius, a thirteen-year-old from Belfast.

William Henry Betty had been ten years old when he had been taken to see Mrs Siddons play in Belfast, and had been so overcome, according to his propagandists, that he announced to his father 'with a look of such enthusiasm, and voice so pathetic, that those who heard him will never forget the expression, "that he should certainly die, if he must not be a player".'[13] Whatever the truth of this story, his father had certainly done everything to push him forward. With the help of a former prompter from the Belfast theatre, who coached him, Betty, an exceptionally good looking and precocious child, had carried out a series of engagements in the Irish and provincial theatres. Within two years he had acquired an enormous following, and by the summer of 1804 both major London theatres were competing for his services. Both Harris and Sheridan were cynical, but Bettymania had already reached such a pitch that neither felt they could afford not to present the prodigy whom his father, playing one theatre against the other, had booked to appear at both Covent Garden and Drury Lane. Kemble, cautious enough to look over the property they were acquiring, went with Harris' son Henry to see Master Betty play in Leicester. The young William Charles Macready, then a schoolboy, was in a box close by. 'I remember John Kemble's hankerchief strongly scented with lavender', he wrote, 'and his observation in a very compassionate tone, "Poor Boy! he is very hoarse!" '[14]

Kemble's compassion, even if genuine at the time, soon gave way to other feelings. Obliged by his position as manager and part proprietor to give the public what they wanted, he had the mortification as an actor, for twenty years the leader of his profession, of

161

being swept off the stage by a thirteen-year-old. He must have known it would not last – adolescence, at the least, would rob the child of his appeal, while his acting, remarkable though it was, showed the marks of careful coaching rather than an understanding of passions he was too young to feel. Master Betty, according to his instructor, 'possessed a docility even greater than his genius; for whatever he was directed to do, he could instantly execute and was certain never to forget'.[15] But this was an opinion voiced later; for the moment, he was presented as a child of nature, untutored and guided by the light of inspiration. The public, in the grip of an infatuation, hailed him in hyperbolic terms; the Young Roscius, wrote the painter Northcote, divided the world with Bonaparte.

Master Betty's first appearance in London, as Achmet in a forgotten tragedy called *Barbarossa*, took place at Covent Garden on December 1st, 1804. From one o'clock onwards the crowds began to gather round the theatre, filling the piazza on one side of the house and the length of Bow Street on the other. So great was the crush when the doors were opened that those who had failed to find a place inside were in danger of suffocation from the press of those behind. Soldiers had to be called to clear the entrances, while within the theatre those who had found places in the boxes defended them by force against their rightful occupants while others, less successful, dropped down from above into the already overflowing pit. The heat was so intense that more than twenty people fainted, and the uproar so great that when Charles Kemble came to give the prologue the audience, impatient to see their idol, howled him into inaudibility.

Master Betty's first entry, dressed in 'white linen pantaloons, a close and rather short russet jacket, trimmed with sable, and a turban hat', was greeted with tremendous applause, but though most of the audience remained in raptures throughout his performance, experienced observers, among them Mrs Inchbald, who was watching from the Kembles' box, were sceptical. 'I hate all *prodigies*', she wrote ' – partly, I fancy, because I have no faith in them. Under this prejudice I saw the first performance and was so disgusted by a monotony, a preaching-like tone, that I gave up my place at the end of the 3rd Act, and walked behind the scenes where myriads of critics were

162

gathered, to listen to their remarks. Here some vociferated that Garrick was returned to the stage; whilst others whispered "The Bottle Conjurer is come again". But as all that is said for him is in a *loud* voice, and all against him in a *low* one, praise must go forth and criticism be scarcely heard.'[16]

All dissenters indeed were forced to remain silent. When the highest in the land, from the Royal family to Pitt, and Charles James Fox, who described him as finer than Garrick, were united in their praises, professional actors could only hold their peace. Mrs Siddons, wisely disdaining to compete, remained almost entirely absent from the stage during Master Betty's heyday; she was in any case far from well, confined to her bed for weeks with painful rheumatism. Kemble's health too kept him away from the stage: during most of the winter he was suffering from a bad cough – 'I fear it is fixed on his lungs', wrote Mrs Inchbald, 'for such coughing I never heard, and nothing stops it but opium – opium in doses that appear to me frightful.'[17] In any case, he had no intention of appearing on the stage with Master Betty, though poor Cooke, for reasons of poverty, was forced to do so.

Master Betty's heyday, though glorious, was short-lived. Within five months of his first appearance the intense enthusiasm he had generated – enthusiasm, that according to his biographer, Giles Playfair, had a clearly sexual element – was beginning to die down. Before then, however, he had played in some of Kemble's leading roles, Hamlet and Rolla among them (though Hamlet, said Kemble, 'he should *not* have attempted'), been painted by Opie and Northcote, and drawn crowds outside his lodgings to read the daily bulletins on his health, when not surprisingly, considering the strain of so much exposure and adulation, he fell briefly ill.

Master Betty's fall from favour, as the world of fashion withdrew somewhat shamefacedly from its infatuation, was hastened by the departure of Hough, the former prompter from Belfast, who had quarrelled with his father. Hough's instruction, though glossed over at the time, had been an essential element of his success: without his skilful coaching Master Betty's deficiencies as an actor soon became obvious. His appearance as Richard III at the end of his first season confirmed the point. The contest between Cooke and Kemble was still fresh in the public mind. Even his most devoted supporters were forced to admit that he came a poor third.

By the beginning of Master Betty's second season, Kemble, who whatever the profits the Young Roscius had brought to the theatre had been outraged by his success, was able to stage a counter-attack. His weapon was a second so-called prodigy, an eight-year-old girl called Miss Mudie. Her appearance in *The Country Girl*, three weeks before Master Betty was due to re-appear, was greeted with such hisses that the child was driven from the stage, but she had served her purpose in discrediting the introduction of children in parts intended to be played by adults. Leigh Hunt, who at the age of twenty had just begun his career as a theatre critic, had no doubt of the folly of 'Rosciusism' as he called it. 'The approaching fate of Master Betty', he wrote just before the boy's return, 'will determine the character of the public judgment. Some persons will favour his attempts from the childish motive of encouraging a child where he should not be encouraged, many from not having gazed on the prodigy before, and more from having praised him before. The un-prejudiced and discerning will say, that the season for his encourage-ment is not yet arrived. Let us admire children as children and men as men.'[18]

Master Betty's second London season was not a success. He was not re-engaged for the third, though he continued to draw large audiences in the country for some years. His story to some extent was a tragedy – of talents burnt out before they had time to develop – but it was a tragedy with consolations. During his first season in London he had made some £10,000, earning more (£50) in one night than Kemble did in a week. He was able to live in modest comfort on the fruits of his labours for the rest of his life, retiring from the stage after several unsuccessful attempts at a comeback in 1824.

For Kemble the whole episode had been deeply humiliating. The cartoonists made mock of his discomfiture. A picture of Pegasus fly-ing swiftly through the air showed Master Betty firmly astride, whilst Kemble, sitting behind, is in imminent danger of falling off. 'Zounds', says Kemble, 'how he cuts and spurs away. If I don't take great care he will certainly have me off', whilst Master Betty, serenely guiding Pegasus, replies, 'Never fear Sir – we shall agree very well – but when two ride on a Horse – one must ride behind you know.'

The public's return to sanity and Kemble's reinstatement in their favour were signalled by another cartoon in which a recumbent John Bull is being helped to his feet by Kemble and Mrs Siddons, while a diminutive Infant Roscius flies away in alarm. 'Ah! My good friend Mr Kemble, how do you do? Mrs Siddons – I am happy to see you', says John Bull. 'Mercy on me what Enchantment have I been under!! Is that the Pigmy I was so much attach'd to, why he appears now no bigger than a pinshead!! and I declare I thought him as tall as the Monument!!'

XVII

The episode of Master Betty, so mortifying to his elders, had not affected Mrs Jordan. As a comedy actress she had nothing to fear from the young tragedian, and she was able to watch the discomfiture of Kemble and Mrs Siddons with a certain satisfaction. The Duke of Clarence, who shared his mistress's dislike of Kemble and who prided himself on his discrimination in dramatic matters, took a particular interest in the boy. He escorted him to a sitting with James Northcote, who was painting him as Hamlet, keeping up a string of jokes at Northcote's expense to amuse him. He gave a supper for him at Saint James's Palace, and when Master Betty, exhausted by over-work, fell ill, he invited him to recuperate at Bushy Park, his home in Richmond. Mrs Jordan, indulgent to her royal lover, did not question his enthusiasm for the boy, which soon waned as the tide of fashion drew away. However, when amongst the spate of 'prodigies' who sprang up in the wake of Master Betty, a Master Wigley, aged four and a half, was engaged to play the bugle at Drury Lane, she is said to have remarked on entering the green room one evening, 'Oh, for the days of King Herod!'

Mrs Jordan's position as the leading comic actress of the day was still secure, but constant child-bearing, for she now had thirteen children living, had taken its toll of that once slender shape which had so delighted her audiences in 'breeches' parts. Her figure, as Hazlitt put it, had become 'large, soft and generous like her soul'; the time had come, her admirers thought, to give up the Romps and Little Pickles of her younger days. In other parts she continued to enchant.'With a spirit of fun, that would have out-laughed Puck himself', wrote William Charles Macready, who played with her when she was over fifty, 'there was a discrimination, an identity with her character, an artistic arrangement of the scene that made all appear spontaneous and accidental, though elaborated with the greatest care. Her voice was the most melodious I ever heard, which she could vary by certain bass tones, that would have disturbed the gravity of a hermit; and who that once heard that laugh of hers could ever forget it? The words of Milman would have applied well to her – "Oh, the words laughed on her lips!" '[1]

That laugh – 'so rich, so apparently irrepressible, so deliciously self enjoying, as to be at all times irresistible'[2] – still echoes down the years, but for Mrs Jordan, in this latter stage of her career, much of the joy of acting had departed. Like Mrs Siddons she drove herself on for the sake of her family. She had her elder daughters by Daly and Richard Ford to establish in the world; the Duke of Clarence's affairs were in a permanent state of disarray; not only her children but her brothers and sisters laid claims on her purse. 'My professional success through life has, indeed, been most extraordinary', she wrote to her biographer, James Boaden, 'and, consequently, attended with great emoluments. But from my first starting in life, at the early age of fourteen, I have always had a large family to support. My mother was a duty. But on brothers and sisters I have lavished more money than can be supposed; and more, I am sorry to say, than I can well justify to those, who have a stronger and prior claim to my exertions. With regard to myself (as much depends on our idea of riches), I have certainly enough; but this is too selfish a consideration, to weigh one moment against what I consider to be a duty. I am quite tired of the profession. I have lost those great excitements, vanity and emulation. The first has been amply gratified; and the last I see no occasion for; but still, without these it is a mere money-getting drudgery.'[3]

Drudgery her work had often become, and she had frequent bouts of ill health, but though she withdrew from the stage for two seasons, in 1806–7 and 1809–10, it seems that the Duke of Clarence had no desire to see her give up earning. His debts were mounting up; in the end it was lack of money and his desire to better his position by a favourable marriage that would lead him to abandon her.

*　　*　　*

With Master Betty banished from the field, Kemble was able to return to his former position at the pinnacle of his profession. He opened the season of 1805–6 as Zanga in Young's tragedy *The Revenge*, a production got up with especial care. 'It is in characters that are occupied with themselves and with their own importance', wrote Leigh Hunt, 'it is in the systematic and exquisite revenge of Zanga, in the indignant jealousy of Othello, and in the desperate ambition of King John, that Mr Kemble is the actor. There is always something sublime in the sudden contemplation of great objects, and perhaps there is not a sublimer action on the stage than the stride of Mr Kemble as Zanga, over the body of his victim, and his majestic exultation of revenge.'[4]

Leigh Hunt, who had begun his career as a theatre critic by attacking Master Betty, was far from uncritical of Kemble. He acknowledged his merit in certain characters, but he waged a determined campaign against his 'vicious orthöepy', the quirks of pronunciation that made him say 'varchue' for 'virtue', 'bird' for 'beard', and 'aitches' for 'aches'. The question of 'aitches', indeed, was becoming something of a *cause célèbre*. An elaborate revival of *The Tempest* in the following year enjoyed an excellent run – perhaps, as Kemble's biographer Herschel Baker suggests, because everyone was eager to hear him say the famous word. 'Night after night', wrote Walter Scott, 'he menaced Caliban with *aitches*, and night after night was for so doing assailed by a party in the pit with a ferocity worthy of Caliban himself. One evening he felt himself, from indisposition, unwilling to sustain the usual conflict, and on that occasion evaded a drawn battle by omitting the line entirely. It was curious enough to see how the critics, as he approached the place where they expected to hear the obnoxious line, resembled

"greyhounds in the slips,
Straining upon the start";

the puzzled countenances which they displayed as speech after speech was made without the expected game being roused; – and the blank look of disappointment when the close of the scene announced to them how Kemble had, for the evening, eluded their resentment without bending to their authority.'[5] In general, however, Kemble was unperturbed by the opposition of the pit, and the actor Charles Mathews recalls meeting him behind scenes one evening while the audience was still loudly hissing his 'aitches'. 'Umph', said Kemble, coolly taking a pinch of snuff, 'how these good people think they are right.'[6]

Mrs Siddons, after a year of absence while the Master Betty craze was at its height, had returned to partner her brother in some of his great roles – acting Volumnia to his Coriolanus, Elvira to his Rolla. 'The Drama, justly directed, is the School of Virtue', wrote an admiring commentator, 'and Heaven has fixed its seal on the forms, the faces, the minds of these two, its chosen disciples.'[7] Despite such claims, however, there was no doubt that while Kemble maintained the classical splendour of his face and figure, Mrs Siddons, like her rival Mrs Jordan, was becoming extremely fat. Rheumatism too had made her movements stiffer; towards the end of her career, when she knelt to the Duke in *Measure for Measure*, it took two attendants to raise her to her feet again. Though only two years older than her brother, ill health and sorrow had aged her faster; and the spring of 1808 brought her a further blow, when in the course of a visit to Edinburgh she received the news of her husband's death. He was sixty-four, they had been married for more than thirty years, and whatever their differences had been at times, their last meetings had been peaceful. Mrs Siddons had spent six weeks with him, only a month before his death, and had left him in seemingly good health with plans to spend part of the summer with her at her cottage at Westbourne. From there, as soon as she had recovered enough to travel from Scotland, she wrote sadly to Mrs Piozzi:

> How unwearied is your goodness to me, my dear friend . . . There is something so awful in this sudden dissolution of so long a connexion that I shall feel it longer than I shall speak of it. May I die the death of my honest worthy husband! and may those to whom I am dear, remember me when I am gone as I remember him, – forgetting and forgiving all my errors, and recollecting only my quietness of spirit and singleness of heart . . . My head is still so dull with this stunning surprise that I cannot see what I write. Adieu! dear soul! do not cease to love your friend, S.S.[8]

*　　*　　*

William Siddons had gone. Ineffectual though he had often been, he had been Mrs Siddons' support throughout her professional life, and had shared, however half-heartedly, in its vicissitudes. But he was not to be at her side in one of its worst calamities, when six months later, on the night of September 30th, 1808, Covent Garden was totally destroyed by fire. Some thirty people perished in the conflagration which was said to have been caused by a piece of wadding fired from a musket in *Pizarro* which had lodged unnoticed in the scenery. The loss to the theatre, not only of the building but of valuable properties, was almost incalculable, while Mrs Siddons herself lost her entire theatrical wardrobe. 'Of all the precious and curious dresses, and lace, and jewels, which I have been collecting for these thirty years, not one article has escaped', she wrote to a friend. 'The most grievous of these, my losses, is a piece of lace which had been the toilette of the poor Queen of France. It was upwards of four yards long, and more than a yard wide. It never cou'd have been bought for a thousand pounds, but that's the least regret. It *was* so interesting!'9

But her chief concern was for her brother. He had sunk almost all his savings in the theatre and still owed money on his original investment; at the age of fifty-one, he had all to begin again. Kemble's first reaction, however, according to Boaden, who hurried round to see him as soon as he heard the news, was typically grandiloquent. Mrs Kemble was in tears on the sofa, Charles Kemble, who had just returned from the fire, sat attentive nearby, while Kemble, totally absorbed, was standing before the glass endeavouring to shave himself. 'Nothing', wrote Boaden, 'could be more natural than for Mrs Kemble to feel and think of their *personal* loss in this dreadful calamity. Her husband, I am convinced, while I saw him, never thought of *himself* at all. His mind was rather raised than dejected, and his imagination distended with the pictured details of all the treasures, that had perished in the conflagration. At length he broke out in an exclamation, which I have preserved as characteristic of his turn of mind:

' "Yes, it has perished, that magnificent theatre, which for all the purposes of exhibition or comfort was the first in Europe. It is gone, with its treasures of every description, and some which can never be replaced. That LIBRARY, which contained all the immortal productions of our countrymen, prepared for the purposes of representation! That vast collection of MUSIC, composed by the greatest geniuses in that science, – by Handel, Arne and others; – most of it manuscript, in the original score! That WARDROBE, stored with the costumes of all ages and nations, accumulated by unwearied research, and at incredible expense! SCENERY, the triumph of the art, unrivalled for its accuracy and so exquisitely finished, that it might be the ornament of your drawing rooms, were they only large enough to contain it! Of all this vast treasure nothing now remains, but the ARMS OF ENGLAND over the entrance of the theatre – and the ROMAN EAGLE standing *solitary* in the market place!" '

Kemble's reaction, in its way, was as much in character as Sheridan's when, by a coincidence so extraordinary that many people at first refused to believe it could have been an accident, Drury Lane was levelled to the ground by fire in the spring of the following year. News of the disaster arrived at the House of Commons where Sheridan was taking part in a debate, and it was suggested that the House should adjourn; but Sheridan, with quiet composure, refused to allow his private misfortune to interrupt public business. Later, having left the House, he sat drinking wine with Michael Kelly in the Piazza Coffee House, watching the theatre on which his whole fortune depended collapsing in flames. Someone remarked on his calm but Sheridan, witty even in calamity, made his famous reply: 'May not a man take a glass of wine by his own fireside?'

Sheridan's position, in fact, was far worse than Kemble's. As chief proprietor of the theatre, his loss was proportionately greater. He had not, as Kemble had, the resource of a regular profession; he stood too high in the world to accept as Kemble, as an actor, could, the help of such noble patrons as the Duke of Northumberland who had offered Kemble a loan of £10,000 without security on hearing of his misfortune. Drury Lane had been on the brink of bankruptcy before the fire and was besides gravely under-insured. Though Sheridan would receive some payment for its patent, the destruction of the theatre spelled his financial ruin and indirectly, since he had depended on it to pay his political expenses, the end of his political career. The task of reconstruction was taken over by a committee, headed by the banker Samuel Whitbread, who expressly excluded Sheridan from taking part in the direction of the theatre. His long association with Drury Lane had come to an end.

The disentangling of Drury Lane's financial affairs and the raising of money to rebuild it was a long and complicated process; it was four years before the theatre re-opened. The building of the new Covent Garden, meanwhile, had gone on apace. £50,000 had been raised by public subscription, almost as much was received from the insurance, and on December 30th 1808, only three months after the fire, the new foundation stone was laid by the Prince of Wales. All the actors and actresses attended the ceremony, which took place in the pouring rain. Mrs Siddons, magnificent in black ostrich feathers, was in torments of anxiety for her brother, who having been ill for nearly a month, had got up for the occasion and was standing bare-headed in his court dress, the water soaking his pumps and thin silk stockings. But the day had a splendid finale for Kemble, when at dinner that evening the Duke of Northumberland presented him with his cancelled bond for £10,000 with the request that he regard it as a gift. The ducal munificence, gratifying though it was, was the subject of some derision in the press; a cartoon by Gillray showed Kemble, Charles and Mrs Siddons outside Northumberland House, Kemble's hat outstretched for money, with the caption: 'Theatrical mendicants relieved. "Have pity upon all our aches and wants".'

In September 1809 the new Covent Garden was completed. De-signed in the neo-classical style by the architect Robert Smirke, it was slightly larger than the former theatre and included a number of improvements: the space between the rows of seats was somewhat wider, the galleries were a few feet nearer the stage. But the cost of putting it up had been far greater than expected, and the proprietors found that even when the house was full the theatre, if run on the old system and at the old prices, was bound to make a loss. It was there-fore decided to operate on a new plan by turning the third tier into private boxes, each with its own little ante-room, whose rent for the season, it was hoped, would bring in an important new revenue. At the same time the traditional one-shilling or upper gallery was re-placed by a series of less commodious 'pigeon-holes' beneath the roof, while the prices of admission in the rest of the house were raised, the boxes from six to seven shillings, the pit from three and six to four. The proprietors, feeling themselves entirely justified in demanding these higher charges, anticipated no trouble when they announced them, and Kemble in a sanguine mood prepared for his opening performance in the new theatre. His reception on that evening dealt him a blow as unexpected as it was shattering, and ushered in what was probably the longest period of disturbances in the history of the theatre, the three months of the so-called OP or Old Prices riots.

XVIII

The causes of the OP riots in fact went far beyond the question of raised prices for admission. The installation of a tier of private boxes, cut off from the rest of the theatre, was a further provocation. The arguments against them were ostensibly on the grounds of morality – loose women could enter by the private staircases, debauchery flourish in the ante-rooms – but the real objection was to the suggestion of privilege which the exclusion of the public from the third tier implied. Class antagonism was in the air, and so too was the chauvinism which fuelled the third grievance of the rioters – the engagement, at a very high salary, of the famous Italian singer Madame Catalini, whose wages, they claimed, had forced the entrance prices up.

Kemble, who had only shared in the decisions which were to rouse such furious opposition, bore the full brunt of them in public. Seldom before or since has an actor been exposed to such execration. His first appearance when, on the opening night of the new Covent Garden, he stepped forward to deliver the inaugural address, set the tone for all that followed.

There had been crowds outside the theatre all day and the doors were besieged at opening time, but this was only to be expected when the new decorations, neo-classical within as without, were being seen by the public for the first time. For several days there had been paragraphs in the press complaining of the new prices, and Kemble had been warned there might be trouble brewing; but he had brushed aside the fears of his friends and Boaden who met him in the street that afternoon found him in a calm and sanguine mood. The evening's programme began with the National Anthem which was received without incident; then Kemble, dressed in his costume for *Macbeth*, which was to follow the address, made his appearance on the stage. He was greeted by an immediate uproar:

'Off! off!' 'Old prices!' were the cries;
'No Catalini!' and 'No rise!'
What hissing, yelling, howling, groaning!
What barking, braying, hooting, moaning!
The people bellowed, shouted, storm'd,
The actors in dumb show perform'd.
Those in the pit stood up with rage,
And turn'd their backs upon the stage.[1]

Kemble's gestures, said a press report next day, 'were imploring but in vain . . . The play proceeded in pantomime; not a word was heard, save now and then the deeply modulated tones of the bewitching Siddons. On her entrance she seemed disturbed by the clamour, but in the progressive stages of her action she went through her part with perfect composure. Kemble appeared greatly agitated, yet in no instance did his trouble prevent him from carrying on *the cunning of the scene*. Perhaps a finer dumb show was never witnessed.'[2]

At the end of the evening the audience, exhilarated by the noise, refused to go home, and continued drumming their feet and yelling for the manager, till two magistrates arrived and attempted to read the Riot Act from the stage. Their appearance was treated as a new incitement; seats were broken up, and a cry of 'Dowse the glims' led a rush to extinguish the lights. The arrival of Bow Street runners and the arrest of several ringleaders prevented further damage being done, but it was two in the morning before the crowd dispersed. *The Beggar's Opera* the following night met the same reception. 'Whenever there is Danger of a Riot', Kemble had noted, 'always act an Opera; for Musick drowns the Noise of Opposition', but the formula this time was ineffective. On the third night it was Cooke's turn to face the hurly-burly:

Though Mr Cooke King Richard play'd
None listened to a word was said.
'Twould not have mattered much, I ween,
Had he, this night, as usual been –
That is, had he been non se ipse
Or, in plain English, had been tipsy.[3]

At the conclusion of the after-piece Kemble, in his capacity as manager, came forward to address the audience. He was greeted with applause which changed to hisses when he attempted to explain the proprietors' position – the great expenses incurred in the building of the theatre, and the narrow margin on which it had operated even before the fire: 'I declare to you, on my honour, and would not tell a lie for all that the theatre is worth – that for the last ten years the proprietors have not received six per cent for their money – money vested in a property of so fluctuating and precarious a nature as this is.'[4] His explanations were shouted down; amidst yells and groans, and ribald references to his attack on Miss De Camp, he withdrew defeated from the stage.

Riots were nothing new in the history of the theatre, and Kemble had confronted angry crowds before. But the strength of class hatred in the protests against the private boxes was something hitherto unknown, while the opposition to the new prices themselves was a reflection of the growing dissatisfaction with the patent system and the monopoly enjoyed by Covent Garden and Drury Lane. A hard core of the rioters, lawyers and professional men, encouraged by the radical press, felt themselves genuinely justified in attacking the presumption of Covent Garden in seeking to press its privileges still further. A far greater proportion, with no reasoned grudge against the management, were simply swept along in the enjoyment of the nightly demonstrations. OP banners and placards hung from the tiers of the theatre, from which the box-holders had fled. OP badges were sported on hats and button-holes. OP dances, when the audience, beating rhythmically with their sticks and feet, chanted the letters in unison, formed a torturing accompaniment to the performances on stage. Toyshops were sold out of penny whistles; watchmen's rattles, coachmen's horns and once a protesting live pig added their sounds to the clamour. The authorities, incredibly supine, seemed powerless to control the disorder. The management, in desperation, called in trained pugilists, led by the champion boxers Dan Mendoza and 'Dutch Sam', to combat the mob, but this ill judged measure only added to the public wrath:

The drama's laws are now abus'd
And Kemble's desperate band
Of hired ruffians, ragged Jews,
With him go hand in hand.[5]

Mrs Siddons, after her reception on the first night, refused to appear on stage again, but Kemble continued to stand his ground, confronting the audience night after night and attempting vainly to reason with them. The services of Madame Catalini – 'Madame Cat' or 'nasty Pussy' as the audience dubbed her – were dispensed with in favour of an English singer, Mrs Brunton. The theatre's books were offered for inspection to an independent committee, which showed, as the management had maintained, that the theatre would be running at a loss had the old prices been maintained. But the audience were out for blood, their indignation as true-born Britons aroused by the hiring of Mendoza, and the arrest of various ringleaders. 'King John' or 'Black Jack' must be brought to his knees. Kemble's haughty manner, his air of lofty superiority, were an irresistible challenge to the vulgar. His classical features were distorted in numerous placards and cartoons, now with the caption 'Mr Kemble's head aitches', now showing him disporting himself with the nobility and ladies of light virtue in the private boxes.

I can't those private boxes rob
Heigh ho says Kemble.
With Lord O'Shabble I drink nob and nob,
And I'm hand in glove with my Lord Thingumbob,
With his rowley, powley, gammon and spinnage,
I am, says manager Kemble.[6]

It became the habit for the rioters, when the evening's entertainments were over, to go round to Kemble's house, breaking windows and alarming those within with yells and war whoops. Kemble, with an intrepid simplicity which was characteristic, was at first resolved to 'go and talk with them' when he heard his own name called for, but was dissuaded by his brother Charles who rightly feared that darkness, confusion and the inflamed state of the mob might bring about some catastrophe. 'Poor Mrs Kemble, I am told', wrote Mrs

Inchbald to a friend, 'and no wonder, is nearly dead with terror',[7] and Mrs Siddons, at about the same time, gave a pathetic picture of the strains they were living under:

My appearance of illness was occasioned entirely by an agitating visit that morning from poor Mr John Kemble, on account of the giving up of the private boxes, which I fear must be at last complied with. Surely nothing ever equalled the domineering of the mob in these days. It is to me inconceivable how the public at large submits to be thus dictated to, against their better judgment, by a handful of imperious and intoxicated men. In the meantime, what can the poor proprietors do but yield to overwhelming necessity?

Could I once feel that my poor brother's anxiety about the theatre was at an end, I should be, marvellous to say, as well as I ever was in my life. But only conceive what a state he must have been in, however good a face he might put upon the business, for upwards of three months; and think what his poor wife and I must have suffered, when, for weeks together, such were the outrages committed on his house and otherwise, that I trembled for even his personal safety; she, poor soul, living with ladders at her windows, in order to make her escape through the garden in case of an attack. Mrs Kemble tells me his nerves are much shaken.[8]

In the end, as Mrs Siddons had foreseen, the proprietors of Covent Garden were forced to capitulate. The arrest of one of their number, a lawyer Henry Clifford, had given the rioters a leader; he had promptly sued the Covent Garden box-keeper, James Brandon, who had brought him before the magistrates, for false imprisonment and assault, and at the end of a trial which became a *cause célèbre* had been awarded damages of £5. 'I *hate* mobs of all kinds', wrote Walter Scott, deploring the riots, 'but I fear disciplined mobs, especially those with leaders such as Clifford who has just knowledge enough to keep him within the verge of the law, talent enough to do mischief and no capacity whatever to do the slightest good.'[9] With Clifford as its chairman an OP banquet (tickets 12s.6d.) was arranged at the Crown and Anchor tavern; some three hundred people attended, and Kemble, having been assured that he would be offered no insult, presented himself before them at the end. The rioters set out their terms. Madame Catalini had already been dismissed, the theatre's accounts had been laid before the public, but more concessions must be made – a reduction in the number of private boxes, a return to the old prices of admission for the pit though not the boxes, a withdrawal of all legal charges against the rioters, and finally the dismissal of James Brandon, whose courageous resistance to the rioters, Henry Clifford among them, had drawn their especial fury. To all, except the dismissal of Brandon, Kemble immediately agreed; Brandon had been a faithful servant of the theatre for forty years, and he could not recommend his co-proprietors to turn him away. But even Brandon had to be sacrificed: when Harris brought him forward at the theatre later that evening, he was pelted from the stage, and on the following night Kemble was compelled to announce he had been dismissed. His cup of humiliation was still not full: before the clamour from the audience would die down, he had to abase himself further with an apology on his own and his partners' behalf for introducing 'improper persons', presumably Mendoza and his fellows, into the theatre. With this a great placard with the words 'We are satisfied' was raised from the pit and so, on December 15th, 1809, after sixty-seven nights of disturbances, the OP riots came to an end.

*   *   *

It is pleasant to record that Brandon, having been dismissed for too faithfully serving the theatre, was re-instated to his office shortly after – though not before a public apology from the stage. But Kemble's troubles were not entirely over. At the beginning of the following season, there was renewed rioting when it was discovered that the number of private boxes had not been sufficiently reduced. There had been a genuine misunderstanding over this. Drury Lane, now in the process of rebuilding, had applied to have a greater number of private boxes than that agreed by Covent Garden with the OP rioters, and at the end of the previous season Kemble had appealed, as he thought successfully, from the stage, to be allowed the same number as their competitor. But the public were having none of it. Kemble's attempts at an explanation were greeted with cries of 'No shuffling'; new pamphlets, placards and lampoons were prepared and the whole saturnalia seemed due to start again, till the management hastily agreed to abolish the excess boxes. The alterations, together with those previously made, and the great expense of rebuilding, had a serious effect on the theatre's finances. The decline of Covent Garden, which when Kemble first bought into it had been a tightly controlled and well run enterprise, may be said to have commenced with the OP riots and their consequences.

Meanwhile, once the riots had subsided, Kemble, with stoical determination, set himself to restoring the theatre's position and his own. He had stood the storm manfully, but there was no doubt that he had felt its humiliations very deeply. In dealing with the rioters his unbending manner had been a disadvantage, and he had perhaps been slow to gauge the public mood. 'He shuts himself up too much', wrote his friend Thomas Lawrence, 'and it leads to self confidence and little subtleties of conduct and reserves in Trifles, that, long continued in, produce their last certain effect – an impression on the Minds of others that seems to justify the harsh opinion given of him.'[10] But these faults of manner and the error of bringing in hired pugilists aside, he could rightly feel that he had been disgracefully ill used, and it was not surprising that, in the words of Walter Scott, his favourite art lost some of its attractions for him. His health, too, was not what it was: the asthmatic condition against which he had always had to struggle had grown worse, and gout, the consequence of years of excess, was a recurrent plague. He did not allow his ailments to keep him from the stage, dosing himself with vast quantities of opium in order to perform, even after his worst attacks. Sometimes his fellow players would find him groaning when he came off stage. 'I am very sorry to see my poor husband in such pain', said Eliza O'Neill, who was playing the erring Mrs Haller to his Stranger, when she found him thus one night, Kemble, tortured though he was, replying equally in character: 'Yes, you are a dear creature and *deserve forgiveness*.'[11]

Cooke, increasingly drunk and unreliable, had left Covent Garden for an engagement in America, but Mrs Siddons was at Kemble's side for some of his best parts – Macbeth, Hamlet, Wolsey. The public, as if to demonstrate their unpredictability, took him back to

their hearts as though the riots had never taken place. In two revivals, as Brutus in *Julius Caesar* and Cato in Addison's tragedy of
that name, he added new laurels to his crown. If Coriolanus remained
his highest achievement in the Roman vein, his Brutus and Cato fell
not far short of it. 'Other performers might excel Kemble in the full
burst of instant and agitating passion to which the person represented is supposed to give the reins upon any natural impulse', wrote
Scott, 'but we cannot conceive of anyone delineating, with anything
approaching the same felicity, those lofty Romans, feeling and partly
exhibiting, yet on the whole conquering the passions of nature by
the mental discipline to which they had trained themselves. Those
who have seen Kemble as Cato bend over the body of his slain son,
and subdue the father to assume the patriot, or have heard him
pronounce the few words in Brutus,

> No man bears sorrow better – Portia's dead

will at once understand our meaning – to others we almost despair
of explaining it.'[12]

As manager as well as actor Kemble exerted himself to the full.
A young actor, Charles Mayne Young, who played Cassius to his
Brutus, bid fair to replace Cooke, if not to rival Kemble in tragedy.
On the comic side the company was strong. The immortal Joe
Grimaldi, at the height of his fame as a clown, drew in crowds in the
pantomime of *Mother Goose*. Lewis had retired, but actors such as
Quick, ideally cast as a 'busy, strutting, money getting citizen; or a
crusty old guardian, in a brown suit and bob wig',[13] Munden, never
better than when portraying the 'variable fatuity of intoxication',[14]
and Fawcett, the jolliest of hunting squires, gave life and colour to
the indifferent comedies of the day. Charles Kemble, less powerful
than his brother in tragedy, but infinitely superior in comedy, was a
gay and graceful Charles Surface in *The School for Scandal*. (Kemble's
own appearance in the part some years earlier had been a disaster;
Sheridan praised him slily for his *execution* of the role.)

Elaborate spectacle was a continuing attraction. *Blue Beard* was
revived in an extravagant new production which brought sixteen
white horses on the stage. 'The dressing-rooms for the new company
of comedians', complained Genest, 'were probably under the

orchestra, for in the first row of the pit the stench was so abominable that one might as well have sitten in the stables.'[15] An elephant 'from the banks of Ganges' was introduced in a pantomime to the disgust of serious theatre-goers and of Kemble himself. But the elephant, like the horses, was extremely popular, and his partners thought the £900 they had paid for it well spent.

For two years after the riots Kemble gave his best to the theatre, striving to hold the torch of tragedy high amidst these rival attractions. The young Lord Byron, just back from his travels abroad, described himself as 'living quietly, reading Sir W. Drummond's book on the bible and seeing Kemble and Mrs Siddons',[16] and a few days later, on December 15th, 1811, wrote of him in *Coriolanus*: 'He was glorious and exerted himself wonderfully.'[17] But though Kemble's powers, despite bouts of ill health, seemed unabated, it was becoming clear that his sister's were on the wane. Her movements had become stiffer, her voice at times seemed to fail her altogether. Even so great an admirer as Thomas Lawrence felt it was time she should retire. 'He saw her last night in Lady Constantine [sic] in *King John*', wrote his friend, the painter Joseph Farington, in September 1811, 'a character in some degree favourable to her person which is now become very large, but her powers in acting are not what they were. In one passage Her voice sunk when it should have been raised to a high pitch. This he remarked to Kemble who played King John & with whom He supped that evening. Kemble replied that she had not power to express the passage properly, Her voice failed from lack of strength.'[18]

Though Mrs Siddons had often spoken of her desire to leave the stage and her longing for a quiet retired life, the prospect, when it drew close, appalled her. 'I feel', she wrote to Mrs Piozzi ten days before her final performance, 'as if I were mounting the first step of a Ladder conducting me to another world.'[19] She played fifty-seven times, recreating almost all her famous roles, in her last season. For her final performance, on June 22nd, 1812, she chose, inevitably, *Macbeth*.

'The house was crowded in an extraordinary manner in every part', wrote Farington. 'Persons of high distinction were in the uppermost Boxes – Ladies as well as gentlemen . . . When Mrs

Siddons walked off the stage in Her last scene where she appears as walking in her sleep, there was a long continued burst of applause, which caused Kemble & c. to conclude that it was the wish of the Spectators that the Play should stop. The Curtain was dropped and much noise was continued. One of the Performers came forward to request to know whether it was the pleasure of the audience that the play shd. stop or go on.

'A tumult again ensued, which being considered as a sign that the Play shd. stop, some time elapsed till at length the Curtain was drawn up and Mrs Siddons appeared sitting at a table in her own character. She was dressed in white Sattin and had on a long veil. She arose but it was some time before she could speak the clapping and other sounds of approbation rendering it impossible for Her to be heard. She curtsied and bowed, and at last there was silence. At 10 o'clock precisely she began to speak Her farewell address which took up Eight minutes during which time there was profound silence. Having finished, the loudest claps, & c, followed, & she withdrew bowing & led off by an attendant who advanced for that purpose ... Her appearance was that of a person depressed & sunk in spirits, but I did not perceive that she shed tears. J. Kemble came on afterwards to ask whether the Play shd. go on? – He wiped His eyes, and appeared to have been weeping. The play was not allowed to go on.'[20]

So ended the career of one whom the theatrical historian Brander Matthews describes quite simply as 'probably the greatest actress the world has ever seen'. She was fifty-seven. 'Nothing ever was, or can be like her', wrote Byron, who saw her only in her splendid sunset. Hazlitt, who as a student fifteen years before had first felt the quickening power of her genius, was better fitted to express the void she left behind her:

Who shall give us Mrs Siddons again? . . . Or who shall sit majestic in the throne of tragedy – a Goddess, a prophetess and a Muse? . . . Who shall stalk over the stage of horrors, its presiding genius, or 'play the hostess' at the banquetting scene of murder? Who shall walk in the sleepless exstacy of the soul, and haunt the mind's eye ever after, with the dread pageantry of suffering and

183

guilt? Who shall make tragedy once more stand with its feet upon the earth, and with its head raised above the skies weeping tears and blood? That loss is not to be repaired. While the stage lasts, there will never be another Mrs Siddons![21]

XIX

Mrs Siddons had retired. She had been the soul, as Kemble had been the brains, of their great partnership and he wept, when she left the stage, as he would not do at his own departure. His career was not yet at an end but his sister's retirement marked the moment to withdraw for a time from Covent Garden – perhaps, as Walter Scott remarked, to make the public appreciate his absence, but also to recuperate his health. To the best of his ability he had put the affairs of the theatre in order; for two seasons he would confine his interest in it to drawing his dividends while he himself set out on a leisurely programme of provincial engagements interspersed with long visits to the houses of his noble friends.

Meanwhile in London Drury Lane, after four years of financial wrangling, had risen from its ashes. In October 1812 the new theatre, designed by Benjamin Wyatt, was opened to the public. Lord Byron had written the opening address, but though his poem paid graceful tribute to Sheridan the former proprietor was not present at the ceremony. Excluded from the management by Whitbread, who resolutely refused to allow him any hand in the theatre's affairs, he regarded the consolatory offer of a box for himself and his wife as an insult; he did not set foot in the theatre till 1815, the year before his death, when he was persuaded to come and see Edmund Kean in a performance of *Othello*. Nor had he been fully paid for his share of the concern; Whitbread had deliberately withheld £12,000 to cover claims from the old theatre. Indirectly this cost Sheridan his parliamentary seat in the election of 1812 and led, since he was no longer immune as a member of Parliament, to his arrest and temporary confinement in a debtors' prison. Though Whitbread obtained his release Sheridan blamed him bitterly thereafter.

Deprived of his twin anchors, the theatre and politics, Sheridan's last years were melancholy ones. His wit and brilliance could still blaze forth in company but they were more and more obscured by drink and ill health. 'I have seen poor Sheridan weep, and good cause had he', said Byron, recalling these years to Lady Blessington. 'Placed by his transcendent talents in an elevated sphere without the means of supporting the necessary appearance, to how many humiliations must his fine mind have submitted ere he arrived at the state in which I knew him, of reckless jokes to pacify creditors of a morning, and alternate smiles and tears of an evening, round the boards where ostentatious dullness called in his aid to give a zest to the wine that often maddened him, but could not thaw the frozen current of their blood.'[1] It was not till his death in 1816, and his funeral in Westminster Abbey, that the glories of his great days, the days when the screen scene in *The School for Scandal* set the theatre in an uproar, or his oration at the trial of Warren Hastings held his audience breathless, were regained.

*   *   *

Mrs Jordan, formerly the brightest ornament of Drury Lane, did not return for the opening season of the new theatre. 'The theatrical committee of Drury Lane', said a paper, 'are at variance as to the terms upon which she is negotiating for an engagement, and the lady finds she can employ herself better in a provincial ramble than even at a brilliant theatre in the metropolis.'

Mrs Jordan was still driven by the need for money. She had heard the news of Mrs Siddons' retirement with envy. 'I long to make my *last* appearance, more than ever I did to make my first',[2] she wrote wistfully. But since the burning of Drury Lane her circumstances had changed dramatically with her separation, after twenty years of domestic happiness, from the Duke of Clarence in 1811. The Duke's financial affairs, with his children growing up and their futures to be provided for, had become increasingly embarrassed. At the same time his brother's accession as Prince Regent early that year gave him hope that the terms of the Royal Marriage Act could be adjusted; marriage with some great heiress might provide a solution to the otherwise insoluble problem of his debts. The prospect was less disturbing than it might have been some years before. Mrs Jordan, however devoted a companion and delightful an actress, was unquestionably fat and nearing fifty.

The idea of an advantageous marriage was crystallised by his meeting, in the summer of 1811, with a certain Miss Catherine Tylney-Long, young, good-looking and possessed of some £40,000 a year. Attracted by her income as much as her charms, the Duke was soon paying suit to the lady while Mrs Jordan was carrying out a series of provincial engagements. Her letters to the Duke while she was on tour show her to have been oblivious of impending disaster, though as mistress to a royal duke she must always have been aware that reasons of State, or even of convenience, might one day put an end to their relationship.

In October 1811, on the last day of a stay in Cheltenham, where she was to perform for the manager's benefit as Nell in *The Devil to Pay*, she received a letter from the Duke asking her to meet him at Maidenhead to arrange the terms of their separation. The blow, according to Boaden, was entirely unexpected, but Mrs Jordan, shattered though she was, insisted on going through with her performance. Arriving at the theatre weak from tears and a succession of fainting fits, she struggled through her part till they came to the scene where Jobson, one of the characters, accuses the conjuror of making her 'laughing drunk'. Mrs Jordan attempted to laugh but burst into tears instead, whereupon the actor playing Jobson, with great presence of mind, changed the text and exclaimed, 'Why, Nell, the conjuror has made thee crying drunk', and so carried her through the scene.

The Duke's courtship of Miss Tylney-Long was unsuccessful. With ten children, a mistress of twenty years' standing and a multitude of debts, his royal lineage was an insufficient attraction and she refused him. But the separation from Mrs Jordan, which his pursuit of Miss Tylney-Long had precipitated, was accomplished, and having failed with one heiress he was soon on the track of another. Bluff and insensitive, he seemed almost unconscious of the suffering he had caused: to Miss Tylney-Long's aunt, in the course of his courtship, he had written breezily: 'Mrs Jordan has behaved like an angel and is equally anxious for the match.'[3] To his credit he did his best to make suitable financial provision for Mrs Jordan, but money was always short and the debts and extravagances of her daughter by Daly, whose husband was facing bankruptcy, forced her again on the exhausting but lucrative undertaking of a provincial tour. It was in the course of this that the young actor William Macready saw her, and his memoirs record not only his impression, already quoted, of her acting, but of the professionalism which lay behind it. 'At rehearsal I remarked, as I watched this charming actress intently through her first scene, how minute and particular her first directions were; nor would she be satisfied till by repetition she had seen the business executed exactly to her wish. The moving picture, the very life of the scene was perfect in her mind, and she transferred it in all its earnestness to every movement on the stage.'[4]

Typical too was the actress's kindness to the young man, when he nervously commenced his opening scene with her; her grave and emphatic 'Very well indeed, sir' at a speech which pleased her restored his confidence and self-possession.

In February 1813 she returned to play in London, but it was Covent Garden, not Drury Lane, which was the setting. The management had offered her handsome terms: '£50 per night for 30 nights – and a Benefit. There never was such terms *given* for so *many nights*',[5] she wrote to her son.

The audience hailed her first appearance with great applause; only *The Times* next day, in an indirect attack on the Duke, sounded a brutally dissenting note:

Is not the public forced to find an alternative for this degraded woman's appearance in the decline of life, either in her own vile avarice, or in her viler breach of stipulation by those who should never abandon her to poverty? We cannot believe the latter is the case; and if the former, what share of public approbation should be permitted to one for whom it is impossible to feel any share of personal respect? Whose sons and daughters are now strangely allowed to move among the honourable people of England, received by the Sovereign, and starting in full appetite for Royal patronage, while their mother wanders, and is allowed to wander, from barn to barn, and from town to town, bringing shame on the art she practises, and double shame on those who must have it in their power to send her back to penitence and obscurity.

The attack rebounded in Mrs Jordan's favour. Other papers hastened to her defence; and when, in the course of her next appearance, one of the characters addressed her with the sentence, 'You have an honest face, and need not be ashamed of showing it anywhere', the house raised such a roar of approval that she burst into tears. She had always defended the Duke in private. '*Money, money* or the want of it has, I am convinced, made *him* at this moment the most wretched of *men*; but having done wrong he does not like to retract . . . His distresses should have been relieved before',[6] she wrote to Boaden. Now in a letter replying to *The Times* she defended him, and herself, in public: he had provided for her generously, she wrote, and it was only to secure her future in the unhappy event of his death that she had, with his consent, returned to her profession. The reception of the letter confirmed the affection in which she was held by the public. 'I have had the most complete triumph over the rascal in the *Times*', she wrote to her son, 'his scurrility has been of service to me as an actress, and my letter has done me more honour as a woman than I can describe to you. The noise it has made is beyond everything, and the compliments and congratulations I have received in consequence of it are unbounded. When I went on last night in Rosalind they bravoed several times before I spoke – this I own was very flattering.'[7]

It was perhaps her last great triumph in a career which had become increasingly burdensome. She had not recovered, and indeed never would, from the shock of her separation; her health was failing her; she longed to see more of her children. But the disastrous affairs of her eldest daughter and the claims of a family seemingly incapable of living within its means drove her on, and the season at Covent Garden was scarcely over before she set off once more on the weary round of the provincial theatres.

*   *   *

While Mrs Jordan, beset with financial worries, continued unwillingly in her profession, Mrs Siddons, now that the curtain had fallen on her career, faced the anti-climax of retirement. She had her youngest daughter and Patty Wilkinson for companions, friends to visit and entertain, but nothing could make up for the glories and excitement she had known. Time lay heaviest in the evening; it was then, she told Samuel Rogers, that she would think, as she sat at home, 'Now I used to be going to dress; now the curtain is about to rise',[8] and to Tom Moore, years later, she spoke of the desolation she had felt on leaving the stage. Her niece Fanny Kemble, an actress in her turn, described the 'vapid vacuity' of Mrs Siddons' later years, and her apparent deadness and indifference to things, which she attributed less to age and failing health than to the withering influence of the overstimulating atmosphere of excitement and admiration in which she had passed her life. 'Certain it is', added Fanny, 'that such was my dread of the effect of my profession upon me, that I added an earnest petition to my daily prayers that I might be defended from the evil influence I feared it might exercise upon me.'[9]

For a time Mrs Siddons found some solace in giving readings from Shakespeare and Milton, at first in public and later to chosen guests in her own home. Haydon, in his diary, gives an amusing description of one such occasion, at which Thomas Lawrence was present. The play chosen was *Macbeth*, and there had been an interval for tea after the third act:

> While we were all eating toast and tinkling cups and saucers, she began again. It was like the effect of a mass bell at Madrid. All noise ceased; we slunk to our seats like boors, two or three of the most distinguished men of the day, with the very toast in their mouths, afraid to bite.
>
> It was curious to see Lawrence in the predicament, to hear him bite by degrees and then stop for fear of making too much crackle, his eyes full of water from the constraint; and at the same time to hear Mrs Siddons': 'Eye of newt and toe of frog', and then to see Lawrence give a sly bite, and then look awed and pretend to be listening.[10]

Mrs Siddons' readings were carefully staged. Dressed in white, with her dark hair *à la grècque*, she stood at a writing desk on which lights were placed, with a large red screen behind her. She spoke mostly from memory, donning her spectacles from time to time to refer to her text, and using these mundane articles so gracefully that they seemed an essential part of her performance.

Save on a very few occasions she resisted all appeals to return to the stage. Her most sustained reappearance was in 1815, when she played for ten days in Edinburgh to raise money for her daughter-in-law, wife of Henry Siddons who had died that spring. His death had shaken her deeply. 'I don't know why', she wrote to a friend, 'unless that I am older and feebler, or that I am now without a profession, which forced me out of myself in former afflictions, but the loss of my poor dear Harry seems to have laid a heavier hand upon my mind than any I have sustained.'[11] She was greatly agitated upon her first appearance, but a critic expressed the general opinion of the audience when he wrote: 'Mrs Siddons not only is, but looks older than when she was last before us. But in this single observation everything inauspicious to her efforts is included and exhausted.'[12]

Less well received was her return, in the following year, at the request of Princess Charlotte, as Lady Macbeth to her brother's Macbeth. The occasion brought forth Hazlitt's famous protest:

Players should be immortal, if their own wishes or ours could make them so; but they are not. They not only die like other people, but like other people they cease to be young, and are no longer themselves, even while living. Their health, strength, beauty, voice fails them; nor can they, without these advantages perform the same feats, or command the same applause that they did when possessed of them. It is the common lot: players are only *not* exempt from it. Mrs Siddons has retired once from the stage: why should she return to it again? She cannot retire twice from it with dignity; and it is to be wished that she should do all things with dignity. Any loss of reputation to her, is a loss to the world. Has she not had enough of glory? The homage she received is greater than that which is paid to Queens . . . She was not only the idol of the people, she not only hushed the tumultuous shouts of the pit in breathless expectation, and quenched the blaze of surrounding beauty in silent tears, but to the retired and lonely student, through long years of solitude, her face has shone as if an eye had appeared from heaven; her name has been as if a voice had opened the chambers of the human heart, or as if a trumpet had awakened the sleeping and the dead. To have seen Mrs Siddons, was an event in every one's life; and does she think we have forgot her? Or would she remind us of herself showing us what *she was not*?[13]

He deplored the falling-off, the slow and laboured speech, the seeking for effect, which he found in her performance, but in Kemble's Macbeth on the same evening he saw no diminution of his powers. 'Too much praise', he wrote, 'cannot be given to Mr Kemble's performance of Macbeth. He was "himself again" and more than himself. His action was decided, his voice audible. His tones had occasionally indeed a learned quaintness, like the colouring of Poussin; but the effect of the whole was fine. His action in delivering the speech "To-morrow and to-morrow", was particularly striking and expressive, as if he had stumbled by an accident on fate, and was baffled by the impenetrable obscurity of the future. In that prodigious prosing paper, the Times, which seems to be written as well as printed by a steam-engine, Mr Kemble is compared to the ruin of a magnificent temple, in which the divinity still resides. This is not the case. The temple is unimpaired; but the divinity is sometimes from home.'[14]

Kemble's return to Covent Garden, after his two years' absence, on January 15th 1814, had been a triumphal occasion. The whole pit rose spontaneously to greet him, and a circlet of laurel was flung on the stage at his feet. He was playing Coriolanus, and the pride which he assumed for the character must for a moment have been submerged in that of the actor. But if on that evening, the OP riots forgotten, Cooke and Master Betty no more than episodes in the past, he still stood unassailed as the head of his profession, it was almost for the final time. On January 27th, Edmund Kean made his first appearance at Drury Lane. Within a month he had taken the town by storm and the public, fickle as a Roman crowd, had turned from their old idol to the new.

*   *   *

The advent of Edmund Kean marked a turning point in the history of the stage; as in art, so in the theatre, the neo-classical style was replaced by the romantic. The transition was by no means cut and dried: there was much that was romantic in Kemble's acting and still more in Mrs Siddons', but there was always an underlying unity in their playing, a subordination of the parts to the whole. Coleridge's well-known statement that Kean's acting was like 'reading Shakespeare by flashes of lightning' catches the unevenness as well as the fiery brilliance of his genius. In contrast to the consistent and cumulative intensity with which Kemble would build up a character Kean's performances were remarkable for the swiftness and vehemence of his transitions and the dazzling variety of his resources. His acting, seemingly spontaneous, was in fact as carefully prepared as Kemble's, so much so that when rehearsing on a new stage he 'accurately counted the number of steps he had to take before reaching a certain spot, or before uttering a certain word; these steps were justly regarded by him as part of the mechanism which could no more be neglected than the accompaniment to an air could be neglected by a singer'.[15] Few of those carried away by the seemingly irresistible force of emotion he generated, however, were aware of the underlying technique; for the romantics his acting was all impetuosity and passion. 'His style is quite new, or rather renewed, being that of Nature',[16] wrote Byron, and it was the contrast between nature and art that was constantly adduced in comparing Kean with Kemble.

Mrs Siddons was beyond comparison; for Byron she was worth Kean and Kemble put together, and even Hazlitt, greatly as he admired Kean, set Mrs Siddons above him, if only for the effortless grandeur of her playing. Kemble, colder and more studied, was a different matter:

> Precise in passion, cautious ev'n in rage,
> Lo Kemble comes, the Euclid of the stage,
> Who moves in given angles, squares a start,
> And blows his Roman beak by rules of art.[17]

In almost every way he seemed the antithesis of Kean, and in the remaining years in which he held the stage critics never tired of measuring one against the other, the new generation of romantics inevitably favouring Kean. Physically Kean was distinctly at a disadvantage, slight and insignificant in stature; only his brilliant dark eyes gave a hint of the powers he could unleash on stage. Kemble, tall and statuesque, still strikingly handsome despite his age, seemed made for the classical parts he had taken as his own, and in these, even in the eyes of Kean's most devoted admirers, he remained supreme. In other parts, notably Richard III, it was Kean who bore away the honours: if Kemble's Richard had been forced to give place to Cooke's, it was extinguished by Kean's. 'By Jove, he is a soul', wrote Byron. 'Life – nature – truth without exaggeration or diminution. Kemble's Hamlet is perfect; but Hamlet is not nature. Richard is a man and Kean is Richard.'[18]

If it was not true, as Leigh Hunt would have it, that Kemble faded before Kean 'like a tragedy ghost', it is certain that Kean's coming hastened the end of his career. During Kean's first season, when the crowds were flocking to Drury Lane, revivifying the theatre's fortunes, Kemble pursued his stately way at Covent Garden in the roles he had perfected over so many years. But it was soon clear that his star was waning, not that there was any falling off in his own performances, but because the novelty and tempestuous energy of Kean's approach had captured the mood of the age. 'Our styles of acting are so very different', he told Boaden judiciously, after a secret visit to Drury Lane to see Kean in *Richard III*, 'that you must not expect me to like that of Mr Kean; but one thing I must say in his favour – he is at all times terribly in earnest.'[19]

Kemble's own achievement was secure. For thirty years he had dominated the stage, imposing his own character on an era. The moment was coming for him to step down and over the next two years, with characteristic calm and dignity, he would prepare himself to do so.

XX

1814, the year of Kean's first performance at Drury Lane, saw Mrs Jordan's last appearance on the London stage. For another year she struggled on in a variety of provincial engagements but her health, weakened by the hardships of touring, was failing her, and her family and financial anxieties were worsening. Two sons in the army had been censured for bringing unproved charges of negligence against their commanding officer in France; they were to be transferred in disgrace to regiments in India. Mrs Jordan bade farewell to them for the last time, early in 1815. The follies and extravagances of her eldest daughter, now separated from her husband and entirely dependent on her mother, had eaten heavily into her resources. But the crowning blow came when Edward March, the husband of Mrs Jordan's second daughter, for whom she had signed blank promissory notes, revealed that he had filled these in for sums far beyond what she could possibly pay, while he himself, facing bankruptcy, was in no position to redeem them.

The problem might not have been insoluble: some arrangement might have been made with the creditors and, apart from any earnings she might still gain on the stage, she had an assured income from the Duke of Clarence. But the possibility of imprisonment for debt, a terror since the time, long ago, when Daly had attempted to have her arrested, prevented her from thinking rationally. She determined to flee to France, out of reach of the law, till the business could be settled. Neither the Duke's financial adviser, anxious to spare his master embarrassing publicity, nor her son-in-law, weak and irresolute in the crisis he had created, attempted to dissuade her; and neither, once she reached France, made a serious attempt to sort out her affairs so that she could return home free from the fear of arrest. The Duke, though he must have been aware that she was in difficulties, seems to have been ignorant of their extent, which was kept from him by his adviser.

The story of Mrs Jordan's last months makes melancholy reading.

Living in rooms in Saint Cloud with one companion, a former governess to her children, she waited vainly for news from March or the Duke's adviser that it was safe for her to return. Cut off from her children, who wrote to her from time to time but whose distance from her was the greatest anguish of her exile, her health and spirits gradually gave way. Towards the end her skin became discoloured – possibly from jaundice – and she would pass whole days sighing on the sofa, her one source of hope and interest the arrival of the post. She died in June 1816, unattended by any of her family. The funeral expenses were paid by strangers, and it was a sympathetic Englishman who had met her in France before her death who put up the headstone for her grave. The inscription, in Latin and English, was composed by the theatrical historian Genest. After commemorating her pre-eminent talents on the stage and her charity in private life, it gave her age and the date of her death, and concluded simply: '*Mementote, lugete* – Remember and weep for her.'

*   *   *

In the months before her death, an English visitor, Helen Maria Williams, paid several calls on the great actress. Perfectly lucid – in contradiction to those who said that after her arrival in France she showed signs of mental disorder – Mrs Jordan talked of her past in the theatre, of her own acting, and of the exhilaration for an actor, of applause. 'It is impossible for anyone to picture the satisfaction arising from popular applause', she said. 'Conceive for an instant an actor in full health, perfectly satisfied with his own conception of a character, having previously established his fame with the public. He executes every scene with becoming spirit, progressing in perfectability of acting in proportion to the rounds of applause that greet his ears at intervals. The piece at length closes, and as he makes his bow, incessant peals of approbation salute him. Place such a scene, Miss Williams, before your imagination, and then judge what internal exultation must animate the frame – yes, stimulate the senses to delight bordering upon extasy.'[1]

She remembered too, less happily, her ancient grievances against the Kembles. The years had toned down the bad feeling between them but had not erased the memory. 'As for jealousy and ill nature',

196

she said, 'I had an awful share to encounter in the progress of my public life, and from quarters pursuing a different walk, consequently the last who ought to have manifested their spleen towards me. For a considerable time, I met their shafts with good nature, but finding such conduct increase rather than otherwise, I banished my smiles and had recourse to reserve, until, the attacks becoming too frequent for further endurance, I was compelled to make my grievances known in another channel . . .'[2] The other channel of course was Sheridan.

Now Sheridan was dead and Kemble, whose disputes with Mrs Jordan had punctuated his career as manager, was entering the final stage of his career. In the summer of 1816 he made his farewell visit to Dublin, previously the scene of some of his greatest successes. But Kean had been there the preceding summer, acting for several weeks to overflowing houses; Kemble's last performance in the city that had seen his rise to fame took place in a theatre that was only half full. He had chosen Othello as his final role, a part in which Kean particularly excelled. Kemble had seen Kean's performance. 'If the justness of conception', he had commented, 'were equal to the brilliance of the execution it would have been perfect; but the thing was a mistake; the fact being *that Othello was a slow man.*'[3] But his own performance, according to Macready who saw him then for the first time, though faultless in his reading of the part, was unlit by any spark of energy or passion. He did little more than walk through the role. Perhaps he was unwell, perhaps out of humour with the sparseness of the audience; the spectators who had applauded him heartily on his first entry let the final curtain fall in silence.

Back in London for the autumn, Kemble began what was announced as his last season. 'As his meridian was bright, so let his sunset be golden',[4] wrote Hazlitt. But the continued triumphs of Kean overshadowed his last performances, and though he kept a respectable following, it was Kean that the crowds flocked to see. Hazlitt, who so clearly saw the merits of both, made his famous lament: 'We wish we had never seen Mr Kean. He has destroyed the Kemble religion and it is the religion in which we were brought up. Never again shall we behold Mr Kemble with the same pleasure that we did, nor see Mr Kean with the same pleasure that we have seen

Mr Kemble formerly. We used to admire Mr Kemble's figure and manner, and had no idea that there was any want of art of nature. We feel the force and nature of Mr Kean's acting, but then we feel the want of Mr Kemble's person. Thus an old and delightful prejudice is destroyed, and no new enthusiasm, no second idolatry comes to take its place. Thus, by degrees, knowledge robs us of pleasure, and the cold icy hand of experience freezes up the warm current of the imagination and crusts it over with unfeeling criticism.'[5]

Kemble himself was often far from well. Asthma and gout were troubling him and he took medicine before almost every performance. He had had the satisfaction in the previous year of seeing an eight-volume edition of the plays, Shakespeare's and others, which he had revised or altered for the stage, through the press. But the ideals for which he had laboured over the years seemed to be crumbling. The theatre, which he had hoped to see dedicated to Shakespeare, was more and more given over to showy spectacle, his carefully staged revivals set aside by his co-proprietors in favour of more profitable entertainments. 'I do not know what the taste of the world may be with you', wrote Kemble to Talma, who was contemplating a visit to England, 'but our world in London are at present mad for splendid sights at the Theatre and the most impossible extravagances are the most certainly admired. I really do not think we have anything worth your giving yourself the trouble of a journey and a voyage to see – If Voltaire thought our Theatre monstrous in his time, I do not know what epithets he would describe it by now.'[6] But Talma, a consistent admirer, would be in London for Kemble's last performances.

In the spring of 1817 Kemble left London on a farewell visit to Edinburgh. Walter Scott, who attended his final performances there, found his old friend temporarily revived: 'He has made a great reformation in his habits; given up wine, which he used to swallow by pailfuls, – and renewed his youth like the eagle.'[7] His Coriolanus, thought Scott, had never been finer, but it was in *Macbeth*, appropriately enough, that Kemble made his last appearance. Scott had composed the valedictory ode with which he ended the evening and its reception, amidst mingled cheers and sobs from the audiences, visibly moved the veteran actor. Seldom have verses so well matched an occasion, with their glance, as he made his adieus, at the Roman roles in which he had excelled:

> . . . higher duties crave
> Some space between the theatre and the grave,
> That, like the Roman in the capitol,
> I may adjust my mantle ere I fall.
> My life's brief act in public service flown,
> The last, the closing scene, must be my own.

*　　*　　*

The visit to Edinburgh had been a rehearsal for the graver parting now impending. Kemble began his last round of performances at Covent Garden in May. Their attraction proving less than the management had expected, they were given for the benefit of Kemble's fellow actors, with whom, as the end of the season drew near, there were affecting moments of farewell. At the end of *Julius Caesar*, in which he played Brutus to the Cassius of Charles Mayne Young for the final time, he went round to the younger actor's dressing-room to present him with some of the properties he had worn, in memory of their having fought together at the battle of Philippi. 'Well', he said, 'we've often had words together on stage but never off'; then, touched by Young's thanks, he wrung his hand and hurried from the room, saying:

> For this present
> I would not, so with love I might entreat,
> Be any further moved . . .[8]

For his brother Charles' benefit, Kemble made his last appearance as Macbeth, with Mrs Siddons, once more brought out of her retirement, as Lady Macbeth. 'It was manifest', Farington reported, 'that it was time for Kemble to quit the stage. His personal powers are much weakened and His formal measured stiffness more expressed than when He was younger.'[9] Macready, who had made his début at Covent Garden that season, carried away a happier impression of the evening. The first four acts, he wrote, moved heavily, with Kemble 'tame, correct' and ineffective; but in the fifth when the news was brought, 'The queen, my lord, is dead', he seemed struck to the heart. 'Gradually collecting himself, he sighed out, "She should have died hereafter!" then, as if with the inspiration of despair, he hurried out, distinctly and pathetically, the lines:

> To-morrow, and to-morrow, and to-morrow
> Creeps in this petty pace from day to day,
> To the last syllable of recorded time;
> And all our yesterdays have lighted fools
> The way to dusty death. Out, out, brief candle.
> Life's but a walking shadow; a poor player
> That struts and frets his hour upon the stage,
> And then is heard no more: it is a tale
> Told by an idiot, full of sound and fury,
> Signifying nothing –

rising to a climax of desperation that brought the enthusiastic cheers of the close-packed theatre. All at once he seemed carried away by the genius of the scene. At the tidings of "the wood of Birnam moving", he staggered, as if the shock had struck at the very seat of life, and in the bewilderment of fear and rage could just ejaculate the words "Liar and slave!", then lashing himself into a state of frantic rage ended the scene in perfect triumph.'[10]

At last it was time for Kemble's final performance, and on June 23rd 1817, nearly thirty-four years after his first appearance there, he took his leave of the London stage. On this night at least no rival attractions stole the limelight. The boxes had been sold out weeks before, and the orchestra was laid out as stalls, though even on this occasion there were a few empty places in the cavernous reaches of the theatre. It was as Coriolanus that Kemble chose to make his farewell and the audience rose to the occasion as he rose to his greatest role. He played that evening, wrote a spectator, with 'an abandonment of self care, a boundless energy, a loose of strength, as though he felt he needed to husband his powers no longer.'[11] He was applauded rapturously throughout, and when he fell, wrote the *Morning Post* next day, 'the repeated shouts of cheering from all parts of the house were ardent and ecstatic beyond anything of the kind perhaps ever before witnessed'. When he came forward to make his valedictory address there was a shout like thunder of 'No farewell'; a laurel wreath, with a white satin scroll deploring his retirement, was flung from a box into the orchestra and handed to the stage by Talma, who was sitting in the foremost row. Kemble's speech was brief; scarcely able to master his emotion, he hurried it to its close before withdrawing with a long and lingering look.

In the green-room a new ordeal awaited him as his fellow actors gathered round to beg some article of clothing or adornment as a relic of his last performance. To the actor Charles Mathews he presented the sandals he had worn that night, and Mathews, as he bore away his prize, was heard to exclaim, 'I may wear his sandals, but no-one will ever stand in his shoes.'[12]

It was true. There would be no successor to Kemble. His influence would linger on, reflected in the acting of his brother Charles and of Charles Mayne Young, but the future lay with Kean, with a more natural, less heroic style. 'It was as sure a thing', said Leigh Hunt, 'as Nature against Art, or tears against cheeks of stone.'[13] But for over thirty years he had sustained a lofty view of his profession, pursuing it, amidst disappointments and setbacks, with unwearying diligence. To the end of his career he was continuing to study. 'I feel I am only just beginning to understand my art', he said just before its close. His high seriousness had its comic side: there have been few actors more easy to caricature or imitate, and few who have been more pilloried than he was at the time of the OP riots. But in the end his single-mindedness inspired respect, even from those least sympathetic to his style. Like Garrick, he had raised the standing of his profession. 'We feel more respect for John Kemble in a plain coat', said one critic, 'than for the Lord Chancellor on the woolsack.'[14]

A few days after his last performance Kemble attended a banquet to commemorate his departure from the stage. It was a singular honour: even Garrick had had nothing comparable. Lord Holland presided, with Kemble on his right and the Duke of Bedford on his left; three hundred guests, drawn from the highest reaches of rank and talent, were assembled. A commemorative vase had been commissioned from Flaxman, Thomas Campbell had composed a farewell ode, and a silver medal had been struck to mark the occasion, with Kemble's profile on one side and on the other the words, 'Thou last of all the Romans, fare thee well'. It was no wonder that Mrs Siddons, seeing the honours loaded on her brother, allowed herself, in a rare moment of pique, to remark to Samuel Rogers, 'Ah! Mr Rogers, perhaps in the next world women will be more valued than they are in this.'[15]

The formal banquet passed soberly enough. But at a dinner which he gave for his principal actors not long after, Kemble, who for some time had given up drinking, was induced to take champagne. It had not agreed with him, Thomas Lawrence told Farington, and he had been very unwell for several weeks. Kemble's health, in fact, could no longer be relied upon. The asthma which had bedevilled his last years on the stage was growing worse, and he was tortured by a persistent cough. Within a year, driven partly by the desire to find a warmer climate, he left England with his wife to settle, after pausing for some months in Paris, in Toulouse. Here Hazlitt took pleasure in picturing the great actor: 'He is now quaffing health and burgundy in the South of France. He perhaps finds the air that blows from the "vine-covered hills" wholesomer than that of a crowded house; and the lengthened murmurs of the Mediterranean shores more soothing to the soul, than the deep thunders of the pit.'[16]

Economy, as well as health, had sent the Kembles abroad; it was cheaper to live out of England. Of all the fortune amassed during Kemble's years of labour only a relatively small sum, sufficient to procure an annuity of £1,000 a year, remained. The rest had been swallowed up in his investment in Covent Garden, whose affairs were going increasingly badly. Such dividends as he received went to clear the cost of his original investment. In 1820, on the death of his partner, Thomas Harris, he made over his share in the theatre to Charles Kemble. It was a generous gift – Charles had always been his favourite brother, and his natural successor as an actor – but it was one that would eventually bring him close to ruin. Kemble did not live to see his present become a liability. Already, at the time he made the transfer, he felt his time was running out. He had returned to London, on Harris' death, for the last time. Hazlitt, who saw him then, found him much changed. 'His face', he wrote, 'was as fine and noble as ever, but he sat in a large arm chair, bent down, dispirited and lethargic. He spoke no word, but he sighed heavily, and after thus drowsing for a time he went away.'[17] To Mrs Inchbald, on his departure from London, Kemble wrote a farewell letter:

Know, dear Muse,
         " 'Tis our fast intent
To shake all cares and business from our age,
Conferring them on younger strength, while we
Unburthen'd crawl toward death."

In plain prose I have assigned over my sixth part of the property in absolute fee to my brother Charles, and "God give him good on't". When I left you before, dearest, it was to visit Spain, and you managed for me in my absence; now, I think I shall make out my tour to Italy, and end perhaps like an old Roman.[18]

He died just over two years later, in Switzerland, in February 1823.

The Kemble era was over. Mrs Siddons lived on till 1831, already a legend in her lifetime, and one, like Garrick, whose memory would not fade. Kemble, by his own admission, had never been her equal; though with him as her partner she had reached some of her greatest heights. His influence as a manager would last. 'All the truth, all the uniformity, all the splendour of the stage', wrote Boaden, 'came in, but did not die with Mr Kemble.' His image as an actor would recede as his classical style was superseded. It remains for us in the portraits of Thomas Lawrence, embodying a lost ideal of grandeur.

It is common to regret the actor's lot and the fleeting nature of his fame, so aptly expressed by Garrick:

The painter dead, yet still he charms the eye,
While England lives, his fame can never die.
But he who struts his hour upon the stage
Can scarce extend his fame for half an age;
Nor pen nor pencil can the actor save;
The art, and artist, share one common grave.[19]

But the actor perhaps has consolations that other artists lack. Mrs Jordan spoke of the 'delight, bordering upon extasy' that an audience's enthusiasm could bring; and Hazlitt, as though to echo her, once wrote: 'Players, however, have little reason to complain of their

203

hard earned, short lived popularity. One thunder of applause from pit, boxes and galleries, is equal to a whole immortality of posthumous fame.'[20] This reward, and the admiration of his age, had been Kemble's in good measure.

NOTES

Titles abbreviated in the notes will be found in full in the bibliography. Quotations from Boaden, where no numbered reference is given will be found in his *Memoirs of the Life of John Philip Kemble*, those from Campbell in his *Mrs Siddons*, and those from Fitzgerald in *The Kembles*; entries from Kemble's journals from the five MS volumes in the British Museum.

PREFACE
1 Hunt: *Autobiography*, p. 152

CHAPTER I
1 *The Examiner*, October 27, 1816
2 Boaden: *Mrs Siddons*, p. 16
3 August 12, 1775, MS letter, British Museum
4 *Letters of David Garrick*, p. 1026
5 Campbell: *Mrs Siddons*, p. 37
6 Boaden: *Mrs Siddons*, p. 18
7 For this and subsequent quotations by her in this chapter see *The Reminiscences of Sarah Kemble Siddons, 1773–85*

CHAPTER II
1 Lee Lewis: *Memoirs*, I, p. 99
2 Fitzgerald: *The Kembles*, p. 138
3 Johnston: *Life of John Philip Kemble Esq.*
4 Hunt: *Dramatic Essays*, p. 9
5 *The Examiner*, October 13, 1816
6 Wilkinson: *The Wandering Patentee*, II, p. 57
7 Boaden: *Mrs Inchbald*, I, p. 93
8 June 26, 1781, MS letter, Harvard Theatre Collection
9 Boaden: *Mrs Inchbald*, I, p. 171
10 MS letter, Forster Collection

CHAPTER III
1 *Quarterly Review, XXXIV*, 1826
2 John Williams (Anthony Pasquin), quoted by Herschel Baker, *John Philip Kemble*, p. 87
3 Hunt: *Dramatic Essays*, p13.
4 Macready: *Reminiscences*, I, p. 55

5 Campbell: *Mrs Siddons*, p. 117
6 *Reminiscences of Sarah Kemble Siddons*
7 Boswell: *Life of Johnson*, p. 1251
8 *Ibid*, p. 1252
9 Hazlitt: *Conversatious with Northcote, Collected Works*, VI, p. 349

CHAPTER IV

1 Reynolds: *Life and Times*, II, p. 217
2 Boaden: *Mrs Inchbald*, I, p. 174
3 July 17, 1784, MS letter, Forster Collection, Victoria and Albert Museum
4 Campbell: *Mrs Siddons*, p. 145
5 Boaden: *Kemble*, I, p. 345
6 Betsy Sheridan: *Journal*, p. 32
7 For this and the two quotations following see *Reminiscences of Sarah Kemble Siddons*
8 Boaden: *Kemble*, I, p. 212
9 Campbell: *Mrs Siddons*, p. 185
10 *Reminiscences of Sarah Kemble Siddons*
11 Campbell: *Mrs Siddons*, p. 182
12 G. J. Bell, quoted in *Revels History of Drama*, VI, p. 120
13 Hazlitt: *Characters of Shakespeare's Plays, Collected Works*, I, p. 190
14 Campbell: *Mrs Siddons*, p. 187

CHAPTER V

1 *Public Advertiser*, February 3, 1785
2 MS letter, Harvard Theatre Collection
3 Boaden: *Mrs Inchbald*, I, p. 200
4 Fitzgerald: *The Kembles*, I, p. 215
5 *Ibid*, p. 216
6 *Sheridania*, p. 283
7 Boaden: *Mrs Jordan*, I, p. 28
8 *Ibid*, p. 142
9 *The British Theatre*, vol XVI, p. 5
10 Boaden: *Mrs Jordan*, I, p. 72

CHAPTER VI

1 *The Examiner*, October 22, 1815
2 Lamb: 'On Some of the Older Actors', *Works*, p. 404
3 Boaden: *Mrs Jordan*, I, p. 80
4 Betsy Sheridan: *Journal*, p. 77
5 Boaden: *Kemble*, I, p. 204
6 *Ibid*, p. 394
7 Kelly: *Reminiscences*, p. 149

8 *London Magazine*, January 1820
9 Manvell: *Sarah Siddons*, p. 153

CHAPTER VII

 1 *The Examiner*, May 5, 1816
 2 Lockhart: *Life of Scott*, III, p. 107
 3 Macready: *Reminiscences*, I, p. 150
 4 Haydon: *Autobiography and Memoirs*, p. 362
 5 *The Examiner*, May 5, 1816
 6 Ernst Brandes: *Bemerkungen über das Londoner, Pariser und Wiener Theater*, 1786, quoted by Bertam Joseph, *The Tragic Actor*, p. 246
 7 *Dramatic Essays*, p. 118
 8 Campbell: *Mrs Siddons*, p. 241
 9 *Ibid*, p. 250
10 *Quarterly Review*, XXXIV, 1826
11 Moore: *Journals, Memoirs and Correspondence*, V, p. 13
12 Dibdin: *Reminiscences*, I, p. 197
13 Scott: *Quarterly Review*, XXXIV, 1826
14 Hunt: *Autobiography*, p. 149
15 *Morning Post*, March 10, 1789
16 Boaden: *Mrs Jordan*, I, p. 292

CHAPTER VIII

 1 *Quarterly Review*, XXXIV, 1826
 2 *Public Advertiser*, quoted by P. W. Sergeant, *Mrs Jordan*, p. 137
 3 *Ibid*
 4 Taylor: *Records of My Life*, II, p. 126
 5 May 17, 1790, *Thraliana*, p. 769
 6 Boaden: *Mrs Jordan*, I, p. 166
 7 Moore: *Journals, Memoirs and Correspondence*, VIII, p. 6
 8 Stanhope: *Notes of Conversations with the Duke of Wellington*, p. 152
 9 Boaden: *Kemble*, II, p. 76

CHAPTER IX

 1 Boaden: *Mrs Inchbald*, II, p. 290
 2 Boaden: *Mrs Jordan*, I, p. 274
 3 *Ibid*, p. 212
 4 *Piozzi-Pennington Letters*, p. 63
 5 *Ibid*, p. 78
 6 Piozzi: *Thraliana*, p. 850
 7 *Piozzi-Pennington Letters*, p. 74
 8 Piozzi: *Thraliana*, p. 808
 9 *Ibid*, p. 738

CHAPTER X

1 Lord Deerhurst, quoted by Mrs Piozzi, *Thraliana*, p. 876
2 Campbell: *Mrs Siddons*, p. 262
3 *Quarterly Review*, XXXIV, 1826
4 Kelly: *Reminiscences*, p. 207
5 Cumberland: *Memoirs*, II, p. 384
6 Fitzgerald: *The Kembles*, I, p. 309
7 Fitzgerald: *A New History of the English Stage*, II, p. 351
8 Baker: *Kemble*, p. 212
9 Lockhart: *Life of Walter Scott*, II, p. 95
10 Coleridge: *Table Talk*, p. 16
11 *Ibid*
12 *Quarterly Review*, XXXIV, 1826
13 *Ibid*
14 Lady Morgan: *Book of the Boudoir*, I, 100, quoted by Baker, *Kemble*, p. 149
15 Reynolds: *Life and Times*, II, p. 95
16 *Piozzi-Pennington Letters*, p. 120
17 Taylor: *Records of My Life*, II, p. 93

CHAPTER XI

1 Kelly: *Reminiscences*, p. 217
2 Hunt: *Dramatic Essays*, p. 5
3 Baker: *Kemble*, p. 193
4 Colman: Preface to *The Iron Chest* (first edition)
5 *Ibid*
6 *Ibid*
7 *Ibid*
8 *Ibid*
9 Lamb: 'The Artificial Comedy of the Last Century', *Works*, p. 420
10 Kelly: *Reminiscences*, p. 220
11 F. A. Kemble: *Record of a Girlhood*, I, p. 283
12 Ireland: *Confessions*, p. 96
13 *Ibid*, p. 139
14 Campbell: *Mrs Siddons*, p. 270
15 Grebanier: *The Great Shakespeare Forgery*, p. 212
16 *Gentleman's Magazine*, April 1795
17 Ireland: *Confessions*, p. 153

CHAPTER XII

1 Campbell: *Mrs Siddons*, p. 271
2 Piozzi: *Thraliana*, p. 938
3 Manvell: *Sarah Siddons*, p. 362
4 Campbell: *Mrs Siddons*, p. 267

5 Piozzi: *Thraliana*, p. 916
6 Campbell: *Mrs Siddons*, p. 273
7 Roberts: *Samuel Rogers and his Circle*, p. 106
8 Boaden: *Kemble*, II, p. 186
9 Cumberland: *Memoirs*, II, p. 281
10 Aspinall: *Mrs Jordan and her Family*, p. 41
11 Boaden: *Mrs Jordan*, II, p. 13
12 *Ibid*, I, p. 309
13 Fothergill: *Mrs Jordan*, p. 146
14 Boaden: *Mrs Jordan*, I, p. 347
15 *Ibid*, I, p. 351
16 *The Times*, June 25, 1817
17 Knapp: *An Artist's Love Story*, p. 44

CHAPTER XIII
1 Manvell: *Sarah Siddons*, p. 335
2 Knapp: *An Artist's Love Story*, p. 26
3 Goldring: *Regency Portrait Painter*, p. 139
4 *Piozzi-Pennington Letters*, p. 152
5-16 The letters quoted are from Oswald Knapp's *An Artist's Love Story*, appearing in the following order: 5, p. 47; 6, p. 58; 7, p. 74; 8, p. 132; 9, p. 138; 10, p. 145; 11, p. 151; 12, p. 148; 13, p. 169; 14, p. 210; 15, p. 121; 16, p. 135
17 Aspinall: *Mrs Jordan and her Family*, p. 42
18 Knapp: *An Artist's Love Story*, p. 174
19 *Ibid*, p. 158
20 *Piozzi-Pennington Letters*, p. 167
21 Knapp: *An Artist's Love Story*, p. 175

CHAPTER XIV
1 *Piozzi-Pennington Letters*, p. 302
2 Wilkinson: *The Wandering Patentee*, III, p. 89
3 Campbell: *Mrs Siddons*, p. 158
4 *Ibid*. p. 134
5 Kelly: *Reminiscences*, p. 295
6 *Ibid*, p. 253
7 *Ibid*, p. 254
8 Boaden: *Kemble*, II, p. 243
9 Boaden: *Mrs Jordan*, II, p. 16
10 Boaden: *Kemble*, II, p. 239
11 Nov 27, 1800, MS letter, Harvard Theatre Collection
12 Undated: MS letter, Harvard Theatre Collection
13 Boaden: *Kemble*, II, p. 291
14 Boaden: *Mrs Inchbald*, II, p. 47

CHAPTER XV

1 Jan 24, 1803, MS letter, Forster Collection
2 Nov 28, 1802, MS letter, Forster Collection
3 Boaden: *Kemble*, II, p. 365
4 Campbell: *Mrs Siddons*, p. 312
5 *Ibid*, p. 316
6 Boaden: *Mrs Inchbald*, II, p. 75
7 Campbell: *Mrs Siddons*, p. 319
8 *Ibid*, p. 320
9 Galindo: *Letter to Mrs Siddons*
10 *Ibid*
11 *Ibid*
12 Parsons: *The Incomparable Siddons*, p. 227
13 Piozzi: *Thraliana*, p. 1066
14 Campbell: *Mrs Siddons*, p. 331

CHAPTER XVI

1 Fitzgerald, *The Kembles*, II, p. 37
2 Hazlitt: *Characters of Shakespeare's Plays, Collected Works*, I, p. 237
3 Odell: *Shakespeare from Betterton to Irving*, II, p. 96
4 *Ibid*, p. 101
5 *Ibid*, p. 170
6 *London Magazine*, January, 1820
7 Boaden: *Kemble*, II, p. 380
8 *Ibid*
9 Boaden: *Mrs Jordan*, II, p. 151
10 *Quarterly Review*, XXXIV, 1826
11 Kelly: *Reminiscences*, p. 290
12 Fitzgerald: *The Kembles*, II, p. 339
13 Baker: *Kemble*, p. 278
14 Macready: *Reminiscences*, I, p. 15
15 Boaden: *Kemble*, II, p. 396
16 Boaden: *Mrs Inchbald*, II, p. 78
17 *Ibid*, p. 79
18 Playfair: *The Prodigy*, p. 138

CHAPTER XVII

1 Macready: *Reminiscences*, I, p. 63
2 *Ibid*
3 Boaden: *Mrs Jordan*, II, p. 243
4 Hunt: *Dramatic Essays*, p. 5
5 *Quarterly Review*, XXXIV, 1826
6 Mathews: *Memoirs*, II, p. 220
7 Disher: *Blood and Thunder*, p. 49

8 Campbell: *Mrs Siddons*, p. 337
9 Manvell: *Sarah Siddons*, p. 292

CHAPTER XVIII

1 Tegg: *The OP War in Poetic Epistles*
2 Campbell: *Mrs Siddons*, p. 340
3 Tegg: *The OP War in Poetic Epistles*
4 *The Rebellion or all in the Wrong*
5 Tegg: *The OP War in Poetic Epistles*
6 *Ibid*
7 Boaden: *Mrs Inchbald*, II, p. 144
8 Campbell: *Mrs Siddons*, p. 341
9 *Familiar Letters of Sir Walter Scott*, I, p. 156
10 *Sir Thomas Lawrence's Letter Bag*, p. 65
11 Boaden: *Kemble*, II, p. 557
12 *Quarterly Review*, XXXIV, 1826
13 Hazlitt: *London Magazine*, January, 1820
14 Hunt: *Dramatic Essays*, p. 46
15 Wyndham: *Annals of Covent Garden*, I, p. 352
16 *Byron's Letters and Journals*, II, p. 147
17 *Ibid*, p. 149
18 *Farington Diary*, VII, p. 37
19 Campbell: *Mrs Siddons*, p. 345
20 *Farington Diary*, VII, p. 88
21 *London Magazine*, January, 1820

CHAPTER XIX

1 Blessington: *Conversations with Lord Byron*, p. 142
2 Aspinall: *Mrs Jordan and her Family*, p. 208
3 *Ibid*, p. 208
4 Macready: *Reminiscences*, I, p. 63
5 Aspinall: *Mrs Jordan and her Family*, p. 244
6 Boaden: *Mrs Jordan*, II, p. 273
7 Aspinall: *Mrs Jordan and her Family*, p. 249
8 Fitzgerald: *The Kembles*, II, p. 198
9 F. A. Kemble: *Record of a Girlhood*, II, p. 64
10 Haydon: *Autobiography and Memoirs*, p. 229
11 Campbell: *Mrs Siddons*, p. 358
12 *Ibid*
13 *The Examiner*, June 16, 1816
14 *Ibid*
15 Vandenhoff, *Dramatic Reminiscences*, quoted by Bertram Joseph, *The Tragic Actor*, p. 270
16 Byron: *Letters and Journals*, IV, p. 67

17 Fitzgerald: *The Kembles*, I, p. 61
18 Fitzsimons: *Fire from Heaven*, p. 61
19 Boaden: *Kemble*, II, p. 554

CHAPTER XX
 1 Fothergill: *Mrs Jordan*, p. 310
 2 Jerrold: *Dorothy Jordan*, p. 221
 3 Moore: *Journals, Memoirs and Correspondence*, VI, p. 70
 4 *The Examiner*, October 27, 1816
 5 *Ibid*, December 8, 1816
 6 May 14, 1816, MS letter, Folger Shakespeare Library
 7 Lockhart: *Life of Walter Scott*, V, p. 187
 8 Young: *Memoir of C. M. Young*, I, p. 80
 9 *Farington Diary*, VIII, p. 131
10 Macready: *Reminiscences*, I, p. 148
11 Baker: *Kemble*, p. 340
12 Matthews: *Memoirs*, II, p. 404
13 Hunt: *Dramatic Essays*, p. 222
14 *Theatrical Inquisitor*, II, 1813, p. 102
15 Roberts: *Samuel Rogers and his Circle*, p. 110
16 *London Magazine*, July 1820
17 Fitzgerald: *The Kembles*, II, p. 272
18 Boaden: *Mrs Inchbald*, II, p. 269
19 Garrick: Prologue, *The Clandestine Marriage*
20 *The Examiner*, January 14, 1816

BOOKS CONSULTED

AGATE, James: *The English Dramatic Critics*, An Anthology 1660–1932. Arthur Barker, 1932

ASPINALL, A.: *Mrs Jordan and her Family*. Arthur Barker, 1951

Authentic Narrative of Mr Kemble's Retirement from the Stage. John Miller, 1817

BAKER, Herschel: *John Philip Kemble, The Actor in his Theatre*. Harvard University Press, 1942

BERNARD, John: *Retrospections of the Stage*. Henry Colburn & Richard Bentley, 1830

BINGHAM, Madeleine: *Sheridan: The Track of a Comet*. George Allen & Unwin, 1972

BLESSINGTON, Lady: *Conversations of Lord Byron*. Ed. E. J. Lovell Jr., Princeton University Press, 1969

BOADEN, James: *Memoirs of Mrs Inchbald*. Richard Bentley, 1833

BOADEN, James: *The Life of Mrs Jordan*. Edward Bull, 1831

BOADEN. James: *Memoirs of the Life of John Philip Kemble*. Longman, Hurst, Rees, Orme, Brown & Green, 1825

BOADEN, James: *Memoirs of Mrs Siddons*. Edward Moxon. 1839

BOSWELL, James: *Life of Johnson*. Oxford University Press, 1961

BYRON, Lord: *Famous in my Time, Wedlock's the Devil*. Letters & Journals, vols. II and IV, 1814–15. Ed. Leslie Marchand, John Murray, 1975

CAMPBELL, Thomas: *Life of Mrs Siddons*. Edward Moxon, 1839

CHILD, Harold: *The Shakespearean Productions of John Philip Kemble*. Oxford University Press, 1935

COLERIDGE, Samuel Taylor: *The Table Talk and Omniana*. Ed. T. Ashe, George Bell, 1884

CUMBERLAND, Richard: *Memoirs*. Cadell & Davies, 1807

DIBDIN, Thomas: *Reminiscences*. Ams Press, New York, 1970

DISHER, Maurice Willson: *Blood & Thunder*. Frederick Muller, 1949

DOBBS, Brian: *Drury Lane*. Cassell, 1972

DONOHUE, Joseph: *Theatre in the Age of Kean*. Blackwell, 1975

DONOHUE, Joseph: *Kemble's Production of Macbeth*, 1794. Theatre Notebook, XXI, no 2, 1966–7

DUNLAP, William: *Memoirs of the Life of George Frederick Cooke*. Henry Colburn, 1813

FARINGTON, Joseph: *The Farington Diary*. Ed. James Grieg. Hutchinson, 1927

FFRENCH, Yvonne: *Mrs Siddons, Tragic Actress.* Cobden-Sanderson, 1936
FITZGERALD, Percy: *The Kembles.* Tinsley Bros, 1871
FITZGERALD, Percy: *A New History of the English Stage.* Tinsley Bros.,
  1882
FOTHERGILL, Brian: *Mrs Jordan: Portrait of an Actress.* Faber & Faber,
  1965
GALINDO: *Mrs Galindo's Letter to Mrs Siddons,* 1809
GARRICK, David: *Letters.* Ed. D. M. Little & G. M. Kahrl. Vol. III,
  Oxford University Press, 1963
GENEST, John: *Some Account of the English Stage.* Vols VI, VII, VIII.
  Bath, 1832
The Georgian Playhouse: Actors, Artists, Audiences & Architecture, 1730–
  1830. Catalogue of the Exhibition devised by Iain Mackintosh,
  assisted by Geoffrey Ashton. Hayward Gallery, 1975
GIBBS, Lewis: *Sheridan.* Dent, 1947
GOLDRING, Douglas: *Regency Portrait Painter: The Life of Sir Thomas
  Lawrence.* Macdonald, 1951
GREBANIER, Bernard: *The Great Shakespeare Forgery.* Heinemann, 1966
HAYDON, Benjamin Robert: *Autobiography and Memoirs.* Ed. T. Taylor,
  Peter Davies, 1926
HAZLITT, William: *The Collected Works.* Ed. A. R. Weller & Arnold
  Glover. Dent, 1903
HUNT, Leigh: *Autobiography.* Ed. R. Ingpen. Constable, 1903
HUNT, Leigh: *Dramatic Essays.* Ed. W. Archer & R. W. Lowe. Walter
  Scott, 1894
INCHBALD, Elizabeth: *A Simple Story.* Ed. J. M. S. Tompkins.
  Oxford University Press, 1967
INCHBALD, Elizabeth (editor): *The British Theatre* (Collections of plays
  in the Drury Lane and Covent Garden repertoire in 25 volumes.)
  London, 1808
IRELAND, W. H.: *Confessions.* Thomas Goddard, 1805
JERROLD, Claire: *The Story of Dorothy Jordan.* Eveleigh Nash, 1914
JOHNSTON, J.: *The Life of John Philip Kemble.* London, 1809
JOSEPH, Bertram: *The Tragic Actor.* Routledge, Kegan Paul, 1959
KELLY, Michael: *Reminiscences.* Ed. Roger Fiske. Oxford University
  Press, 1975
KEMBLE, Frances Anne: *Record of a Girlhood.* Richard Bentley, 1878
KNAPP, Oswald G.: *An Artist's Love Story.* George Allen, 1904
LAMB, Charles: *Works.* Ed. Charles Kent, George Routledge, 1889
LAWRENCE, Thomas: *Sir Thomas Lawrence's Letter Bag.* Ed. George
  Somes Layard. George Allen, 1906
LEWES, Charles Lee: *Memoirs.* Richard Philips, 1805
LITTLEWOOD, S. R. *Elizabeth Inchbald and her Circle.* Daniel O'Connor,
  1921

LOCKHART, J. G.: *The Life of Sir Walter Scott.* Vol III. F. & E. Black, 1902

London Stage, The: Part 5, 1776–1800. Ed. Charles Beecher Hogan. Southern Illinois University Press, 1968

MACREADY, W. C.: *Reminiscences.* Macmillan, 1875

MANVELL, Roger: *Sarah Siddons: Portrait of an Actress.* Heinemann, 1976

MATTHEWS, Charles: *Memoirs.* Richard Bentley, 1839

MOORE, Thomas: *Memoirs of Richard Brinsley Sheridan.* London, 1805

MOORE, Thomas: *Journals, Memoirs & Correspondence.* Ed. Lord John Russell. Longman, Brown, Green & Longmans, 1853

NICOLL, Allardyce: *A History of English Drama, 1660–1900.* Vols III, IV. Cambridge University Press, 1952

ODELL, George C. D.: *Shakespeare from Betterton to Irving.* Vol II. Charles Scribner's Sons, 1920

PARSONS, Mrs Clement: *The Incomparable Siddons.* Methuen, 1909

PEARSON, Hesketh: *The Swan of Litchfield.* (Letters of Anna Seward.) Hamish Hamilton, 1936

PIOZZI, Hester: *Intimate Letters of Hester Piozzi & Penelope Pennington, 1788–1822.* Ed. Oswald G. Knapp. The Bodley Head, 1914

PIOZZI, Hester: *Thraliana, 1784–1809.* Ed. Katharine C. Balderton. Clarendon Press, 1942

PLAYFAIR, Giles: *The Prodigy: A Study of the Strange Life of Master Betty.* Secker & Warburg, 1967

RAYMOND, G.: *The Life & Enterprises of Robert William Elliston.* G. Routledge, 1857

The Rebellion or All in the Wrong (Account of the OP Riots.) Vernon Hood & Sharpe, 1809

The Revels History of Drama in English. Vol VI. General editors, Clifford Leech & T. W. Craik. Methuen, 1975

REYNOLDS, Frederick: *The Life and Times.* Henry Colburn, 1826

RHODES, R. Crompton: *Harlequin Sheridan.* Basil Blackwell, 1933

ROBERTS, R. E.: *Samuel Rogers and his Circle.* Methuen, 1910

SCOTT, Walter: *Review of Boaden's Life of John Philip Kemble.* The Quarterly Review, XXXIV, 1826

SCOTT, Walter: *Familiar Letters of Sir Walter Scott.* David Douglas, 1894

SERGEANT, P. W.: *Mrs Jordan: Child of Nature.* Hutchinson, 1913

SHERIDAN, Betsy: *Journal, 1874–6 and 1788–90.* Ed. William Lefanu. Eyre & Spottiswode, 1960

SHERIDAN, Richard Brinsley: *Sheridania.* Henry Colburn, 1826

SIDDONS, Sarah: *The Reminiscences of Sarah Kemble Siddons, 1773–85.* Ed. William Van Lennep. Cambridge, Mass., Widener Library, 1942

STANHOPE, P. H.: *Notes of Conversations with the Duke of Wellington.* John Murray, 1888

TAYLOR, John: *Records of my Life.* Edward Bull, 1832
TEGG, Thomas: *The OP War in Poetic Epistles.* London, 1810
WHALLEY, T. S.: *Journals & Correspondence.* Ed. Rev. Hill Wickham. Richard Bentley, 1863
WILKINSON, Tate: *Memoirs of his own Life.* York, 1790
WILKINSON, Tate: *The Wandering Patentee.* York, 1795
WYNDHAM, W. S.: *The Annals of Covent Garden Theatre.* Vol I. Chatto & Windus, 1906
YOUNG, Julian Charles: *A Memoir of Charles Mayne Young, Tragedian.* Macmillan, 1871
ZIEGLER, Philip: *William IV.* Collins, 1971

OTHER SOURCES

BRITISH MUSEUM: MS journals (5 vols.) and letters of John Philip Kemble; MS letters of Henry Bate and Samuel Ireland; newspapers of the period from the Burney Collection; cartoons from the Collection of Political and Personal Satires, 1782–1817.

FOLGER SHAKESPEARE LIBRARY, Washington D.C.: MS letters of John Philip Kemble.

GARRICK CLUB: John Philip Kemble's prompt copies of *Macbeth* and *Coriolanus.*

HARVARD THEATRE MUSEUM: MS letters of John Philip Kemble and Priscilla Kemble.

ROYAL OPERA HOUSE, COVENT GARDEN: Pamphlets and press cuttings relating to John Philip Kemble.

THEATRE MUSEUM: Press cuttings relating to John Philip Kemble and Sarah Siddons.

VICTORIA AND ALBERT MUSEUM: MS letters of John Philip Kemble and Priscilla Kemble in the Forster Collection.

INDEX